Charlotte Chandler is the author of many biographies of famous actors and directors including Groucho Marx, Federico Fellini, Billy Wilder, Alfred Hitchcock and Bette Davis. She lives in New York City.

Further praise for *Ingrid*:

'I can never forget Roberto [Rossellini] or the grace of Ingrid Bergman. Evviva Ingrid, this new book of Charlotte Chandler, for bringing their spirit back to life' Michelangelo Antonioni

'Ingrid Bergman remains one of cinema's greatest stars. Charlotte Chandler's "personal biography" offers us a window into the remarkable life of a remarkable woman' John Landis

'Once again Charlotte Chandler opens the door to the personal life of an iconic movie star. I was bewitched by Chandler's book, almost as much as I was by Bergman herself' David Brown

'I live next door to Ingrid Bergman's old Benedict Canyon house. I've never seen her ghost, but she beautifully haunts Charlotte Chandler's *Ingrid*. On every page, Ingrid says "Boo!"' Arthur Hiller

'Ingrid Bergman. What images just the name evokes! But behind the icon on the screen and the scandal in the headlines was a real, flesh-and-blood woman all of us would have liked to know. Meet her now in Charlotte Chandler's *Ingrid*, a biography more exciting and dramatic than most novels' Sidney Sheldon

'Charlotte Chandler helps the testimonies flow easily and nowhere does she intrude herself' *Sunday Telegraph*

'Ultimately . . . this kind of l   lity of anecdotes, and there are son

ALSO BY CHARLOTTE CHANDLER

The Girl Who Walked Home Alone: Bette Davis, A Personal Biography

It's Only a Movie: Alfred Hitchcock, A Personal Biography

Nobody's Perfect: Billy Wilder, A Personal Biography

I, Fellini

The Ultimate Seduction

Hello, I Must Be Going: Groucho and His Friends

INGRID

INGRID BERGMAN
A PERSONAL BIOGRAPHY

‿ᖴᑎ‿

CHARLOTTE CHANDLER

POCKET
BOOKS

LONDON • SYDNEY • NEW YORK • TORONTO

First published in Great Britain by Simon & Schuster UK Ltd, 2007
This edition first published by Pocket Books, 2008
An imprint of Simon & Schuster UK Ltd
A CBS COMPANY

1 3 5 7 9 10 8 6 4 2

Simon & Schuster UK Ltd
Africa House
64-78 Kingsway
London WC2B 6AH

www.simonsays.co.uk

Simon & Schuster Australia
Sydney

A CIP catalogue record for this book
is available from the British Library

ISBN: 978-1-84739-051-6

Designed by Dana Sloan
Printed and bound in Great Britain by
Cox & Wyman Ltd, Reading, Berks

ACKNOWLEDGMENTS

WITH SPECIAL APPRECIATION

Bob Bender, George Cukor, Federico Fellini, Alfred Hitchcock, Robert Lantz, David Rosenthal, Isabella Rossellini, and Roberto Rossellini.

WITH APPRECIATION

Michael Accordino, Robert Anderson, Claudio Angelini, Enrica Antonioni, Michelangelo Antonioni, Amelia Antonucci, Dennis Aspland, Jeanine Basinger, Peter Becker, Marcella Berger, Sidney Bernstein, David Brown, Kay Brown, Charles W. Bush, Jack Cardiff, Jerry Carlson, Fred Chase, Joseph Cotten, Gypsy da Silva, I. A. L. Diamond, Stanley Donen, Lisa Drew, Mark Ekman, Douglas Fairbanks, Jr., Vera Fairbanks, Jean Firstenberg, Marie Florio, Joe Franklin, Steve Friedeman, Bob Gazzale, John Gielgud, Farley Granger, Cary Grant, Tracey Guest, Dick Guttman, Robert Haller, Harry Haun, Paul Henreid, Arthur Hiller, Pat Hitchcock, Christopher Isherwood, Maria Cooper Janis, Peter Johnson, Alexander Kordonsky, John Landis, Ted Landry, Henri Langlois, Arthur Laurents, Madeleine LeBeau, Johanna Li, Pia Lindstrom, Norman Lloyd, Sidney Lumet, Groucho Marx, Giulietta

Masina, Kevin McCarthy, Mary Merson, Sylvia Miles, Liza Minnelli, Vincente Minnelli, Jeremiah Newton, Arthur Novell, Gregory Peck, Anthony Quinn, Michael Redgrave, Leni Riefenstahl, Robert Rosen, Gil Rossellini, Isotta Ingrid Rossellini, Renzo Rossellini, Victoria Rossellini, Lars Schmidt, Martin Scorsese, Daniel Selznick, Irene Mayer Selznick, Sidney Sheldon, Joe Sirola, Dana Sloan, Liz Smith, John Springer, Jeff Stafford, Rip Torn, Jonah Tully, Paavo Turtiainen, Brian Ulicky, Liv Ullmann, King Vidor, Herman G. Weinberg, Tennessee Williams, Will Willoughby, Fay Wray, William Wyler, and Michael York.

The Academy of Motion Picture Arts and Sciences, the American Film Institute, Anthology Film Archives, the British Film Institute, the Cinémathèque Française, City College of New York, the Criterion Collection, the Film Society of Lincoln Center, illy, the Italian Cultural Institute of New York City, the Museum of Modern Art, the New York Public Library for the Performing Arts, the Potsdam Museum Archives, Turner Classic Movies, UCLA Department of Theater, Film, and Television, and the Jeanine Basinger Collection at Wesleyan University.

To Ingrid

CONTENTS

INGRID

"My mum *had* to tell the truth. It was some kind of compulsion, even an obsession. We did not consider it a lie, well not exactly, if someone called us who we didn't want to speak with, and we asked Mama to say we weren't there.

"She didn't want to do it, and in the end, she told the caller that we *were* there. Her face flushed, and sometimes she blushed as she said we didn't want to speak to the person. It was really funny. Well, actually, it *wasn't* so funny.

"We children learned quickly. Our mother might be Ingrid Bergman, one of the most famous actresses in the world, who could say anything onstage or in a film, but she wasn't an actress in our house."

—ISABELLA ROSSELLINI

PROLOGUE

Ingrid Bergman was not a person who cared about fur, but as she told me, "My experiences with fur, you might say, tell the story of my life.

"The story of fur and me is like one of those films you see about an overcoat and all of the people it belonged to, or a tuxedo that starts out in glory and falls on hard times, or even the yellow Rolls-Royce which starred in one of my films.

"As a little girl, I posed for my father's pictures of me in my mother's fur coat, but I never gave it a thought. I lived in a country where just about everyone had some kind of fur coat. I didn't get cold easily and I never needed fur. The reason, I think, most of the girls I knew looked forward to having their first fur coat was because when you got one, it meant you were grown up.

"I loved my childhood, and I did not think much about growing up. I lived in the present. My father was my best friend, and I only wanted everything to stay the same." Everything did not stay the same, however, and when she was twelve, Ingrid's father died.

About to be twenty-one and using money her careful and caring father had left in trust for her, Ingrid moved into her first apartment, all her own. She was "thrilled" by the increased independence the apartment represented. "It was like being able to fly. Even if you don't *want* to fly, it's nice to know you're free to try."

Ingrid especially liked the privacy, much superior to that offered by her room in her strict Uncle Otto's home, with his wife, Aunt Hulda, and Ingrid's five cousins. She did not mind being alone some of the time. In fact, she said she rather liked it and was pleased to find that she enjoyed her own company.

With the earnings from her film work in Stockholm, the first money she ever had earned, teenage Ingrid bought a leopard coat and a used wind-up gramophone, "not the most practical of purchases," she told me, "but not the *least* practical, either. I think that best describes *me*."

For her twenty-first birthday, Petter Lindström (later Lindstrom), who had become Ingrid's fiancé, gave her a fox stole. "It was what fashionable ladies of the time were wearing," she continued, "quite in vogue at the Grand Hotel in Stockholm, which was where Petter and I had our first date. With him, it was the first time I had ever been inside the Grand Hotel, and there were ladies with fox stoles.

"I don't know if you've ever seen one, but it was a small fur stole which, like a scarf, you wore around your neck. The foxes were biting their own tails, and their open glass eyes stared at you.

"Now I find the style ugly and I am appalled by it, but when the package arrived and I opened it, I almost fainted from joy. All alone in the room, I squealed gleefully. As soon as I put it on, I loved it. It was the most wonderful gift I had ever received. It was like Petter's arms around me. The stole was the height of fashion, quite the rage at that moment, and it was for me a symbol of my being grown up and even sophisticated.

"Of course, I wouldn't be living alone very long. Soon, I would be married to Petter and living with him. I couldn't wait for that moment. I knew I couldn't live without him, and this stole was the token of how great his love for me was.

"I ran to the phone to tell Petter how much I loved his gift, and in my enthusiasm—I had great energy and enthusiasm at that time—I tripped and broke my ankle.

"I had to go to the hospital, where I spent that night. My ankle hurt, but I wasn't much aware of it because I was so happy. I took the box with my fur stole with me, and I hid it under the bed. Then, when I was alone during the night, I took it out from under the bed and put the stole around my shoulders, over my nightgown. I felt so warm and so happy, I sat up most of the night, caressing it and feeling close to Petter.

"I was anxious for my ankle to heal, so I could go dancing with Petter, wearing my stole.

"When I went to America under contract to David O. Selznick, David was surprised, shocked, when I arrived at a party at his home and left my cloth coat on the bed with the pile of fur coats of the other women guests. David said, 'Is that all you have, that cloth coat? Don't you have a mink coat?' I said, 'No, but it's easy to find my coat on the bed when it's time to leave.'

"David said, 'You are going to be an important star. You *must* have a mink coat.' I did not feel that wearing a mink was a measure of my success in my work," but Ingrid went shopping anyway.

She found mink coats very expensive. She was tempted to purchase the least expensive one. She certainly was not going to buy the most expensive because, as she told me, "I wouldn't have felt right spending David's money that way." She need not have worried, because Selznick had no thought of paying for it.

The first time she wore the coat was when she was invited to the next party at the Selznick home. She took it off and put it on a bed already piled high with mink coats. She wondered how she would find hers, especially since she would probably be one of the first to leave. She didn't know many people, and while Irene Mayer Selznick, David's wife, would certainly come by to make her feel welcome and introduce her to people, Irene *was* the hostess, who had her duties and responsibilities to all the guests and couldn't spend long with any one guest.

Ingrid didn't mind sitting alone and watching the party. It was, in fact, what she enjoyed most. She enjoyed the atmosphere of the party, but without the responsibility of having to speak with people. It made her feel "shy" to speak with strangers, and she had at that time less than perfect confidence in her English. She did, however, begin to feel "a little uncomfortable" when people noticed her sitting alone and stared, or worse, when she believed they felt compelled to speak with her.

When it came time to find her coat, she looked at the piles of mink on the bed, but she had no trouble finding hers. It didn't look at all like the others. It was a different color with no sheen, and it looked rather thin.

As she left, Selznick said to her, "What kind of fur is that?"

"David, it's the mink you said I should buy. Don't you like it?" Seeing the look on his face, she knew the answer.

"You must return *that* coat, Ingrid," Selznick chided. "If you wear a coat like that, people will think you aren't a success, and then you *won't* be. Give that coat right back to the store. No one will know you've worn it."

But someone would know she had worn it. Ingrid would know. She had worn the coat, so, of course, she could not return it to the store.

She sold it to a used fur store, taking quite a loss. The eventual purchaser never knew how little used it had been, having spent most of its life out in the world, one night, on the bed of David O. Selznick.

Selznick sent Ingrid as a Christmas gift a package from a well-known furrier. She opened it, expecting to find a mink coat, the sort in which Selznick could be proud of her. The coat was Persian lamb.

Ingrid never quite understood what that meant.

When she left Hollywood and arrived in Rome to meet Roberto Rossellini, he said, "Don't you have a mink coat?" She admitted she didn't have one. "Roberto was surprised," she said. "He told me that *all* the Hollywood stars have mink coats.

"That Christmas, *he* gave me one. I hadn't told him that I didn't have a mink coat because I didn't really want one, but this one was from Roberto, so of course I had to keep it. There was a card in the pocket which said, 'With all my love for always, Roberto.' I decided to keep the card in the pocket, always.

"Every time I wore the coat, I would check the pocket a few times to reassure myself that the card was pushed deep down. I was very careful not to let the card get wet if I wore the coat in the rain.

"Then, one day, the card wasn't there. I found a hole in the pocket and checked the lining, but the card was gone. I think I liked the card *more* than the coat, and I felt a little superstitious about it, as if somehow if I lost the card, I would no longer keep all of Roberto's love, always. And so it was. I did not keep all of it, but I know I kept some of it.

"I didn't wear the coat much. One didn't need a fur coat in Rome. Sometimes Roberto would say to me, 'Don't you want to wear your mink coat?' and I would say, 'Oh, no. I'm too warm,' while really I might be a little cold, but I could never say I didn't love the coat he gave me. Then, he forgot about it.

"Even when Roberto and I ended our marriage, I still felt married to the coat. I couldn't annul my relationship with the coat, though I didn't wear it, and it took up quite a space in my closet. I kept it even after Lars, my third husband, gave me a fur-trimmed coat.

"After many years, I decided to line a raincoat with my mink coat. It was a great success. The fur didn't show much, and I was warm. I thought that one day one of my daughters with Roberto might like it.

"For her twenty-first birthday, I gave the raincoat I'd lined with Roberto's mink to Isabella, who hesitated. I said to her, 'Don't worry. It's all been dead for twenty-five years.' "

Isabella, who in the twenty-first century still owns the coat, told me, "My children think I should bury it in the backyard, in our pet cemetery."

INTRODUCTION

I'll be Mother," Ingrid Bergman said. She picked up the ornate silver teapot and poured.

I was having tea at director George Cukor's Cordell Drive home in Hollywood with Cukor and Ingrid Bergman. Cukor had directed such films as *The Philadelphia Story, A Star Is Born, My Fair Lady,* and *Gaslight,* the film he did with Ingrid Bergman. There was a plate of rich butter cookies on the tea table, which indicated Cukor knew Ingrid well.

Cukor said, "The girl always likes to make herself useful. She has such good manners. Usually. I remember once, when we first met, she talked back to me."

"Oh, George," Ingrid pouted, "I never, *never* would have been rude to you."

Cukor explained.

"I had my way of chatting with actors between takes, giving them little bits of advice, perhaps a bit of encouragement to help them stay involved. On *Gaslight,* I offered some tidbit of un-thought-out wisdom to Miss Bergman here, and she gave me *such a look.* What a look! Then, quite unemotionally, she said to me, 'You already told me that.'

"I said, 'So I did.'

" 'Well, I must be more careful with this young Swedish girl,' I thought.

"Then, I rethought it.

"No, she'll have to be more careful with *me*. She'll have to get used to the way *I* work. She did. And we became the greatest friends."

Ingrid said, "Yes, that's true, except I never said what you said."

"You see?" he said to us. "She hasn't changed a bit.

"Ingrid was not overawed by me, then or now. No reason why she should have been. But some were. I suppose because I was their director."

Cukor said it to me, "Can you imagine that our girl here made films in five languages?"

"And I spoke a bit of Chinese, too, in *The Inn of the Sixth Happiness.*"

He asked her how she managed to speak so many languages so well.

She laughed. "By not speaking them so well. I admit I am very fluent in Swedish. I believe I have been able to speak the other languages as well as I do because I have such a fervent desire to communicate."

I asked her in what language she thought. She answered, "I think in the language I am speaking in. It's the only way."

"And when you are alone and thinking by yourself?" I asked.

"English. It seems strange. Everyone would expect me to think in Swedish, my first language, but from the time I learned English, it became my thinking language. I just found it worked better for me."

Cukor said he could never learn a foreign language because he was too shy. Ingrid was astounded.

"*You*, George? I would have said you never had a shy moment in your life. As for shyness, I am the shyest person in the world. When I was a girl, I was famous for my blushes. If anyone spoke to me or even just looked at me, I changed color. But that was when they looked at Ingrid. Acting, I could be someone else. That someone else had no need to blush. That character was thrilled to have an entire audience watching, even millions."

"I can understand that, my dear. Even as director, I have to play a part, and going into the part of the director allows me to say things that, as George, I would be too self-conscious to say. My public person and my private person are always both there."

"Mine, too," Ingrid agreed. "My private self and my public self are one and the same. They both love being an actress. I feel most like myself when I am playing someone else.

"But sometimes my private self gets in the way by being so very much concerned with finding and holding on to love."

"Looking for love is tricky business," Cukor concluded, "like whipping a carousel horse."

Ingrid said, "The way I see myself in my personal life was best expressed for me by Jean Cocteau: 'The dreamer is the guest of his dreams.'"

Ingrid mentioned to Cukor that he had influenced the choice of a name for one of her twin daughters. "I don't think I ever told you, but I remembered that you had said you liked the name of the French actress Annabella. Do you remember, George?"

He did not appear to remember.

"I was trying to think of a name that began with an I, and the name Isabella popped into my mind. That was how my Isabella got her name."

Cukor, obviously pleased, said, "Well, that makes me rather a godfather. Even if Annabella didn't start with an I, I take full credit."

"You were a godfather to all your actors," Ingrid said. "You always loved actors."

Cukor corrected her. "Not every one of them."

"Roberto [Rossellini] did not like actors," Ingrid continued. "At the beginning, I didn't know that. When he first told me, I didn't believe him. Later, I found out it was true."

"I'm sure that it wasn't true about you," Cukor said.

"That was what I assumed," Ingrid said. "Maybe in the beginning, it *was* true that he didn't mean me. Later, I'm not certain.

"When I worked with my husband, I didn't wish to be thought of by him, or anyone, as his wife. I wanted to be just one of the actors. It was a problem, though, for me that there weren't many actors there. Professional actors, I mean.

"When I first saw *Open City,* I was so thrilled that Roberto was able to get such natural performances, not actor-like performances. I learned on *Stromboli* how he did it. He didn't use actors. His actors weren't actors, only people, well selected. And he had to film them quickly before he ran out of film and money, which he was always short of."

Cukor said, "You adjusted so well to your life in Italy, but there must have been something you missed. . . ."

"Many things, George, but I'll tell you one you would never guess."

"I won't even try."

"Corn on the cob. When I first saw people in America eating it, they looked like they were playing harmonicas. It was so funny-looking, it made me laugh. Then I tried it and I learned right away how to do it. It tasted so much better that way, but it tasted best eaten in private with a bib or a towel, so I didn't ruin my clothes."

After we had tea, Cukor, knowing that Ingrid loved champagne, opened a bottle. We clicked glasses, and Ingrid said, "Here's lookin' at you, kids."

"That little film of yours was done by another Hungarian, Curtiz," Cukor said. "I'm Hungarian, you know. Anyway, my family was."

"Would you believe, George," Ingrid said, "that Bogart and Paul [Henreid] and especially me believed that *Casablanca* was a little picture, a waste of our time?"

"I wish someone had asked *me* to waste my time on *Casablanca*," Cukor said.

"Do you know what I especially love about you, Ingrid, my dear? I can sum it up as your naturalness. The camera loves your beauty, your acting, and your individuality. A star must have individuality. It makes you a great star. A great star."

"I think film is in my genes," Ingrid said. "I *love* the camera. My father had a photographic shop in Stockholm, and from the day I was born, he took pictures of me with a still camera, and movies, too. Sometimes I feel the movie camera is my friend or even a relative.

"I believe my father well might have gone into Swedish films had he lived longer. He might have become a famous cinematographer. He saw unlimited potential in those early cameras. When he used his camera, he and the camera became one.

"George, you worked with Greta Garbo. Can you tell me why she retired from films when she was so young? I could never do that. My vision of myself is very, very, very old in a film playing the oldest woman in the world, or on the stage in a children's theater, cackling in the part of an old witch. Witches are such great fun to do. You're never too old to be a witch. And no one can accuse a witch of overacting."

"In answer to your question, I don't think Miss Garbo ever retired," Cukor said. "That implies a real decision. I don't believe she did that. I think she just waited, and she waited too long. She had grown accustomed to being in great demand, but when the demands were softer, she didn't notice. She wanted the perfect part, but Ninotchkas didn't grow on trees. That's a film my friend Ernst Lubitsch made that *I* would like to have made. 'Garbo laughs' is how it was advertised. Well, of course, she laughed, and of course, she cried. No porcelain figure she!

"I think she was sorry she didn't make more films, but she thought she wanted a holiday. We've all been tired and thought we wanted a long vacation when all we needed was a few days off, but didn't know it.

"I think Miss Garbo wasn't hungry enough. She didn't *need* to work. She'd been a very poor girl in Stockholm, and she had not dreamed big. Then, everything rather came to her. Because of her natural attributes, we all adored her and wanted to help her.

"She earned a lot of money, and it was well invested for her. When she went shopping on Rodeo Drive, it wasn't for dresses or for jewelry; it was for Rodeo Drive. She owned top real estate, fine art, and jewels, too. She didn't *have* to spend much money because everyone wanted to pay her way. But she could be very picky. She was also a bit lazy, I suspect.

"She used to tell me she was thinking about returning to the screen, and I feel she *was* thinking about it. But that's where it stopped. She was doing her thinking on someone's yacht.

"I've always meant to tell you," Cukor said to Ingrid, "I think you were marvelous in *A Woman's Face* in Sweden. When I was making the film here with Joan Crawford, I watched your performance several times."

"George, is it true you thought of using Hedy Lamarr for my part in *Gaslight*?"

"No, I *never* did. From the moment I came to it, I never heard that. I understand Miss Lamarr thought so, but that was before I came to the project.

"I don't know if I made it clear at the time how much I thought of your performance in *Gaslight*. I felt certain you would receive an Oscar nomination at least, and I believed you were going to take home Oscar, which you did."

"You were always encouraging, and I loved receiving my first Oscar," Ingrid smiled, savoring the memory. "It was wonderful, and I owe it to you, and to Charles Boyer and Joe Cotten, and others. So I wouldn't want to give it back, but I do think the Oscar really goes to the part you play more than to the actor or actress. I was lucky to be given the part that won the Oscar."

"The truth is," Cukor said, "a director wins an Oscar for a writer's script and actors' performances. Who helped you most to become an actress, and how did you learn to act?"

"The first part is a simple answer, George. My father. He loved me, he loved the arts, and he constantly encouraged me. I don't know where I'd be without him, but it surely wouldn't be here in your beautiful home today. As for *how*, I began as a little girl, studying acting by watching people. I always felt it was the best way."

Cukor mentioned a book I was writing, about people who loved their work and who did not work just for fame or money, but who did what they did because the creative work was what they *wanted* to do. Ingrid said that was what she really wanted to do. "Me. That's me. I'm one of those. I love to act. I'm never happier. I would pay to do it. Wouldn't you, George? Pay to direct?"

"I'd have to think about that," Cukor said, and then hesitated a few seconds. "I've thought. How much would I have to pay?"

I was introduced to Ingrid Bergman by George Cukor to talk about plans for the Friends of the Cinémathèque Française, an organization in America that could help its founder, Henri Langlois, in his film preservation work. While the Cinémathèque Française was based in Paris, it was appreciated worldwide. Both Ingrid and Cukor were passionate about film preservation.

Ingrid became an early member of the board along with Lillian Gish, Gloria Swanson, Otto Preminger, Fritz Lang, Alfred Hitchcock, King Vidor, Vincente Minnelli, Darryl F. Zanuck, and, of course, George Cukor.

She believed that her films, such as *Gaslight, Casablanca, The Bells of St. Mary's*, would not have problems in being preserved, so that people in the future would have no difficulty seeing them. "We certainly don't have to worry about *Casablanca* being preserved," she said.

She felt, however, that the films of her former husband, Roberto

Rossellini, were threatened and would have great difficulty surviving. "They were 'art films,'" she said, "and so did not have the big-money support and rich champions to look after them. And Roberto was not a diplomat, especially after the film was completed. There were often difficult relationships, bitterness, court cases . . ."

Langlois and Mary Merson at the Cinémathèque Française greatly respected the work of Rossellini. Langlois, calling him "a monumental talent," wanted to safeguard not just the feature films, but the documentaries and every scrap of film cut or discarded from anything Rossellini had ever done. Mary Merson had commented on the man rather than the director. "No woman who met him could resist him, and she had to fall under his spell, helpless."

Ingrid said, "Roberto could not have had greater film fans than those two, but they were always without money. *Rome: Open City* and *Paisan* will always be there. But what about the others?"

"We don't have to sell ourselves on what we're already sold on," Cukor said. "And I don't think we have to sell anyone. We just have to let them know what we're doing."

"And soon. Immediately," Ingrid said. "Films are dying every minute, especially my poor Roberto's work. I'm not worried about my big Hollywood movies. And even my Swedish films are, I understand, safe in Sweden, but the films of Roberto . . . *Rome: Open City* and *Paisan* are in the archives, but maybe some of the prints aren't so very good. The other films, the ones we made together, and all of the others of his, they have been brutally cut by other people. Roberto wasn't powerful enough to get the final cut."

As Ingrid was about to leave, I said that I was so pleased to have met her. She responded, "I feel sometimes people are disappointed when they meet me because they are expecting Ilsa from Casablanca, and instead they get Ingrid from Stockholm.

"I suppose some of me was in Ilsa, because an actress does draw upon her feelings and her experiences when she brings to life a character like Ilsa." She added wistfully, "Ilsa never grows old, nor fat."

Ingrid looked down at the cookie plate, seeing that it was empty. "Oh, George! I've eaten all of your cookies."

"All the better for me," Cukor said.

After she had left, Cukor said, "She has a great sense of fantasy. Sometimes this works in her favor—in the films and on the stage.

"In real life, it may have been her undoing. She has such an innocence and openness to life. She's very trusting. She's a romantic who fell in love intensely.

"Garbo was the most artificial actress anyone could imagine, a style that came from silent films, somewhat from the theater, and it was also her own unique persona. It was well suited to her and to her time until her time was up.

"I liked Garbo very much as an actress and a person, but I loved Ingrid personally and professionally. I would use the word 'stylized' to characterize Garbo; as for Ingrid, she was a natural.

"Three strokes of a hairbrush, and her shining hair was perfect. She washed it herself. No other actress I've ever known would or could do that. Nothing about her was ever 'fixed,' because she had been so blessed that everything about her was perfect."

Cukor had directed Garbo in *Camille* and *Two-Faced Woman*, and she often visited him. After her retirement, Garbo sometimes asked Cukor if he thought she should make another film. He refrained from encouraging her even if he might have been the director. "It would have had to be entirely her decision because it was almost impossible to attain the heights to which she had previously ascended and occupied as her due.

"Garbo was considered very aloof. Everyone agreed, although I must say she wasn't ever aloof with me. It was her personality, true, but there was more to it than that. Take Robert Taylor, who really was a very good Armand to her Camille. He was so handsome and, especially, he was so young, which made believable romantic foolishness. They were always casting Armand too old, which made it hard to swallow.

"Garbo did everything to help Armand for the film, but she didn't seem to want to know Robert Taylor. Well, he was a bit crushed, but she had her reasons, which worked for her.

"Perhaps it was a holdover idea from silents. She liked to imbue her co-star with romantic qualities and to make up stories about him that would help her see the person in the right way. Garbo didn't want to know the real Bob, just in case he might say something like, 'Miss Garbo, it's such an honor to be here with you. I've always admired your work,' et cetera. Ugh! Worse yet, he could have added that he watched her when he was a boy.

"Ingrid, exactly the opposite, knew the names not just of co-stars, but of every bit player and every technician. She knew the names of their children, and she shopped for holiday remembrances or sometimes gave away her knitting. I, myself, have two scarves which I wear, one at a time."

When Ingrid and I continued our conversations in a room at the Beverly Hills Hotel a few days later, she said the first subject she wanted to talk about was Roberto Rossellini and *Open City* and *Paisan,* and the other films she made with him, and that whatever I wrote she hoped I would talk about him, too, and his masterpieces. "He was a very great director, one of the greatest," she said, "and I hope that one day he will be more generally appreciated, as he deserves to be."

Then, her serious tone gave way to a more playful, even mischievous one. "Would you like to see a trick?" she asked me.

She took hold of the tablecloth and pulled it out from under the dishes. I was glad I hadn't poured the coffee yet. The water in the glasses, however, hadn't spilled.

"It's just a trick, you know," she explained. "The important thing is that you do it with certainty. If you think you will break the dishes, you will. Fear makes your hand unsteady."

I asked her how many dishes she had broken before she mastered the trick.

"Not many. I learn quickly. I never break any dishes anymore. Once this kind of trick is mastered, it is for forever, like riding a bicycle or swimming.

"Tell George [Cukor]. He'll think it's funny. Tell him how well I did it, and that I promise I will never do it at *his* house. His dishes are too beautiful. And he doesn't have the right kind of table."

One

ᖗᖘᖙ

INGRID AND SWEDEN

The story of Ingrid Bergman began in Stockholm with the romance of her parents.

Justus Samuel Bergman was born in 1871, the thirteenth of fourteen children. His father, Johan Bergman, was a music teacher and organist in Kronoberg, a southern Swedish province. Justus left home at fifteen, supporting himself at jobs in shops while studying painting and singing. In 1889, he went to America, staying with an aunt in Chicago. When he returned to Sweden, he worked in art supply shops, where at the time photography materials were sold, and Justus became fascinated by the new medium.

He liked to take his easel with him into a Stockholm park and paint. It was while he was there one afternoon in 1900 that he met the lovely Frieda Adler, known as Friedel, only sixteen and from Kiel, Germany, who stopped to see what he was painting. She was visiting Stockholm with her parents.

The young girl was impressed by Justus Bergman's work and by the artist himself. He was attracted to Friedel. Justus, who spoke enough German to communicate with her, was almost thirteen years older than she.

Friedel came again and again to watch Justus paint. She loved his work, and she realized that she loved him. He knew he loved her. As it came time for Friedel to leave and return to Germany, Justus pleaded his position with her father.

For her German parents, however, he had no position at all, nothing to offer their daughter. She was too young to marry, and this was certainly not a worthy match. He was too old for her. He was a foreigner. He had no bank account of consequence. He didn't have a flat of his own, but was staying with relatives. He didn't have the right kind of family. As an unsuccessful artist, he offered practically no potential for supporting their daughter and the children she would have. It was absolutely impossible.

It was, however, *not* impossible—only very difficult. Justus gave up his dream of being an artist and became a Sunday painter instead of a seven-days-a-week artist. Now passionate about photography, he opened a photography shop, which became a very successful business. He scrimped, saved, and led a meager personal existence in order to put everything into a bank account.

During those years, which seemed endlessly long to Friedel, she waited faithfully, wearing Justus's ring on a chain around her neck, hidden under the jabot of her blouse. At night, she wore it outside her nightgown. When her parents discovered that she was secretly wearing Justus's ring, they were extremely displeased. They were determined that she should have a prosperous husband, as did her two sisters.

At the end of more than seven years, Justus produced his bankbook, and Friedel's parents could not help but be impressed. They relented and consented to the wedding, which took place in 1907.

Friedel went to live in Stockholm, where it was *she* who was a foreigner. She and Justus were wondrously happy. Also artistically talented, Friedel painted for pleasure and hand-colored photographs for customers.

They hoped for children to complete their perfect happiness. When they learned that Friedel was going to have a child, they were overjoyed. They had been married a little over a year. Their first child, however, died at birth. Four years later, their second child died after living a few weeks. After that, there was a certain sadness that would creep into the expression of Friedel, and she took on an aspect of maturity that replaced her girlish quality. Each time, Justus was disconsolate over the loss of a dearly desired child.

Then, in 1915, Ingrid was born, a beautiful healthy baby. She was named after the Swedish royal princess, who was age two. Her parents were ecstatic. Justus Bergman began taking photographs of their baby from the day she was born. "I was perhaps the most photographed child in Scandinavia," Ingrid commented to me. Renting an early movie camera to film her in motion, he took moving pictures of her sitting on the ample lap of her proud and happy mother. Friedel had grown plumper.

When Ingrid was two, Justus filmed the beautiful little girl who loved the camera as she walked with her mother.

Then Friedel became ill. What was at first diagnosed as a simple stomach ailment turned out to be a serious liver problem. Ingrid was sent to stay with an aunt and uncle, so she wouldn't see her mother in pain, suffering so terribly. There was no respite from the increasing agony, and then from the grief when Friedel died.

Ingrid returned to live with her father. Aunt Ellen, who lived nearby, visited daily to help her brother with the care of his daughter and his home. She sometimes stayed with them.

"I had a wonderful childhood," Ingrid remembered. "I believed that my life with my father was perfect. He was everything to me, and I was everything to him. People would say, 'She must miss her mother terribly.' But I didn't, because for me she was very abstract. She was a photograph. I couldn't remember her as a living person. She was always frozen in a picture frame.

"Sometimes I would see children with their mothers who didn't seem to love their mothers the way I would have loved mine if I could have known her. I knew I would have loved her very much, and she would have loved me very much. I knew my father loved her, and he missed her terribly.

"She was beautiful. I could see that in the photographs, and my father had told me what a wonderful person she was, how much she wanted me and wanted to stay with me, but she couldn't.

"Much later, I understood that I had been living with an ache, but it began so early and was so constant, I was not aware of it. It was just a part of me, missing my mother, and I assumed someday it would go away. I don't think it ever did, though it was covered over by many other feelings. One can only have so many active feelings at any time.

"When I was grown up and saw my mother move for the first time on film, at first it made me sadder to see her so full of life, as she was in the moving pictures taken by my father. Then, it made me happier. It enriched my life, because it gave me a precious image."

Ingrid is seen, at two, in her father's film, playing with her mother, and then alone, at three, putting flowers on her mother's grave.

The film was restored by David O. Selznick shortly after Ingrid's arrival in America. Learning that she had the film of her mother, he had had his best technicians prepare it, not only so that she could see it, but so that it would be preserved for her to see in future years.

"When Father took so many pictures, I remember him telling me that some of those young people he photographed would be famous one day, and he would have the photographs he took. Well, he took hundreds of photographs of me, but that was because I was his daughter, his only child. Also, I suppose I was photogenic, and I really did enjoy it. I liked posing for pictures, and it was an opportunity to be with my father, doing something which pleased him, which I wanted to do, and making him proud of me. I understood it must be something I was good at, and my father always gave me confidence. It was with my father that I learned to perform for the camera. The child in his photographs who became famous was his own daughter—me."

Every summer, Ingrid's father took her for a holiday in Hamburg with her German grandparents and her two aunts, Elsa and Luna, her mother's sisters. "My grandfather and grandmother were strict and there was no laughter," Ingrid said.

"I spent most of my time with my Aunt Mutti. Her name was really Elsa, but I called her Aunt Mutti. Mutti is a nickname for 'mother' in German. I was really calling her Aunt Mother, because she was the closest to a mother I knew.

"She had married a Frenchman who was very rich. He spent most of his time in the Caribbean where he had coffee plantations. Once he took their two sons with him, and one of them died of a tropical disease. She lived alone in their big house on the Alster, and her husband didn't come there much.

"Aunt Mutti was young and pretty, and she said she wished she had a little girl, like me. Her home was beautiful and luxurious, and I loved staying with her, but I was only truly happy when my father came for me.

"Aunt Mutti loved to shop, and she would dress up for the experience. She had the most beautiful clothes I had ever seen, and so many of them. I liked to look at them. And she loved accessories, shoes, purses, scarves, jewelry. She liked to have me wear one of my best dresses, always a dress she bought me. They were a little too grown-up and too stylish for my life in Stockholm, and too different from what the other girls in school wore. They weren't very practical dresses, but I don't think Aunt Mutti was very practical. But she *was* strong. She seemed very soft and feminine, but I think she was also very strong. Everyone looked at her when she did a promenade, because she was so beautiful. She was very funny and a good companion. She wasn't strict, but then there wasn't really much to be strict about with me because I only wanted to be a good girl, and I was.

"There was one thing she did sometimes that I didn't enjoy. It's when she had the saleswoman take out everything to show her and then after it was out and piled up, she said, 'Thank you. I don't see what I want,' and she left with me, and the saleswoman had to put back all those dresses and blouses and skirts and belts. She had tried so hard and then was totally rejected. I thought she must be very hurt. I silently made up my mind that when I had money and went shopping, I would always buy something, even if just a small thing. If I didn't find what I wanted, I could always buy something for a gift."

When Ingrid was nine, Greta Danielsson was employed by Justus to be Ingrid's governess. The year was 1924, and Ingrid's father was fifty-three. Greta was eighteen and really more of an older sister than a governess for Ingrid. She was a music student who dreamed of being an opera singer. Soon, the attractive eighteen-year-old music student was living there. Aunt Ellen, disapproving of the arrangement, stayed away from the apartment except on Sunday mornings when she came to take Ingrid to church.

"I liked Greta," Ingrid said. "No, I *loved* her.

"She had a wonderfully happy disposition and her company made my father happy. He loved me very much, but he was lonely, and he needed something more than just me.

"It was his nature to be a happy person, but after my mother died, he wasn't truly happy, but he always acted in good spirits for me. He was a brave man, and he wanted me to have a good childhood, which I did, until he got sick.

"Greta had a lovely singing voice, and she played the piano. Our house was filled with music. In the evening Greta played, and the three of us sang."

Justus, Greta, and Ingrid went swimming together in the summer. Greta loved the cinema and took Ingrid to see movies, especially romantic ones. Sometimes when they liked a film particularly well, they stayed and saw it again. Afterward they shared some special sweets at one of the local shops.

Ingrid, who felt shy with most people, never felt shy with Greta. It was wonderful for Ingrid to escape her shyness.

"When we all had dinner together, my father laughed more. He seemed so much happier, the three of us laughed all the time, sometimes at things that weren't very funny. Dinner was so much fun."

Greta would be giggling at the dinner table, and after a while, Ingrid noticed her father and Greta holding hands. Far from being jealous, Ingrid was delighted, though her aunts were not. They strongly disapproved of fifty-three-year-old Justus's "scandalous" relationship with a woman less than half his age.

"My family tried to turn me against Greta. They said she was a bad person, but I always defended her. They didn't dare say my father was a bad person, because they wouldn't have dared say that in front of me. They thought I should mind he was seeing someone after he had had such a wonderful wife, my mother, but my mother had died almost seven years before, and my father needed the love of someone besides his daughter."

Eventually, Aunt Ellen and Justus's other relatives prevailed, and Greta stopped living with Ingrid and her father. Since Greta studied voice at a nearby music school, she visited often with Ingrid and Justus.

When Greta moved out of Justus Bergman's home, she was greatly missed by Ingrid. Several years afterward, Ingrid learned from Greta that Justus had wanted to marry her, but she felt his family's opposition would make their life together too difficult.

• • •

When Ingrid was twelve, her father told her that he had stomach cancer. She didn't really understand what that meant, certainly not the full implications of what he was telling her. He showed her an X-ray and said that soon he would be unable to eat. Ingrid was certain he would find a cure.

He told her that he was going to Bavaria to see a doctor who had achieved miracles. Part of the reason her father left was he didn't want his young daughter to see him suffering.

Greta went with him and stayed with him through the terrible ordeal. Ingrid said, "I loved her for that."

Justus Bergman returned to Stockholm to say goodbye to his home, his friends, his family, and especially to his young daughter, for whose future he had tried to provide, as best he could.

Aunt Ellen and Uncle Otto, and Otto's wife, Hulda, as well as others in Justus's family, felt that it was wrong to permit Greta to be there at Justus's bedside.

Friedel's sister, Elsa Adler, "Aunt Mutti," came from Germany to be there, and she ordered the family to permit Greta to be at the bedside. It was what Justus wanted. It was what Ingrid wanted. Greta sat at one side of the bed, Ingrid at the other. Justus was able to see them, and say goodbye to the people he loved most, to the two people who loved *him* most. Justus Bergman died on July 29, 1929, at the age of fifty-eight.

"My father was a sentimental person, and he believed that there was more to life than any of us could really know. He was not a formally religious person, but he was spiritual in his own way.

"He told me that he had felt a great sense of loss when his father died. He always carried with him a small photograph of his father, and when he was troubled and didn't know what to do about something, he would consult the picture and try to get help from his father, to know what his father would have advised him to do. He said it didn't always work, but sometimes he could sense, almost hear, what his father would have said to him. It always made him feel better, and he drew strength from the picture and his father's love.

"Though I didn't carry a photograph of my father, I always had the picture of him in my head. There was no day I didn't think of him and share my triumphs or my failures, my joys and my sorrows with him."

After the death of Ingrid's father, Greta disappeared from Ingrid's world. A few years later, by chance, Ingrid met her and learned that her friend was studying music and singing, and working as a film extra.

"It was no surprise," Ingrid told me, "because Greta was *so* beautiful. It was easy for her to fit into all kinds of films, except where her beauty was a problem, because it called too much attention to her. The people making the film couldn't have their beautiful extra be the focus of all the attention.

"Greta told me about her work. She would be filmed in a nightclub, at a party, or in a grand hotel. It fascinated me, and I asked her if she could arrange for me to visit the set one day. She did better than that. She got me a day's work. Only later did I understand that it was easier for her to get me a job as an extra than it was for an extra to get permission to bring a visitor as a guest on the set.

"When I arrived for my first day, there were several young women there, older than I. I was fifteen. We were told what our parts were. We were to look sick, hungry, and very cold, practically frozen. None of us had any lines.

"There was a lot of time and attention put into our makeup. It was not a glamorous makeup job. Far from it. Some of us were white-faced, like we had frozen to death. I was done in yellowish pasty makeup, which photographed as though I still had a little life in me. I learned then something about how much preparation was necessary for films.

"As we were called to do our scene, girls lost in the snowstorm, I wondered if I should shudder as the camera was on me.

"I thought of asking my question, but the camera was rolling, and within a few minutes, it was all over.

"We were released and told we could leave. But I didn't want to leave. It was so exciting, I wanted to stay in that world. There was so much to learn, and I wanted to know everything about making movies. I wanted to stay, and I found the answer. I left my yellow makeup on, so everyone would think I was still waiting in my makeup to do a scene. Why would anyone else be wandering about with a yellow face?

"When I left the building, I received ten kronor. I wore my yellow face all the way home, as I walked through the streets. I wore it like a badge because it meant I was a film actress, if on the bottom rung.

"I was clutching my first money I had ever earned in my life. Imagine! I had been paid to do what I loved.

"It may sound pretentious, but I wanted to do something worthwhile with my life. But I didn't have a calling, except this one thing, acting. People have told me that it *was* important, that entertaining people, bringing them pleasure, was worthwhile.

"What made it hard to believe was because I loved it so much, that somehow doing it seemed selfish to me."

After the death of her father, Ingrid went to live with her Aunt Ellen, who was conscientious in carrying out her responsibilities toward her brother's daughter, though without the warmth or joy Ingrid had known with her father.

Ellen did not leave her upper-story apartment very much except to shop for groceries and to attend church services every Sunday, to which she always took Ingrid.

"I wasn't very close to Aunt Ellen in life, but I became very close to her in death," Ingrid told me. "I held her in my arms as she died." It was a vivid and unhappy memory that haunted Ingrid throughout her life.

"I had only been living with her for about six months after my father died. Aunt Ellen, my father's sister, had never married and was very religious. The most terrible thing that could have happened in her life would have been for someone to think I was *her* child, since she was an unmarried lady. She was very prim and proper, but kindly.

"I hadn't adjusted at all to my father's death. I never really did. I think of him as my guardian angel watching over me."

One night Ingrid was alone with Aunt Ellen, and her aunt began having trouble breathing. She asked for Ingrid to read to her from the Bible. Then, as her breathing became even more difficult, she sent Ingrid to the phone to call the family for help.

Ingrid called her Uncle Otto, and his son, her cousin Bill, answered. She was supposed to throw the key down from the upper-story window when he came, as they had always arranged it, but she panicked and forgot to open the window so she could hear him calling. Ingrid couldn't understand why it was taking so long for him to come and help. He lived only a few blocks away. Then she remembered and threw down the key to her waiting cousin. It was too late.

"For months afterward, I relived Aunt Ellen's death in a dream," she said. "In my dream, everything happened exactly as it had in reality, but I saved Aunt Ellen. I opened the window and heard cousin Bill calling. I threw the key down in time, and my cousin or my Uncle Otto came running up the stairs and rushed in. Then, the dream became confused, but my aunt was taken to the hospital.

"When I would wake up, I looked around, and I saw I wasn't at Aunt Ellen's. I was in the bedroom at Uncle Otto's, and I hadn't been successful in saving Aunt Ellen, after all.

"I wanted desperately to be able to go back in time and throw the key out the window sooner, but there was no way I could do that. Though they all reassured me that there was nothing anyone could

have done, my head believed them and knew there was nothing anyone could have done. But, in my heart, I wondered. . . ."

After the death of Aunt Ellen, Ingrid went to live with Uncle Otto and
Aunt Hulda, and their children, three much older male cousins and
two girls closer to her own age. Margit was a little older than Ingrid,
and Britt, a little younger. Britt and Ingrid immediately became best
friends.

As young girls, they swam together and took evening walks in
downtown Stockholm, where it was perfectly safe for them to be out
alone. Ingrid was given the best room in the house, while the others
had to share rooms.

Aunt Hulda held the family together, and their previously strained
economic position was helped by the arrival of Ingrid. Not only did
she have her inheritance, but Uncle Otto took over the management
of her father's profitable photography shop. In her private room,
Ingrid was able to have her mother's piano and her father's desk and
photographs, and paintings by her father.

Since Hulda was dedicated to the education of her three sons for
professional careers, it was not a home with time for gaiety, and there
was no semblance of the kind of joyful childhood Ingrid had experienced with her father.

The practical Uncle Otto and Aunt Hulda believed that Ingrid
should prepare to become a secretary or a salesgirl while waiting to
become a wife. They did not approve of her ambition to be an actress.

For Otto Bergman, there was disgrace attached to being an
actress, but she was so determined, he couldn't deny her the chance.
He was Ingrid's guardian and responsible for the money her father
had provided for her future. Her future had become the present, and
Uncle Otto knew his brother would want Ingrid to have her chance.
The difference, however, was that Ingrid knew her father would have

given her many, many chances, and he would have devoted himself to her studying acting, dance, elocution, whatever it took for her to win a place at the Royal Dramatic Theater School.

Uncle Otto exacted a promise from his niece, which created tremendous pressure. If she went to the competition and failed to win a place for which so many were competing, then she would not try again. Ingrid felt she had to promise. She believed she would succeed. She had to. Failure would mean the end of any meaningful life. It was too terrible even to contemplate.

The Royal Dramatic Theater School required each actor to submit three pieces which he or she could do. The judges would then select two of those. If an individual failed either test, a big brown envelope, the sign of failure, would be awaiting the aspiring individual at the door.

Ingrid had guessed that the other young girls who were trying out would all attempt heavy drama, the most tragic parts possible, trying to break hearts. She decided she would do comedy.

She opened with a leap onto the stage, a bold peasant girl teasing a boy who is not onstage, but whose lines are heard from offstage.

The jury seemed not to be amused at all, not even to be paying attention. Ingrid heard them whispering even while she was performing. Then, after her first reading, she was dismissed without the judges giving her the chance to do her second reading. Actually, before she had finished her first reading, she was told she could leave.

Ingrid, more than half a century later, recalled her heartbreak.

"As I walked off the stage, I was in mourning, I was at a funeral. My own. It was the death of my creative self. My heart had truly broken. As I went into the street, Stockholm, my home which had always seemed very beautiful to me, was no longer beautiful. I couldn't even see it because my eyes were filled with tears.

"Not only did I not win a place, they didn't think I was even worth listening to, or watching.

"The only answer seemed to be suicide.

"I could never imagine how anyone could commit suicide. I loved life too much. It seemed to me that people who committed suicide didn't understand that whatever it was that day that made them feel so terrible might not *always* make them feel that way, but they wouldn't ever find that out if they put an end to their lives. But this was different. This was the end of all of my hopes and dreams, because I had promised Uncle Otto that if I failed, I would not try again."

When Ingrid went to look at the dark waters of the canal, fortunately she saw how dirty they were. "They were filthy. I was utterly revolted, so I went home.

"I only wanted to be alone to cry into my pillow.

"No one could help. No one could find words that could reach through to the depths of my soul where the pain was. No one except my father, who had died.

"I tried to think what he would have said to me to give me perspective, to make me feel better. He could always make me feel better. He had such warmth, such joy in life. Maybe it wasn't the words, but his feeling for me that always made me feel good."

At home, Ingrid's two girl cousins were waiting for her. They told her that a friend of hers had called. He was an aspiring actor, and he had been at the tryouts.

He had received his white envelope and had asked the guard if Ingrid Bergman had picked up her envelope and what color envelope she had received. He was told that she'd left without picking it up. Everyone had wondered why. Didn't she understand? Didn't she *care?*

Ingrid asked him if he knew what color *her* envelope was. He did indeed.

"I *flew* out," Ingrid said. "I ran all the way to pick up my *white* envelope."

The porter had waited for her. He understood full well what a white envelope meant to hopeful young actors.

"I was so excited," Ingrid recalled, "I tore the message inside in my excitement getting the envelope open.

"It was only many years later, when I was living in Rome, I met one of the members of the jury, Alf Sjöberg. It was my moment to know something I had wondered about for years. I had never been able to imagine what had happened. I asked him why they had stopped me so early in my readings.

"'We loved your security and your impertinence,' he said. 'We loved you and told each other that there was no reason to waste time. We had dozens to see who were going to be difficult decisions. We didn't need to waste any time with you. We knew you were a natural and great. Your future as an actress was settled.'"

Ingrid said she could remember, even as he spoke casually to her, "the pain I had felt that night until I returned home to learn about my white envelope, on the night that changed my life."

During her first few months at the Royal Dramatic Theater School, Ingrid could not have been happier with everything she was learning. She said that for all of her life, she was pleased when she felt she was learning new techniques that would help her to become a better actress.

After only a few months there, Ingrid was selected by Alf Sjöberg to be in the new play he was preparing, *Ett Brott* (A Crime), by Sigfrid Siwertz, and starring Edvin Adolphson. This was totally against procedure at the school, where the girls were supposed to spend three years before they had this kind of opportunity. Sjöberg insisted, and Olof Molander, the head of the school, relented.

Ingrid was thrilled, but "the girls who had served their time," Ingrid remembered, "hated me. It was a strange feeling, knowing that I was being hated. One never gets adjusted to that feeling."

Ingrid said that as she left school, some of the girls hit her. They were not punished. She was. She was taken out of the play, but the older girls still hated her. She had been chosen.

"One is most impatient when one is very young and has all the time in the world," Ingrid said, remembering how her loss of the part brought her to the realization that not only would she be expected to study for three more years, but that then she would have two years of bit parts. She understood the frustration of the older girls.

"It came to me I might use up some of an actress's best years. I craved the real thing. I felt I could learn more by doing than by studying how to do it.

"I wasn't popular in school. I wasn't popular with boys. Too tall. Too serious. Too shy. And I wasn't popular with girls, either."

Ingrid was so shy that she sometimes would blush when someone merely asked her name. There were members of her family who thought she was well on her way to becoming an old maid. Her Aunt Hulda, however, tried to be encouraging, reassuring her, "You're not a bad-looking girl."

"If you can believe it, but remember this was a different time. It was only after my eighteenth birthday that I went out on my first real date," Ingrid told me.

On a blind date arranged by her cousin Margit, Ingrid, her date, the cousin, and the cousin's boyfriend went to lunch at Stockholm's Grand Hotel. "It was my first time at the Grand Hotel. It was the grandest luxury hotel of the city, where the rich who came from all over the world stayed."

Ingrid immediately liked the tall, handsome, polite Dr. Petter Lindström, but she remembered being extremely self-conscious with this "man of the world," as she then saw him. She found herself not really listening to him, only thinking about what he might be thinking about her. She said almost nothing.

"I knew he would be disappointed in me, but he was very polite and didn't show his disappointment. He was an older man, but not *too* old, nine years older. It seemed like more, but not because he *looked* old.

"I liked his name, too. Petter. It was one of my favorite names. It was *his* invitation, and he paid the bill. *And* he had a car."

Dr. Lindström was already a successful dentist in Stockholm, with plans to become a doctor. His goal was to become a surgeon.

Ingrid was surprised when he asked if he might call and invite her to another lunch at the Grand Hotel. She said yes. There were many lunches after that.

When summer came, the students were advised to go on studying at summer programs in other countries, especially Russia. "That was out of the question, not because of money, because I had my own money from my father, and my 'Uncle' Gunnar had told me I could always go to him." Gunnar Spångberg was her father's best friend.

"The truth was, I couldn't bear to be away from Petter. I was too desperately in love. The idea of being away from him for even a day was too terrible.

"I was never in love like that before, and I was never in love in quite that desperate way again.

"Now I can't remember how it felt to be unable to be away from someone for one or two days. What an incredible dependence! But there it was.

"I had a whole summer of days to fill in Stockholm while Petter worked. He never missed a day of work and was totally concerned about his patients. I didn't want to waste the time. I remembered how I had loved making films when at fifteen I was an extra."

Spångberg, who was a successful florist, was one of those who kept a watchful eye on Ingrid. "He had a wonderful flower shop, and whenever I went there with my father, he always gave me a flower.

"When my father went away to die, Uncle Gunnar was always there for me, to give me advice when I wanted some, even when I didn't know what question to ask. What he gave in abundance was encouragement, which was what my father would have given. I think that was what I really needed. It wasn't what was said. It was more what was unsaid.

"Being with him gave me a feeling of support. But the greatest thing he gave was all of that encouragement, so I believed whatever I wanted could come true. I only had to prepare myself to be ready for good things. Uncle Gunnar had strength like a pillar.

"He never said things like other people say that keep you from even trying, like, 'You know how terrible the odds are,' or, 'All of the most beautiful girls try,' and worse yet, they have a look on their faces which says a wordless, 'You poor thing, how could you think *you* could do that?' All the while, there was Uncle Gunnar to say that I should be an actress, that it was 'my destiny.'"

Ingrid was fourteen when Uncle Gunnar gave her a handsome leather-bound diary with a metal lock, which had her name embossed on it so there could be no mistake as to whom it belonged. For a number of years it remained her closest confidant. She called it "Dear Book."

"Uncle Gunnar told me if I wrote down my thoughts, I would have a record of them which would, years later, surprise me. I learned that even the next day, I might be surprised by what was important to me the night before.

"I had put down thoughts I didn't even know I was thinking. The act of having written them down, then of seeing them written down, usually placed it in my memory, forever.

"I could tell my diary all of my hopes and dreams and feelings. I never had to tell my dreams to anyone because I could tell my diary.

"I never felt the need to lock it. No one in my family would ever have looked in it."

Ingrid went to Uncle Gunnar for assistance, not with money, but with connections. She knew that the artistic director at the Svensk Filmindustri was an enthusiastic flower purchaser who also attended

Uncle Gunnar's Sunday suppers. Uncle Gunnar had the most beautiful flowers, the freshest, and he had a regular Sunday evening salon supper attended by Stockholm's artistic elite. Even as a child, she had been there many times, often reciting poems she had memorized. Uncle Gunnar's flowers lasted days longer than those in other floral shops, and no one who came to his delicious Sunday suppers, with their good talk and entertainment, would want to lose his or her place there. The artistic director wouldn't ignore Uncle Gunnar, Ingrid thought, and she was correct.

An appointment was made for Ingrid, and she chose to present poetry. She felt comfortable doing this because she had been reading poems aloud at social gatherings since she was four years old.

On the day of her screen test, Ingrid left home quite early, as she always did to be certain that she would never be late for an appointment. It was what she did throughout her life.

On the way to what she sensed might be an important turning point in her life, she got off the tram and visited the graveyard where her parents were buried. She sat on a bench and explained the situation to her father and asked him to help her. Never having really known her mother, Ingrid did not speak with her.

No one else being available to direct Ingrid's screen test, Gustaf Molander, who was the brother of the director of the Royal Dramatic Theater School and one of Sweden's most famous film directors, did her test himself.

When Ingrid's test was screened for her the next day, she was depressed by what she saw, but the director, Molander, recognized her unique quality, and he felt he had found his next star.

In the film, *The Count of Monk's Bridge,* Ingrid plays a maid in the hotel, pursued by Edvin Adolphson, who stars in the film as well as directing it. Adolphson had noticed Ingrid when she was being considered for *Ett Brott.* "Good luck was so important in my life," Ingrid said.

"There are so many factors which contribute to your achieving your goals in life. For instance, look at me. My good luck was to be born in Stockholm, very close to the theater, which gave me my chance for a life in theater, and in film. Stockholm was a great place to be born and to pursue a life in the arts. Of course, what was most important was that I had the greatest father in the world."

For her first film role, Ingrid was cast in the small part of the ingenue. This was a loosely plotted comedy reminiscent of the style of René Clair's *Under the Roofs of Paris*.

Munkbrogreven (The Count of Monk's Bridge, 1935)

Monk's Bridge is in Stockholm's bohemian section. The Count of Monk's Bridge (Valdemar Dalquist) is a likable rogue who leads a group of vagabonds in their daily quest to get as drunk as possible without working. Sweden's strict liquor laws make this difficult, and illegal, which seems only to inspire greater ingenuity on the part of the Count and his followers.

Their daily routine is interrupted by the appearance of an unknown jewel thief in the area. The police suspect them. The most likely suspect, however, is a mysterious stranger named Åke (Edvin Adolphson) who has taken up residence in a cheap hotel where the beautiful young Elsa (Ingrid Bergman) works. She lives there, and her aunt operates the hotel.

Åke and Elsa fall in love, but their future together seems unpromising until the real thief is apprehended, and Åke, it turns out, is an investigative reporter.

Adolphson was shocked by Ingrid's fearlessness. He told her she was impudent, a word she had heard before and always took as a compliment. She didn't appear to be at all nervous and, for the most part, it was because she wasn't. She took her performance very seriously, but she enjoyed herself. Adolphson and Ingrid became good friends.

Offered a film contract, Ingrid decided on a career on the screen instead of the stage, at least for the next few years. There was a difficult parting at school when she announced that she would not be returning, that she was doing the unthinkable, choosing cinema over theater.

Ingrid was saddened by the anger and turmoil. She hadn't expected it. She simply wanted to depart with the good wishes of all. She never liked to quarrel and preferred to dwell on what was good in any experience or relationship, if possible. Later in life, she realized that the rage she had encountered, especially on the part of the school director, Olof Molander, was actually a compliment to her talent.

She remembered the strange feeling she had, because just such a short time before, winning entrance to the school had seemed to her more important than anything else in the world.

Ingrid was too busy, however, to ponder it all very much. Her contract had provided money for acting training, and her second film, *Bränningar*, was ready to begin shooting.

Bränningar (*Ocean Breakers*, 1935)

A fishing village's newly ordained minister, Daniel Nordeman (Sten Lindgren), feels doubts about his being right for the ministry. These doubts are more than confirmed when he seduces parishioner Karin Ingman (Ingrid Bergman), the beautiful young daughter of a fisherman. Later, a remorseful Daniel rushes out during a stormy night to seek guidance from the Lord, and is struck by lightning. As a result, he loses his memory and is taken away for treatment.

Regaining his memory, he returns to the fishing village to find that Karin has given birth to his child, although she has not revealed that he is the father. In a sermon he admits his sin to the whole village, and then resigns as their minister. As a humble farmer, he seeks forgiveness for his sins.

Ingrid had her first experience with people wanting *her* autograph, and she loved it. She received many compliments, and she told herself firmly that she must not "grow a big head." It was a favored admonition of Petter's, "Don't grow a big head." She enjoyed the love scenes with Sten Lindgren, and he told her he did, too.

Ingrid was rushed into her next film, *Swedenhielms*, which was directed by Gustaf Molander, as would be most of her Swedish films. She described Molander as "a master of serious comedy."

The theme of *Swedenhielms* is a familiar one in European drama: What happens to a wealthy bourgeois family with aristocratic pretensions when they lose their wealth but not their taste for the luxuries and status that accompany it? The Swedenhielm family, heirs of a banker, have added aristocratic honor and professional achievement to their basic values.

Ingrid's part is small, but important. She plays a rich girl who loves the Swedenhielms's son and accepts the family as it is, whatever their social or economic status.

Swedenhielms has the quality of a stage play that has been "opened up," exactly what has been done. It is based on a Swedish play by Hjalmar Bergman, no relation to Ingrid.

Swedenhielms (1935)

Widower Rolf Swedenhielm (Gösta Ekman) is a brilliant Swedish scientist who has spent most of his inheritance trying to perfect a patent that he hopes will win a Nobel Prize. His disdain for money is shared by his three grown children, Rolf, Jr. (Björn Berglund), Julia (Tutta Rolf), and Bo (Håkan Westergren). Bo borrows money from a moneylender so that he can marry Astrid (Ingrid Bergman), perfectly confident that his father will win a Nobel Prize.

The family has been held together for years by Marta Boman (Karin Swanström), a plump, industrious housekeeper, who always manages to come up with some kronor in emergencies. When it appears that Rolf will not win a Nobel Prize, Bo's pride will not allow him to marry Astrid because she is rich. She does not feel that her money should be held against her.

All seems lost, until a phone call announces to Swedenhielm that he *has* won a Nobel Prize, after all. Far from being ecstatic, as he always assumed he would be, he feels let down. He had expected it to be the answer to everything.

A new dark cloud appears when Eriksson (Sigurd Wallén), the moneylender, shows Rolf proof that his son Bo has forged his father's signature to borrow money. Eriksson sells the forged IOUs to Rolf, because what he really wants is the satisfaction of showing more compassion than was shown him by Rolf's father, a banker, who sent him to prison as a young man for embezzlement. Eriksson's revenge consists of showing Rolf that it could happen to someone in his own family. Rolf is devastated by the realization that his son Bo could lose that which was of the utmost importance to a Swedenhielm, his honor. Honor means more than even a Nobel Prize.

Rolf's pride is saved, however, when the housekeeper, Boman, admits that it was she who really forged the IOUs to keep the family going and to finance Rolf's experiments. At the Nobel ceremonies, Rolf receives his prize from the King.

This was Ingrid's first Gustaf Molander picture and her first picture with Gösta Ekman, her personal idol and Sweden's premier actor. At twenty, Ingrid was already a Swedish film presence. It was a joy for her to work with Molander, and she was thrilled and amazed because he seemed to concentrate his attention on her.

Molander had been working as a screenplay writer at Svensk Filmindustri since 1919, and had become one of the company's leading directors toward the end of the silent era. One of his earliest films as a writer was the Swedish classic *Terje Vigen* (1919), based on the Henrik Ibsen poem and directed by Viktor Sjöström (later Victor Seastrom in Hollywood). Forgiveness and redemption were favorite themes of Sjöström's, and Molander stresses them in *Swedenhielms*. In *Terje Vigen,* it is the hero who forgives and is redeemed. In *Swedenhielms,* it is the villain.

The Swedish film industry in which Ingrid Bergman received her early training was one of the most advanced, technically and artistically, outside of Hollywood. There was no reluctance on the part of most of the important Swedish stage actors to work in films, thus Ingrid in her third film found herself playing scenes with the renowned Gösta Ekman.

At first Ingrid had worried that she might have to wait too long between films, but the opposite occurred, and she needed every bit of her abundant good health and energy to work constantly. "Fortunately," she told me, "I had a wonderful memory for lines."

When she first learned that she would be cast opposite Gösta Ekman, Ingrid, who was not nervous when filming, was suddenly nervous, "not professionally," she said, "but personally." Just thinking about it made her blush. Ingrid had always blushed easily, *too* easily, in her opinion, and it embarrassed her. She feared it might embarrass Ekman.

As a girl, she had admired him from afar, and she was not alone. He was a romantic ideal and idol. "I dreamed of Gösta Ekman. He was married. He had a son almost my age."

When she met him, he more than lived up to her dreams. She was inspired, and he did everything he could to help her. He encouraged her and praised her work, and Ingrid said she was "divinely happy." She felt she always did her best work with people who believed in her talent. "But then," she said, "doesn't everyone?"

"I loved Gösta Ekman," Ingrid told me. "I think every woman did, but not every woman had the opportunity to perform with him.

"When I was a girl wanting to be an actress, I was dreaming of acting with him. It seemed it would be divine. It was more divine than I could ever have imagined then.

"Looking back, I suppose I really was a little in love with him. Well, more than a little. I couldn't help it. Nothing happened. He was much older.

"Later, it came to me that Petter was a little jealous, maybe more than a little.

"I talked about Gösta all the time. I was filled with excitement and babbling about how wonderful an actor Gösta was. 'You must be tired of hearing all of this,' I said, but I think he was more tired of it than I knew.

"I learned that it's generally not a good idea to talk too much about how wonderful another man is when you are talking with a man. A woman can love her husband and still feel attracted to another man. Men feel that way. Why can't a woman?"

With trepidation, Ingrid attended the premiere of *Monk's Bridge*. She was hopeful, but the reviewers failed to praise her. Somewhat dismayed as she read negative reactions, she was reassured by Ekman, who told her that for an actress it was better to be noticed, even if not in the way she preferred, than not to be noticed at all. She remembered his words all her life, but was never sufficiently convinced. She never adjusted to the idea of ignoring negative reviews or relishing them because they show more attention then just being ignored.

For *Swedenhielms,* Ingrid *was* praised. With a year and a half of film work, by 1936, Ingrid had received recognition by the Swedish press, and even American *Variety* took note.

Ingrid's next film, directed by Gustaf Edgren, was controversial outside Sweden. Adultery is treated with some tolerance, even sympathy, and an abortion is part of the plot. The film could not be released in the United States until six years later and only after significant cuts had been made.

Valborgsmässoafton (Walpurgis Night, 1935)

At the same time crusading newspaper publisher Frederik Bergström (Viktor Sjöström) is editorializing against Sweden's falling birth rate and a national lack of interest in family life, his daughter Lena (Ingrid Bergman) is hopelessly in love with a married man. He is Johan Borg (Lars Hanson), for whom Lena works as a secretary. His wife, Clary (Karin Kavli Carlsson), denies him conjugal relations out of fear of becoming pregnant.

When Clary does become pregnant, she has an abortion without telling Johan. A blackmailer appears, threatening to tell her husband unless she pays him. In a struggle for the incriminating medical records, she accidentally shoots him, and then kills herself. The story is exploited by Frederik's newspaper, creating a scandal. Johan joins the French Foreign Legion.

When he finally returns to Sweden, Johan finds Lena waiting, anxious to start a family with him.

Walpurgis Night refers to the eve of May Day, when witches come together from all over the world to celebrate. Ingrid, who was always interested in witches, thought it a good title.

The film that followed, *On the Sunny Side,* provided an opportunity to be directed again by Gustaf Molander. Ingrid admired his light touch with comedy, but what he did was never trivial. She felt he had a genius similar to that of Charlie Chaplin. Ingrid was not only certain of Molander's greatness, but also of his warmth, sincerity, generosity, and his special appreciation of her. "He said to me, 'Learn your lines and be yourself.'" His perfect confidence in her gave her a sense of security that reminded her of the way she had felt with her father.

When the film played in New York City, it was reviewed by *Variety* and *The New York Times*. Both publications noted Ingrid as someone to watch. She was already a familiar face in European films.

> ### På Solsidan (On the Sunny Side, 1936)
> Bank clerk Eva Bergh (Ingrid Bergman) desires to follow in the footsteps of her artist father, but lacks the talent for anything but the social part of the life of the artist. While she is enjoying life with Stockholm's bohemian group, she meets a wealthy gentleman, Harold Ribe (Lars Hanson), who offers her marriage and security on his country estate. She accepts, but not without fears that she will be bored when away from the excitement of the city. After the marriage, she invites her friends to leave the city for a weekend. She finds that her values coincide more with those of her husband.

Ingrid could easily identify with her character's admiration for her artist father. She always looked for aspects of the character she was playing with which she could identify.

In March 1936, Otto Bergman died, and Ingrid was grateful for Petter's sympathetic presence in her life. Elsa Adler (Aunt Mutti) was impressed by Petter when Ingrid brought him to Hamburg that year on a visit to introduce him to her German family. Petter, however, was alarmed by what he saw in Germany. After three years, the Nazis were firmly entrenched, and their ominous presence could be felt everywhere.

While she was there, Ingrid was told that Joseph Goebbels had expressed interest in her as an actress for German films, especially after he learned that her mother was German. The German studio

UFA was then one of the major film production centers of the world and was controlled by Goebbels.

"Petter and I, like good Swedes, liked to walk, and on Saturdays when I wasn't working, we would go for very long walks in the woods.

"I would fix our meal, assorted sandwiches, different kinds of cheese, little cakes, butter cookies, and I would pack it all attractively and put it in a knapsack on my back. It didn't weigh very much until after we had walked for hours, and then, those sandwiches started to seem heavy.

"Petter had a knapsack, too, and his was very, very heavy when we started out, but he never opened it. I didn't understand.

"So I asked Petter, 'What do you have in that sack that you never open?' He opened the knapsack and showed me. There were five large, heavy bricks. I still didn't understand. Petter, seeing the look on my face, explained, 'I am building muscles.'

"Petter was a natural athlete, and he believed in doing everything to keep fit. He enjoyed physical activity and was an excellent skier.

"He was a marvelous dancer," Ingrid remembered, "much better than me, and he never got tired, or so it seemed. I always tired first.

"For Petter, everything was sort of an endurance thing. Maybe he got tired, but just would never admit it."

As the date of their wedding approached, Petter encouraged Ingrid to go to Aunt Ellen's place to see what might be there that they could use to start their own married life. They would need such things as good pots and pans, silverware, utensils, sheets, goose-down pillows, blankets, and other useful household goods.

Ingrid had not been able to bring herself to go alone and look through the property that her Aunt Ellen had left, as well as everything that she had left with Aunt Ellen. With Petter's encouragement, she was able to do so. There she found one of the great treasures of her life, her mother's letters to her father before they married.

Friedel, Ingrid's mother, had made it clear in her letters during the years before her marriage that, much as she loved Justus—so much that if they could not be married, she would never marry anyone else— there was one thing she could never do. She wanted him to understand that she would never be able to bring herself to pose nude for him.

The letters her mother had sent her father were "so beautiful," Ingrid told me, "that I cried all night, as I came to know my mother as a girl, long before I was born, passionately in love with my father, as he was with her.

"I had to hold the letters carefully and direct my tears in the opposite direction so they wouldn't fall on the letters and stain them."

She told me she envied the love and passion and dedication to their love felt by her parents. She hoped she would have that with Petter, but without the tragic part.

The letters were so important because they allowed Ingrid to know the mother she hadn't known and couldn't remember. Ingrid told me she had felt some guilt at the time, like being an eavesdropper. She was reading her mother's most intimate thoughts, but she couldn't help herself. She felt compelled to do it, and afterward, she believed her mother would have wanted to share her feelings with her daughter, who was just about to marry.

Ingrid, however, felt it would be wrong to share her mother's most intimate feelings with another person, even Petter, but she didn't know what she could say to him should he ask if he could read her mother's letters. There was no way she could say no to him. She felt it was right for her to open her own heart totally to the man she loved and was going to marry, but she felt troubled about revealing her mother's most private thoughts that had been intended only for the man her mother loved so desperately, Ingrid's father.

Ingrid stayed up all through the night reading the letters, and she read much of the next day. That evening when Petter came to take her to dinner, he didn't ask about the letters, nor did he ever mention them.

Ingrid attributed this to Petter's great sensitivity and respect for her privacy. In later years, she wondered if the letters just hadn't interested him.

Petter was not one to cling to the sentimental past. He liked to live in the present and the future in terms of goals. Ingrid believed he thought she handicapped herself with the weight of too much sentimental baggage.

Ingrid's picture of her mother would be complete one day when, in Hollywood, she would see the carefully restored bit of surviving film taken by her father that showed her mother with her, and allowed her to see her mother moving, not only as a still photograph.

"Petter was an older man, but that didn't bother me. I may have been more attracted to him because I was so young and really innocent for my years. I'd never gone out with men. I'd never even gone out with boys. He wasn't really old, just older. It was like having a big brother, and every girl who doesn't have one would like a big brother.

"Then, as I fell in love with him, he didn't seem like a brother at all. I felt very romantically about him. Sometimes it was almost like an illness. It's difficult to explain unless *you* have felt that way. It was certainly a dependency. I can't recapture the feeling now; I can't even describe it. I can't even remember it exactly.

"I do remember whatever happened I couldn't wait to share it with Petter. Sharing it with Petter seemed more important than what had happened. I don't remember exactly when it stopped being that way between us. The feeling I know was stronger before we married, and just after.

"At that time, in the months looking forward to our marriage, I couldn't imagine life without him. I just knew that if he had died, *I* would have died."

Ingrid's next film was written for her by Molander and Gösta Stevens. Gösta Ekman was again signed for the lead. Since Ekman was appearing in the theater in the evenings, the film's production schedule required shooting around his performances, with rehearsals by day and filming after midnight until they finished. It was important to have Ekman, and Ingrid enjoyed the challenge, but it was a grueling schedule, especially for Ekman.

Intermezzo (1936)

When internationally acclaimed violinist Holger Brandt (Gösta Ekman) returns to Sweden after an extended tour, his longtime accompanist, Thomas Stenborg (Hugo Björne), announces his retirement. Needing a qualified replacement, he chooses Stenborg's talented young pupil, Anita Hoffman (Ingrid Bergman), who is also the piano teacher of his beloved young daughter, Ann-Marie (Britt Hagman). Anita is flattered, even tempted, but declines because she hopes to win a scholarship to study abroad.

Carried away by the attentions of her idol and the music, "Rustle of Spring," she has an affair with him. Later, she feels guilty about their clandestine relationship, and she decides to end it and leave Stockholm.

Confronted by his wife, Margit (Inga Tidblad), Holger admits he is having an affair and that he is in love with the young pianist. He and his wife agree to separate.

At the train station, Holger asks Anita to reconsider her decision to leave. She decides to stay, as his accompanist and mistress.

Vacationing in Switzerland after a European tour, the couple is apparently happy, but Anita is troubled. She notices how taken Holger is by a young girl who resembles his daughter. When his manager arrives with the divorce papers, Holger is reluctant to sign them, and is only interested in hearing about Ann-Marie and his son Åke. Understanding what his family means to him, Anita reluctantly leaves him when she is offered a grant to study in Paris.

Holger returns to Stockholm feeling he has lost not only Anita, but his family, as well. He visits his daughter's school. Seeing him, Ann-Marie is so happy, she runs in front of a car and is struck.

Holger comes out of the hospital emergency room where his wife is waiting for news of their daughter. When he tells her that Ann-Marie will be all right, Margit says softly, "Welcome home, Holger."

Katharine (Kay) Brown, who was head of David Selznick's East Coast office, saw *Intermezzo* in early 1938. She was impressed by Ingrid, and contacted Selznick, suggesting the possibility of his remaking this film in English with her. Later, Brown became one of Ingrid's closest friends.

After Selznick had bought the rights and arranged for Ingrid to come to Hollywood for the remake, he suffered some uneasy moments. He noticed that she wasn't billed as the lead actress. She wasn't even second or third, but fourth. Brown explained that in Sweden actors were usually listed in order of appearance.

Intermezzo repeats the redemption-through-forgiveness theme of other Molander films. Holger's wife forgives him, as does his son, and his daughter is just happy to have her father back at home.

Ekman died a year and a half later at the age of forty-seven. Ingrid remembered that he had seemed tired when filming late at night after his theater performances, though at the time it seemed only natural. She wrote in her diary that she had no words for her grief.

"I was a virgin when I married, not because I gave it any importance," Ingrid told me. "My virginity wasn't something I especially treasured. It wasn't anything I thought about, and I don't think any of the boys around were very intent on claiming that prize.

"Before Petter, I had no suitors, and I didn't mind a bit. In fact, I was glad, because I have never liked to say no to anyone, so I was glad when they didn't ask me out. I needed all of my time and energy to prepare myself as an actress. I could not imagine any greater thrill than acting.

"There was no boy in school to whom I was attracted, perhaps it was because they were boys and seemed too young, and that was strange, because in those days *I* was young for my years.

"I think my innocence and naïveté were a great part of my attraction for Petter and why he wanted to marry me. At the time of our first dates, I was worried that I couldn't be attractive to him because I wasn't sophisticated.

"I had offered to go to bed with Petter during our long, long engagement. We *were* going to be married, after all. He wouldn't consider it. He said we should take long walks in the cold instead. I felt it was because he respected me so much.

"I believe that, but after we married, I sometimes wished he *hadn't* respected me so much.

"I was shy, but I expected with Petter I would lose all of my inhibitions and find an intimacy beyond my imagination. I believed that life was a search for the kind of romantic intimacy shared by my parents. They had been forced to wait more than seven years to be together, but for true love, it was worth it.

"I discovered that Petter, who was so wonderfully outgoing and, I thought, the least shy person I knew, was shy, too. It surprised me to find when he made love that he was so decorous. I think he was very concerned about abandoning himself and losing his dignity, seeming a fool in front of me. Perhaps he thought about how we would feel facing each other in the morning. He cared so much about what everyone thought of him, and I believed that included me, even in our marital bed.

"I thought that this would pass and that with a love like ours, any nervousness would pass, that we would grow to be as close physically as we were in every other way. I assumed that passion grows. I was wrong.

"Perhaps it was because we had come to know each other too well before we married, becoming almost like a brother and sister. Petter seemed happy and satisfied with our physical love, so I was happy that I made him happy, and maybe that whole side of life had been exaggerated."

Ingrid and Petter were married in his hometown, Stode, on July 10, 1937. She had wanted to be married on the seventh day of the seventh month of a year with a final seven in it. Seven was her mother's lucky number, but preproduction work on *Dollar* delayed the wedding three days. As was the Swedish custom, they had exchanged rings a year earlier. That ceremony had taken place in the same small Hamburg church where her parents had been married.

"The one thing Petter didn't want was any sort of publicity at our wedding," Ingrid told me. "So he became very upset when he saw a young lady hiding in the bushes of the front yard of his parents' home, waiting to take a photograph. I didn't remember ever before having seen him so upset. He was about to send her off with some angry words when Papa Lindström appeared on the porch and, very amiably, rebuked his son for not being more hospitable to the young lady. Then, he invited her into the house for some coffee. Petter's family had lovely manners. I was very fond of them."

The young woman with the camera was Barbro Alving, and it was her first assignment as a reporter. "Imagine. Her very first assignment! She was very nervous about it. It was my very first wedding, and I was nervous, too, so we could sympathize with each other. Later, she became known as Bang and had a career as a very well-known Stockholm columnist. We became friends and saw each other in the years that followed.

"Perhaps I should have been warned by Petter's so-extreme reaction to publicity and the press, but I assumed he was just nervous, because it was his wedding day, too.

"Petter's career was even more demanding than mine, and he was equally dedicated to his work. He loved his dental practice and his dream of being a surgeon as much as I did my life being an actress. I worked long hours when I worked, but there were periods of time between when I was free to be a good wife, and later, a mother. There was no such time-between for Petter. A doctor is always on call. For an actress, plays close, films wrap."

After she was married, Ingrid took an extended leave from filmmaking, more than a year. During this time, she returned to the theater to star with Edvin Adolphson in *Jean,* a political satire by Hungarian playwright Bus Feketes. Then she returned to the film studios for *Dollar,* a comedy directed by Molander.

Dollar (1938)

Actress Julia Balzar (Ingrid Bergman) and financier husband Kurt Balzar (Georg Rydeberg) are close friends with two other wealthy couples whose chief concern is, who is being unfaithful with whose spouse? When one of the husbands, Louis Brenner (Kotti Chave), loses heavily while gambling, Julia steps in to save him by selling shares of her husband's company without telling him. Realizing that such a large sale of securities will substantially affect the market, another husband, Ludvig von Battwyhl (Håkan Westergren), buys them up, also without telling Kurt. Julia is grateful, but it does compromise her with the other two wives, who are now convinced both of their husbands have been having affairs with her. Especially suspicious is Brenner's wife, Sussi (Tutta Rolf).

While the couples are on holiday at a ski lodge, the distraught Sussi loses her way in the snow and is rescued by a wealthy American skier, Mary Johnstone (Elsa Burnett). As Mary comes to know the three couples, she registers disgust at their petty grievances, but in doing so, reveals Julia's stock transactions to Kurt. All is forgiven, and Mary joins the group when she marries the lodge clerk, Dr. Johnson (Edvin Adolphson).

Ingrid wanted to do *A Woman's Face,* but the studio wanted her to do *Only One Night.* She agreed that if they would let her do *A Woman's Face,* she would appear in *Only One Night,* which she considered "an entertainment film that was not all that entertaining." Though *Only One Night* was shot before *A Woman's Face,* it was released afterwards.

En Enda Natt (Only One Night, 1939)

When circus roustabout Valdemar Moreaux (Edvin Adolphson) learns that he is the illegitimate son of wealthy aristocrat Magnus von Brede (Olof Sandborg), he tries to adjust to his rightful heritage but finds it difficult. What isn't difficult is adjusting to von Brede's beautiful young ward, Eva (Ingrid Bergman). He falls in love with her, almost forgetting Helga Mårtensson (Aino Taube), the earthy circus owner he had lived with before.

Valdemar gets drunk and tries to seduce Eva in the same rough manner he had made love to Helga, but is repulsed. Realizing that there is too great a difference between the life he was used to and the life he is now expected to lead, he returns to the circus, and to Helga, whom he marries.

In the movie Ingrid wanted to make, *A Woman's Face,* her character has a disfigured face after one side of it is badly burned in a fire. Ingrid wanted desperately to do this film, but there were many who told her she would ruin her career if she allowed herself to appear ugly on-screen. They wanted her to have only a suggestion of disfigurement, but that would not do for Ingrid. She was determined to look her worst, and she persuaded Molander that she was right. "Make me as ugly as possible," she said.

Ingrid chose the perfect person to create her deformity in a realistic way. She did not like the work of the makeup people "because their touch was too light. They weren't accustomed to making an actress look ugly."

She turned to Petter. He created a brace that fit inside Ingrid's mouth and forced her cheek to protrude. "It was so great," she told me, "that it made me *feel* ugly.

"That was wonderful for me as an actress. Petter was a genius. Makeup alone couldn't do it, he said, and then he did such a masterful job, that the way I looked was rather frightening for both Petter and me."

During a break, Ingrid decided to go out for a snack. Seeing an enticing goat's cheese in the window of a store, she entered. As she was waiting and studying some black bread to go with it and a tub of fresh sweet butter, she noticed some of the customers staring at her. They seemed horrified. Others averted their gaze. It was not a reaction to which Ingrid was accustomed. She had never before had the experience of people pitying her for the way she looked.

Ingrid had forgotten that she left the set still wearing her makeup, including her cheek brace. She realized that the makeup was truly effective. "Thank you. I'll be back," she mumbled, and rushed out of the store.

"I learned a valuable lesson that day," Ingrid said. "We all live in different worlds, and *I* am one of the luckiest people ever. Some people are so terribly tested by life. From the first days I could remember, I had known only smiles and compliments."

En Kvinnas Ansikte (*A Woman's Face*, 1938)
Anna Holm (Ingrid Bergman), embittered by her badly scarred face, has become the leader of a group of blackmailers. She is accustomed to being rejected by men, so when a handsome aristocrat, Torsten Barring (Georg Rydeberg), seems attracted to her, she welcomes his advances even as she doubts any man could really want her.

One of the gang's victims is the wife of a plastic surgeon, Dr. Wegert (Anders Henrikson). In a chance encounter, he recommends to Anna an operation to remove the scars.

When the operation is successful, Anna believes Torsten will now be sincere in his desire for her, but she is wrong. What he really wants is her help in murdering his young nephew, Lars Erik (Göran Bernhard), the only obstacle in his way to his inheriting his father's fortune. Because she is so much in love with Torsten, she reluctantly agrees to be an accomplice.

When it comes time to kill the nephew, Anna cannot do it. Her new face has given her a new outlook on life. She is no longer angry, bitter, and filled with hate toward everyone. She is indicted for murder after she shoots Torsten when he tries to kill the boy. She is brought to trial, and the film ends. It is left to the audience to decide what the verdict will be.

Molander didn't know how to end the film. Her beauty restored by plastic surgery, Anna has murdered the aristocratic blackmailer and saved a young boy. By standards of the time in Sweden, she had to be punished for her crime, but that wasn't the ending Molander wanted. He had been unable to decide on the ending.

When Molander asked Ingrid how she thought the film should

end, she suggested Anna Holm go on trial for murder and that would be the end of the film. The audience would have to decide for itself, "each member of the audience for himself or herself."

I asked Ingrid if she knew what the court decided.

"Of course," she answered. "Mercy was shown and my character was freed."

In October 1938, Ingrid went to the UFA studios in Berlin to make a German film, *Die vier Gesellen* (The Four Companions). The director was Karl Froelich, one of the most active and successful directors of this period. He specialized in films about young women, of which this was an example. The half-Swedish, half-German Ingrid, already well known in Europe through her Swedish films, was cast as an ideal German woman. This wasn't unusual. Ingrid was actually more German than many of the most popular "German" actresses of the 1930s. Kirsten Heiberg, Zarah Leander and Kristina Söderbaum were all Scandinavian, Lilian Harvey was English, and Anny Ondra and Lída Baarová (who became Joseph Goebbel's mistress) were Czech.

Froelich was said to be Hitler's favorite director. He certainly was *one* of his favorites. After the war, he resumed making films after having been cleared of being a Nazi.

"I am half-German and German was my second language," Ingrid said, "though I had always lived in Stockholm except when, after the death of my mother, I visited my German grandparents and aunts in the summers. I believed the Germans to be a basically good people. I was not at all prepared for what I saw when I arrived in Berlin to do *The Four Companions*.

"There was an all-pervasive sense of apprehension, of fear in the air wherever you went. My director, Karl Froelich, was a nice man, but he was so fearful, and he conveyed his dread to everyone on the set. And the film was supposed to be a romantic comedy!

"He took me to a huge Nazi rally where Hitler was the main attraction. Everything was organized with a great theatricality. On cue, little children would rush up to the podium with flowers, and everyone would 'Heil' at whatever monstrous nonsense he screamed. It sounded so silly, I couldn't imagine people taking someone like Hitler seriously. But in the whole audience, I was, I think, the only one who wasn't raising my arm and saying 'Heil.'

"Froelich turned to me and said, 'You must say "Heil." They are watching.'

"I said, 'Nonsense. Nobody is watching us. Everyone is watching Hitler. Besides I'm not German. I am a Swedish citizen, I live in Stockholm, and there is nothing they can do to me.'

"He said, 'Yes, but you are half-German, and you never know what can happen. People can have accidents. People disappear. They are everywhere, watching, listening. It could be bad for you.'

"I think what he really meant was that it could be bad for *him*.

"But I never once said 'Heil Hitler' during all the time I was in Germany."

Ingrid was warned that Goebbels was particularly interested in every attractive actress who worked in Germany, that she would be summoned to his office, and that she had to be very careful how she handled it, because he was all-powerful. But she wasn't intimidated.

"I never was summoned by Goebbels," Ingrid said. "I guess I wasn't his type."

Leni Riefenstahl, director of *Triumph of the Will* and *Olympia*, told me that it was Goebbels who first had recognized the great potential in the young Swedish actress—especially when he learned she was half-German. She had also spent fourteen summers in Germany, so she knew the language. After the death of her mother, when Ingrid was almost three, her father had taken her every year to stay with her German relatives.

In *The Four Companions,* she played a German girl, and she spoke her own lines. Had she chosen to do so, Ingrid could have been a star in German films.

Goebbels probably had more than a professional interest in Ingrid. She would undoubtedly have been offered a multiple picture contract for more money than she could hope to receive anywhere except Hollywood.

Riefenstahl said that Goebbels most certainly would have expected Ingrid to share his bed as an unwritten clause in the contract for German film stardom. Riefenstahl, who was nearly one hundred years old when I talked with her at her home near Munich, spoke from personal experience, having turned down such an invitation herself. She said that when Goebbels saw Ingrid on the set for the first time, he had a change of mind and said, "Too tall." Riefenstahl said Magda, Goebbels's wife, was her source for the comment.

Die vier Gesellen (The Four Companions, 1938)

After graduation, four ambitious commercial art students, Marianne (Ingrid Bergman), Lotte (Carsta Löck), Käthe (Sabine Peters), and Franziska (Ursala Herking), start an advertising agency called Die vier Gesellen (The Four Companions). They achieve some success, but it is jeopardized by being dependent on only one company. An employee in that company is Stefan Kohlund (Hans Söhnker), whose marriage proposal is turned down by Marianne at the school's graduation party. If he says something unfavorable about the agency, it can wreck the account. Not knowing that Marianne heads the agency, Hans continues to ask Marianne to marry him.

Soon, three of the four companions start to have doubts about being career women. Two of them drop out to get married, one of them because she has to, while the third decides to become a "serious" painter. Unable to continue on her own, Marianne accepts Hans's proposal.

Ingrid discussed with me how this German project came about. "Petter was a very good husband. I wasn't such a good wife, but I didn't know it, because he took such care of me, and he seemed pleased. I think he was. I was so shy. I don't think I could have had my wonderful career without Petter. I might have been limited to Sweden.

"I was having a little success in Sweden as an actress there, but I did want to act in other countries. I wanted to act in French, but my French wasn't so good. I wanted to act in English, but my English was even less good. But there was German. It was my second language.

"I don't know if Mama ever spoke German to me. If she did, I was too young to remember it. I learned German well, if not perfectly, according to my Aunt Mutti.

"So, when I received an offer to make three films for UFA in Germany, Petter encouraged me to go. I was thrilled and ready.

"This is the best example I can give you of the kind of man Petter was. When I think about him and remember, and I do often, he was my youth and my daughter Pia's father, the image I most often remember is this one:

"I went to Berlin, and they had put me in a luxury hotel, the Adlon. It was very nice, more grand than I had expected, but I wasn't enjoying it. I had felt confident, even happy, looking forward when I prepared to leave for Germany. When I left, Petter had helped me pack and make decisions about what to take. He even watched over what I should wear.

"I always had trouble making decisions about choices I didn't consider very important. I could waste a lot of time deliberating. Well, what I wore didn't make any difference to me, but it would have made a difference when I was in Germany and had all left shoes.

"Perhaps the hotel was *too* grand for me, not cozy. I knew staying in the room was not good for me, so I thought I might find my confidence in the lobby with all of the people coming and going. The people were all speaking German, which I understood, but it was not a comfortable language for me. I spoke and understood 'summer German,' but I was afraid I wouldn't be convincing in a foreign language on the screen, even though I would be given my lines to say. I would have to express emotions I could only feel in Swedish. Little did I know what the future held for me!

"To tell the truth, I was feeling lost, and, even worse, I was ashamed of feeling that way. I thought I should be more sure of myself and independent. I should be more grown up.

"Then, in the lobby, I saw a man reading a newspaper, not exactly reading it, but hiding behind it. I saw only the top of his head, but it was a top of a head with which I was very familiar. It was my Petter!

"He had sensed how I would feel. He knew me so well. It was a very happy moment for me.

"Petter had come from Stockholm to take care of me. He had followed me to Berlin because he thought I would want to talk things over with him and would need him to tell me how to deal with people because that wasn't what I did, but he told me that it must be *our* secret, that I must not tell anyone. He said to me, 'They will not want husbands. They expect you to be a confident young lady who can stand on her own two feet.'

"So, I stood extra firmly for him. 'Remember,' he said, 'I'm here.' I remembered. I never forgot it. It was the moment I remember when I think about Petter. He was my husband, my lover, my father, my brother, my best friend.

"While I was treated royally, Petter stayed in a dingy hotel right nearby which was very cheap. He said it was all we could afford, he didn't mind, and most important, no one should see us together. He told me that most of the people I would be working with would be men, and it was better that they see me as a beautiful, innocent young woman, not as a married matron. Even though I always told the truth and they might know I was married, they wouldn't think about it, and they would fall a little in love with me, needing no encouragement at all. Meanwhile, he would be there for me if I needed him. His presence made me feel very secure. Whenever I think about Petter, that is how I like to remember him.

"We were concerned about our young lives, our careers, our family, our world.

"It was Germany, and the year was 1938."

After seeing the situation there at that moment, Petter was strongly against Ingrid's completing her three-picture contract. She remembered that though many people believed that there wouldn't be any real war or if there was, it would be a limited war and it would be over quickly, Petter did not see it that way. He thought it would be a long war, and it would have lasting repercussions.

"After I completed my work on the film, he suggested we leave Germany and drive in Europe, as it might be quite a while before we could do that again. I, myself, did not need any reason, because it sounded wonderful. "Our baby would be born soon.

"I didn't know Petter was working behind the scenes to see that I didn't go back to Germany to make another film. He told me he did not want me to, but he didn't say it to me as strongly as he felt it. I didn't understand yet how strongly Petter was capable of feeling things. Petter was a very interior person. I did not feel things as deeply as he.

"He believed there was an immediate future for Germany which would tragically affect not only Germany, but all of Europe and beyond.

"Not I. I said to Petter, 'Hitler cannot last. The German people are good people, and they are too smart not to see through this man.' Well, so much for my political judgment."

Ingrid did not see Germany again until she returned to Europe after the war, to entertain American GIs, when she went to Paris, Berlin, and traveled through the ruins of Germany.

• • •

After a driving tour that took them to Paris and Monte Carlo, the Lindströms returned to Stockholm in mid-1938. Their daughter was born in September. She would, one day, become a well-known American television personality, Pia Lindstrom. Her name was an acronym of her parents' names, Petter, Ingrid, and Aron, her father's middle name.

Ingrid had agreed to make the two more films in Germany for UFA while hoping for an offer from Hollywood. Shortly after Pia's birth, Ingrid was approached by David O. Selznick's European representative, Jenia Reissar. She had come to Sweden to secure Ingrid's services and those of Gustaf Molander for a remake of *Intermezzo* starring Leslie Howard. Ingrid was reluctant to sign a seven-year contract, and Molander didn't consider his English adequate for directing in Hollywood. Following Petter's advice, Ingrid finally accepted a one-picture contract at $2,500 a week. Petter would stay with Pia in Sweden while Ingrid went to Hollywood to make the film. She would then return to Stockholm, to make another already-contracted Swedish film and then the two UFA films. The German films were subsequently canceled.

"I was happy to be going to Hollywood," Ingrid told me, "though I wished Petter could come with me. Suppose Hollywood didn't like me? Who would I to turn to?"

Two

֍

INGRID AND HOLLYWOOD

merican ice cream, yummy with its high cream content, is one of
the great delights of America. I couldn't wait to introduce Petter to it.
In tribute to it, I immediately gained two pounds."

Accompanied by Selznick representative Kay Brown, Ingrid arrived
in America aboard the *Queen Mary* on April 20, 1939. She stayed in
New York for eleven days before taking a train to Los Angeles, where
she would film *Intermezzo: A Love Story* and then return to Sweden.

She was thrilled by the lights of Broadway, the theater, the skyscrap-
ers, the museums, double-decker buses, Central Park, and banana splits.

Ingrid arrived in Los Angeles on May 6. She would stay at the
Selznick home in Beverly Hills until a proper residence could be
leased for her during the filming of *Intermezzo*.

"At his house," Ingrid told me, "one of the first things I remember
Mr. Selznick saying to me was, 'Take off your shoes!' It wasn't exactly
the *first* thing he said, but it was the first thing I really remember.

"I said, 'It isn't any use. My shoes are flat!' I knew what worried
him. People were always having that reaction when they met me.
They didn't expect me to be so tall."

She saw the look on his face, and though tempted to do so, she remembered Petter's admonition, "Do not bend your knees."

"I was told a number of times as a girl in Sweden I would have been better off if I hadn't been so tall, but I never wished to be shorter. It was *part* of me. I didn't want to be less of myself."

"I knew Ingrid all my life," Danny Selznick, David and Irene's son, told me. "She was like a member of my family. As she used to remind me, I was three years old when she met me. She was so beautiful. I saw her continuously until I was ten, and Pia was a friend of mine.

"My father had four concerns about Ingrid Bergman. She didn't speak English, she was too tall, her name sounded too German, and her eyebrows were too thick. He also didn't think it was very thrilling that her husband was a dentist.

"Ingrid learned English quickly enough, and *she* was the only one who didn't like the way it sounded. Everyone else thought it was charming. She always was her own severest critic.

"Being tall didn't turn out to be much of a problem. They just avoided wide shots on her with Edna Best [who played Leslie Howard's wife] and the son. Leslie Howard wasn't short.

"She resisted changing her name to Ingrid Lindstrom, which was suggested, because she was already well known as Ingrid Bergman in Europe, and she wasn't at all certain she would be staying in Hollywood. My father agreed with her on the name, Ingrid Bergman, and *he* believed she would be staying in Hollywood.

"The eyebrows stayed. My father was a man who didn't easily take no for an answer, but Ingrid was a woman a man couldn't easily resist."

In those days, actresses' eyebrows were plucked, and sometimes they didn't grow back. "I wouldn't let them do that to me," Ingrid said. "I was ready to go back to Sweden *with* my eyebrows before I would let them take my eyebrows. I had no guarantee they would grow back, and I was attached to them, and they were attached to me."

For the most part, *Intermezzo: A Love Story* closely follows the Swedish film. Selznick had bought all the rights to the film. Some European montage sequences that did not include the stars were taken from the original.

Selznick could make any changes he wanted, but he chose not to tamper with the success of the film. He appreciated not only the artistic achievement, but also the savings that could be achieved by not making too many changes. The scenes involving Ingrid are remarkably alike in both versions—dialogue, shots, settings, and even the camera angles are often the same.

One change combined the accompanist and manager characters, even after both have been introduced. Another change is the setting chosen after the violinist's daughter has been hit by the car. In the Swedish version, she is rushed to a hospital. In the Hollywood version, she is taken home, although the hospital would have seemed a more logical destination.

Molander's effective shadow scene behind the operating room door is eliminated, while the concept of the violinist returning home, both literally and symbolically, is emphasized. Edna Best in the American version says "Welcome home, Holger!" emphatically several times during the course of the film, and Inga Tidblad in the Swedish version says it only once, softly, at the end. Thus the concept of redemption through forgiveness, which is an important theme in other Molander films, becomes secondary to the obligatory Hollywood happy ending.

"A Love Story" was added to the title when exhibitors expressed doubts that "Intermezzo" would be understood by audiences.

William Wyler was to have directed *Intermezzo: A Love Story,* but there was a lot of preproduction arguing about the film. Wyler always had definite ideas about what he wanted to do. He wanted the freedom to explore and the power to make decisions.

Selznick had his own definite ideas about what *he* wanted to do, and was even more determined than Wyler. He did not easily relinquish his power to make final decisions.

Selznick wanted to follow the successful Swedish version as exactly as possible. This was an unthinkable approach for Wyler, not because he didn't like *Intermezzo*, but because this was, in his view, "a disrespectful approach toward a director who was supposed to have some intelligence he could apply." The discussions broke off, and Wyler returned to Goldwyn.

Gregory Ratoff became the director. Ratoff would not argue with Selznick. He would be happy to carry out what he was asked to do.

Many years later, Wyler told me, "*Intermezzo* was one that got away." He regretted having taken such a strong stand "too early in the game." He liked the film that was made. He knew that his would have been different, though he didn't know in exactly which ways. He felt it had been his loss not to have directed the very young Ingrid Bergman and have played a part in her development as an actress, "but then, she did all right without me."

Ratoff, who had worked for Selznick before, spoke with a thick Russian accent. "Can you imagine," Ingrid told me, "it was my first Hollywood picture, I could speak some English, but I understood much less, and my director spoke even worse English than I did! And English was the only language we had in common." Ratoff is perhaps best remembered as Max, the Broadway producer, in *All About Eve*.

Selznick gave Leslie Howard credit as an associate producer on *Intermezzo: A Love Story* as incentive for Howard to accept the part of Ashley Wilkes in *Gone With the Wind*. Howard, though a Hollywood star, really wanted to be a producer, and that was the condition he exacted for being cast in what Selznick was certain was going to be "one of the greatest, probably *the* greatest film of all time."

"My father found actors a perplexing breed," Danny Selznick told me. "Leslie Howard never bothered to *read Gone With the Wind*, because he found it that uninteresting."

"Gösta Ekman couldn't play the violin," Ingrid remembered, "so close shots of him playing were impossible until Molander had a brilliant idea. He had two violinists stand beside him in close-ups, and while Gösta held his arms close to his body, one violinist did the bowing and the other the fingering.

"That's how they did it then with Leslie Howard in the picture. I don't think they had ever thought of that before, but after that, it became the standard practice whenever an actor couldn't play a stringed instrument. I was the one who introduced them to it in Hollywood, from the Swedish *Intermezzo*.

"But they didn't need to have anyone play for me. I can't remember when I couldn't play the piano.

"My father played the piano with me, and when I played for him, it made him so proud and happy that I didn't want to stop. When Greta, a music student, came to be my governess and like an older sister for me, the three of us played and sang. Music made all three of us happy. My father had a great voice, and Greta's voice was beautiful. I didn't have that kind of voice, but I loved singing with them. My father believed I could become a professional opera singer. I think he would have been proud of my little song in *The Bells of St. Mary's*."

Among the difficult pieces Ingrid actually plays are Christian Sinding's "Rustle of Spring" and Edvard Grieg's piano concerto, although the playing heard on the soundtrack is that of a professional pianist. Ingrid's correct fingering made it possible to show her hands.

The theme violin piece, known as "Intermezzo" and important in both films, was written for the original by Swedish composer Heinz Provost. It became a best-selling record, rare for this kind of music.

• • •

American audiences' first view of Ingrid was in the *Intermezzo: A Love Story* trailer with Leslie Howard, a striking scene in which winter becomes spring. Icicles melt, flowers bud, and the couple suddenly realize they are in love. Ingrid later admitted that she actually did have a crush on Gösta Ekman, and perhaps he on her a few years earlier, when they were making the first *Intermezzo*.

"You cannot imagine the impact of that scene when it first showed here," film historian Herman G. Weinberg told me. "I had already seen the Swedish version, and I was deeply impressed by the freshness and vitality of the young Ingrid Bergman. But seeing it with an American audience and sensing their realization that a star had just been born was overwhelming. It was the same feeling I'd had ten years earlier when I first saw [Marlene] Dietrich, in *The Blue Angel*.

"When Ingrid Bergman plays the piano, it is especially moving, because you see it's really she who is playing, and you can empathize with her feelings as her fingers caress the keyboard. I've always believed such feelings, as a love of music, cannot be totally acted, even by a fine actress. I felt she played with her soul.

"*Intermezzo* in both the Swedish and American versions brought to the screen the best elements of the silent film and the sound film."

Intermezzo: A Love Story was a critical and popular success. Critics wrote that the simple plot was enhanced by a new star: Ingrid Bergman. "My father described her as being a combination of exciting beauty and fresh purity," Danny Selznick told me, "and he was right.

"He also described her as the most conscientious performer with whom he had ever worked. She was always ready and prepared, sitting there waiting, and her mind was only on her work. She never thought about overtime, and she even volunteered to be her own stand-in. They didn't have stand-ins in Sweden. She was even concerned about saving money for my father by not spending it where she thought it was unnecessary. She especially didn't like wasting a costume. She thought they could be recycled after a seamstress altered them. Very Swedish.

"My father always liked the *Intermezzo* story, and he wanted to do a remake of it. He had in mind starring Jennifer Jones with Leonard Bernstein."

Ingrid left Los Angeles by train in early August 1939 to return to Sweden. Since *Intermezzo: A Love Story* had not yet opened, she was not certain she would be coming back. She hoped so, because Hollywood had been everything she dreamed it would be.

While she was in Stockholm, *Intermezzo* opened to rave reviews for her performance. Also while she was in Sweden, Germany invaded Poland, World War II began, the Soviet Union invaded Finland, and *Gone With the Wind* premiered in Atlanta, fulfilling all of Selznick's optimistic expectations.

With all thoughts of making any more films in Germany ended, Ingrid started the last Swedish film she had agreed to do, *June Night*. The theme of the film, sexual harassment, was well ahead of its time.

Juninatten (June Night, 1940)

Kerstin Nosbäc (Ingrid Bergman) leads a lonely life as a druggist's assistant in a provincial Swedish town. At the public library, she meets a sympathetic sailor, Nils Asklund (Gunnar Sjöberg). They begin an affair, but she finds they share none of the cultural and intellectual interests that are so important to her.

When she tries to end the affair, he threatens suicide with a gun. Before he can do this, the gun accidentally goes off, seriously wounding Kerstin.

At the trial, she pleads for leniency, and Nils receives a short sentence. The scandal, however, forces Kerstin to leave the town and move to Stockholm, where she changes her name.

As Sara Nardanå, she meets Stefan von Bremen (Olof Widgren), a compatible spirit who brings her the happiness for which she has always longed.

As filming ended in early December of 1939, Kay Brown called Ingrid, relaying to her the chief terms of her new seven-year contract with Selznick. Ingrid was advised to return to the United States. It would have to be without Petter. He had joined the Swedish army as a producer of training films on military dentistry, and to be ready if Sweden needed more from him.

On January 12, 1940, Ingrid and Pia arrived in New York on the SS *Rex* from Genoa. Petter had accompanied them to the Italian port, then returned to Sweden.

The ship had made an unscheduled stop in Lisbon to pick up passengers whose Atlantic flights had been canceled. Some were en route from Casablanca to New York.

Ingrid, Pia, and a Swedish nursemaid would be staying with Kay Brown in her Park Avenue apartment until a film project materialized. Ingrid hoped that her first picture for Selznick on her new seven-year contract would be an adaptation of *Saint Joan* by George Bernard Shaw. Ingrid had been fascinated by Joan of Arc since she was a girl, when she first read about the newly canonized French saint. Meanwhile, Selznick was having second thoughts about the commercial possibilities of a Joan of Arc project, either as a film or onstage, and Ingrid was asked not to talk about it with the press.

After Ingrid had returned from a trip to Los Angeles to appear on *The Lux Radio Theatre* in an adaptation of *Intermezzo,* Kay suggested to Selznick the possibility of loaning her out for an upcoming six-week Broadway revival of Ferenc Molnár's *Liliom.* She would play Julie, the daughter of Liliom, who knows her father only as a spirit.

Molnár, living in New York at the time, expressed some misgivings about an actress playing Julie who was several inches taller than

Burgess Meredith, the actor playing Liliom. There was also the question of her English, which was still heavily accented. Ingrid was more concerned about letting Selznick down by getting bad reviews.

Her American reputation was still tenuous. Although *Intermezzo: A Love Story* had opened at Radio City Music Hall to great critical acclaim for her performance, the picture itself was dismissed as routinely sentimental, and outside the big cities it had been received with little enthusiasm. Her anxiety was heightened by the wartime problems of the European market and thus the limited possibility of continuing her career there if she failed in Hollywood.

Ingrid, however, liked a challenge, as much as she despised boredom. The play opened at the 44th Street Theatre to predominantly rave reviews, particularly for her performance. Also in the cast was Elia Kazan. Ushering at a nearby movie palace was Tom Williams before he became Tennessee.

"In the beginning," she told me, "it was difficult for me to feel I was making direct contact with my audience, because I was Swedish, speaking English.

"I always had terrible stage fright, especially for an opening night. In my dressing room, I imagined myself standing onstage, opening my mouth, with nothing coming out. Somehow I push myself, and suddenly I'm someone else, the character I'm playing. Then, everything is fine."

Working on the stage again, Ingrid was reminded of Gösta Ekman's emphasis on the importance of actors listening to each other. He had told her it was something at which she excelled.

"Listening is very important. I have noticed how often actors don't seem to listen to what the others are saying because he or she thinks they know it all already. When I am talking to actors in a play or a film, it is a terrible feeling if they don't seem to be listening.

"In life, if someone isn't listening to you, you can raise your voice, move closer, attract attention with body language, touch the person, but on the stage or on film, you are limited. You have to just put up with it."

I told her about the occasion when I went with George Cukor to New York University. It really shocked him when the student actors didn't listen to each other. They were standing there reciting, and they knew all the lines that were coming. They didn't realize that reaction can be more important than action. Not listening was what he said most distinguished the amateurs from the professionals.

In June, after Ingrid had completed her six-week run of *Liliom*, Petter arrived in New York for a visit.

"I couldn't wait to show my New York to Petter," she told me. "And I couldn't wait to show Petter to New York. I was certain he would love the sounds of this great city as I did.

"Petter didn't like New York. He hated it. He saw only that the buildings were dirty. He complained his socks got dirty when he walked on the rug in the hotel. He complained about everything.

"I was terribly disappointed. I had wanted to share my happiness with him, but his displeasure was too strong for my pleasure.

"It didn't influence me in how I felt about New York. Maybe it influenced how I felt about Petter."

Petter returned to Sweden to complete his military obligation, while Ingrid and Pia stayed in New York until August, and then went on to Los Angeles. At the request of director Gregory Ratoff, Selznick was lending Ingrid out to Columbia to make *Adam Had Four Sons* with Warner Baxter.

Fay Wray, who had worked with Erich von Stroheim on *The Wedding March*, as well as being legendary for her role in *King Kong*, talked with me about working with the young Swedish newcomer.

"I didn't know Ingrid Bergman well at that time. She was very serious. Her heart was *so* in the film. She treated the film like it was the most important one ever done.

"I knew this was a girl who *had* to be an actress or her heart would surely break. She wasn't working for the money, for fame, for success, even for fun, but because she *had* to be an actress. Mr. Ratoff, who had directed her on *Intermezzo,* was in love with her, I think. He was the one who insisted on her for the part of Emilie, even though the character is French in the novel.

"She was both ethereal and sensual. She seemed more real than reality. She had magic."

Adam Had Four Sons (1941)

As the French governess for the four young sons of Adam Stoddard (Warner Baxter), Emilie (Ingrid Bergman) quickly wins the affection of the boys and their father. Her feeling for Adam is even stronger, though she scrupulously avoids coming between him and his wife, Molly (Fay Wray). After Molly dies, Adam loses his fortune, and he is reluctantly forced to dismiss Emilie, who returns to France.

Years later, after the boys are men, Adam regains his fortune, and he arranges for Emilie to return to the household. One of the sons, David (Johnny Downs), brings home an attractive but unfaithful young wife, Hester (Susan Hayward). Discovering that Hester is having an affair with David's brother Jack (Richard Denning), Emilie tries to shield Adam from heartbreak by taking the blame herself. Eventually, Hester is exposed, and Adam realizes that he still loves Emilie.

Again, Ingrid's performance was praised by the critics, while the film was dismissed as routine. Her next film, *Rage in Heaven,* starred her with Robert Montgomery at MGM.

"I should have been overjoyed when Mr. Selznick loaned me out to MGM," Ingrid told me. "After only a couple of years in Hollywood, I was working at the same studio as Garbo. I saw her many times, but I was hesitant to speak to her. Once in a while, I followed closely behind her. I hoped she might speak to me, but she never did. I didn't know if she knew who I was or not. Everyone knew who *she* was. She was always careful not to make eye contact with people. She looked past you without seeing you. I didn't speak because I was shy. It never occurred to me that the reason she was so aloof was that Garbo was shy, too.

"I didn't like the picture I was working on, and I disliked the director, Woody Van Dyke. My co-stars, Robert Montgomery and George Sanders, felt just like me, only I made trouble by complaining to the director myself. Mr. Selznick pacified me by saying the magic words, 'Ingrid, think of Joan of Arc.' He didn't want me to get a reputation for being hard to get along with so early in my Hollywood career. I don't know if I was any easier to get along with because of what he said, but I never stopped thinking of Joan of Arc.

"Just before we started shooting *Rage in Heaven,* Robert Montgomery asked me to forgive him if he wasn't at his best. He said he was tired, but the studio wouldn't give him any time off." Although he actually had been inordinately busy in 1941, Montgomery was faced with suspension without salary by MGM should he make good his threat to take an unauthorized holiday after doing Alfred Hitchcock's *Mr. & Mrs. Smith.*

Based on the writing credits alone, *Rage in Heaven* should have turned out better than it did. It was from a novel by James Hilton, author of *Lost Horizon* and *Good-bye, Mr. Chips.* The screenplay was by Christopher Isherwood and Robert Thoeren. Isherwood wrote the *Berlin Diaries,* which became *I Am a Camera* and *Cabaret,* and Thoeren was best known for co-writing *Fanfaren der Liebe,* which inspired Billy Wilder's *Some Like It Hot.*

Rage in Heaven (1941)

When mentally unbalanced Philip Monrell (Robert Montgomery) assumes control of his family's factory, he makes conditions so unbearable that the workers strike. During the strike, he tries to kill his best friend, Ward Andrews (George Sanders), after he has made the life of his young wife, Stella (Ingrid Bergman), intolerable because of his erroneous suspicion that his wife and friend are having an affair.

The deranged Philip ingeniously commits suicide in a way that makes it appear that Ward has murdered him. Ward is found guilty, and he is sentenced to hang.

As Ward awaits execution, a Parisian psychiatrist, Dr. Rameau (Oscar Homolka), rushes to London after he recognizes Philip as an escapee from his mental institution. He and Stella search for a confession by Philip, intended to be found after Ward's execution. They find it and Ward is saved.

I was seated next to Christopher Isherwood at one of George Cukor's dinners in the early 1980s. Isherwood spoke about Ingrid Bergman.

"She was absolutely the most beautiful being I ever met, male or female. I don't go that way, you know, but I'm sure I could have made an exception for Ingrid Bergman. She was irresistible. It was more than how she looked outside. She radiated being that way inside, too.

"I believe she was quite aware of the effect she had on people, though she didn't flaunt it. Instead, she made *you* feel as if you, too, were beautiful and endlessly fascinating. It wasn't false, either, though I suspect she well knew what she was doing. She was a real pro.

"On the set, there were these people who would take advantage of the familiarity she seemed to inspire. But if they did something like pinching her on her bottom, she just smiled at them, almost a wink, like she was one of the boys in the locker room, too. And in a sense, she was. While being perfectly ladylike and feminine, she had balls, too.

"I admired her deeply. She was a generous spirit, which is rare, but ever rarer, she was sui generis."

Except for continuing praise for Ingrid, *Rage in Heaven* went virtually unnoticed until five years later, when MGM rereleased it. In 1946, most people assumed it was a new Ingrid Bergman film because so few of them had seen it in 1941 when she was new to American audiences. By 1946, Ingrid was the number one female box office star. She had made only one film that year, Alfred Hitchcock's *Notorious,* and audiences, eager to see her in anything, rushed to see *Rage in Heaven.*

The film played at New York City's Capitol Theatre, not only *not* a second-run house, but a great movie palace. The second time around, audiences turned out because it was "an Ingrid Bergman film."

After completing *Rage In Heaven,* Ingrid was approached by Victor Fleming about being in his upcoming *Dr. Jekyll and Mr. Hyde* for MGM. Ingrid was enthusiastic about appearing in the film, but not in the part she was offered.

Ingrid wanted the bad girl part of Ivy, the barmaid, but it was planned that she play Beatrix, the young lady to whom Dr. Jekyll is engaged. She was typecast in what seemed to her a dull part with which she could do little.

She argued with director Victor Fleming that she *could* be a tart, but Selznick argued forcefully that it would ruin her career. Ingrid, remembering the same admonitions when she did *A Woman's Face* in Sweden, reminded Selznick that he had let that property slip through his fingers, and the rights had been snapped up immediately for a Joan Crawford picture.

She persuaded Fleming, who told several of his friends how much in love with her he was, to make a screen test of her as Ivy. This convinced Fleming, Selznick, and everybody else. Lana Turner was cast against type as the good girl versus Ingrid's bad girl, and the film was an enormous success.

Dr. Jekyll and Mr. Hyde (1941)

Dr. Henry Jekyll (Spencer Tracy) promotes theories about the dual nature of man so revolutionary that his future father-in-law, Sir Charles Emery (Donald Crisp), breaks off Jekyll's engagement to his daughter, Beatrix (Lana Turner), and takes her abroad.

Jekyll rescues a barmaid, Ivy Peterson (Ingrid Bergman), from a street attacker, and takes her to his lodgings. There, his medical ethics prevent him from accepting her seductive offers, but after she has left, he becomes obsessed by her.

After drinking a chemical potion he has developed to isolate good from evil, he becomes Mr. Hyde, a man who is not bound by moral inhibitions. As Hyde, he finds Ivy, and they begin a brutal sadomasochistic affair.

Ivy consults Dr. Jekyll for the injuries she has received in this relationship, not realizing that he is also Mr. Hyde. Later, when he becomes Mr. Hyde, he murders her.

Jekyll now finds himself unable to control his two opposing natures, even without the potion. He increasingly becomes Mr. Hyde. Beatrix returns, and Jekyll tries to warn her of Hyde. When her father intervenes, Hyde kills him.

Jekyll, now entirely Hyde, is cornered by the police after a chase, and mortally wounded. As he dies, Hyde's distorted face returns to the smooth features of Dr. Jekyll.

Just before Christmas 1941, Petter arrived in Los Angeles after having crossed the Atlantic in six weeks on a freighter. In America, he changed his name to Peter Lindstrom. The couple celebrated their reunion with a skiing holiday in Sun Valley, Idaho. Ingrid's thoughts were already on a part she desperately wanted, that of Maria in *For Whom the Bell Tolls*.

"Petter Lindstrom was very handsome," Danny Selznick remembered. "Beautiful blue eyes. Very Nordic. And he was high-strung. I wouldn't describe him as nervous, but high-strung. Very handsome, very poetic, and very tender with Ingrid. And obviously controlling.

"I think that one can now realize, given his really very sensitive nature, how devastating it was for him to have his wife be this woman who was being made love to on-screen by all these handsome men, and who was becoming an icon of world cinema. You know, there comes a point where you have to let go. You have it today, people who are married to famous stars who are not famous themselves. He was 'Mr. Ingrid Bergman,' so to speak. People like this have to adjust to being the consort of these mythic figures.

"She had that natural thing, but the word 'natural' had to be reinvented for her.

"Of course she was so naturally natural, but not in any ordinary way. The point is, she was a totally free spirit, and her husband, Petter, couldn't control that. I *believe* he admired it. Probably it was an aspect of Ingrid he had loved about her. But the more famous she became, the freer she became, the more it was out of his control, and there was nothing he could do about it. Frankly, I felt sorry for him, because I could see that the man loved her, but could no longer influence her as he had. I mean, she worshipped him in early years. She obeyed him, and she respected him and loved him, but as the world embraced her, she was like a character in an Ibsen play. She couldn't stay, you know, like Nora in *A Doll's House*, cooped up in her Benedict Canyon doll's house for many more years. It was inevitable that something was going to explode, I thought.

"God, she was beautiful! There is no one I have ever met, of any age, of any generation, that took one's breath away at every meeting the way she did. The complexion, the lips, the cheeks, the ears, the nose, the eyes, the body of a goddess. And she was just completely unselfconscious. *Completely* unselfconscious.

"Today, if the stars are beautiful, people are pawing them, and they don't like it. They're kind of nervous. The big female stars of every era have beauty that is partly natural, partly manufactured. Ingrid's was only natural."

After *Dr. Jekyll and Mr. Hyde,* Ingrid appeared in a West Coast stage production of Eugene O'Neill's *Anna Christie,* produced by the Selznick company, that later played in New Jersey. She was also heard on radio as Jenny Lind in a *Cavalcade of America* radio program. The rest of the time she spent in Rochester, New York, with Pia and Petter, who was now working toward his degree at the University of Rochester Medical School. Because of the help of Selznick, Dr. Lindstrom had several choices of schools, but the medical school at the University of Rochester was willing to accept more of his Swedish credits.

In April 1942, Ingrid was informed that Selznick had arranged for her to be in *Casablanca* at Warner Brothers. She was not pleased.

"I was never so talented in selecting for myself the best or the most successful films, although I dreamed of being independent and successful enough to do so. A film I definitely would *not* have selected was *Casablanca,* and it is my best-loved, best-remembered film. Everywhere I go, people ask me or *tell* me about *Casablanca.*

"I would never have guessed it. I couldn't understand why. Many years later, I decided to see what all the fuss was about.

"Now, I understand. I was wrong."

At the time, however, she didn't believe it was going to be a good film, and she didn't particularly like her part, which she felt didn't call on her to do very much.

What made her feel most insecure about the film—and Ingrid didn't like feeling insecure just before a film—was that she didn't have a full script, only a part of one, and she had been told there might be changes. Most critical for her was that it had not yet been decided which of the two leading men she would be with at the end of the film. She didn't know if she would be with Paul Henreid or Humphrey Bogart. She felt fairly certain it would be Humphrey Bogart because he was the bigger star, and he certainly had the bigger and more interesting part in the film.

Most of all, she didn't *want* to be Ilsa in *Casablanca*. She wanted to be María in *For Whom the Bell Tolls*.

And Humphrey Bogart didn't really want to be Rick.

Ingrid told me that as soon as she learned she would be working with Bogart, she tried to see some of his films so she would feel she knew him, at least his screen persona. Diligently, as Ingrid did everything related to her acting work, she stayed through two and even three showings of some of his films.

Ingrid didn't really know Bogart, although she had met him. Then, when she had lunch with him, they did not have instant rapport. "We didn't have the same taste in food, and certainly not the same interest in it. He ate very little and ate it very fast." Ingrid remembered that the only subject they found in common was how much they both wanted to get out of *Casablanca*.

"That was not very constructive, because, of course, we never did anything about it, except go to the set and hit our marks and do our best."

Being with him made her feel very tall. Bogart, however, didn't seem to be at all self-conscious about height or his lack of it.

Ingrid had suggested the lunch because she was looking for encouragement about *Casablanca*. Bogart was the wrong person for that. He didn't make the usual comment about how glad he was to be working with her. Ingrid liked having the best possible rapport with everyone on the set, all of the actors, the crew, and certainly those with whom she would play important scenes. She did not have that desired relationship with him.

The romance between Humphrey Bogart's Rick and Ingrid's Ilsa lives as long as people will watch films. The relationship between the two actors was considerably less passionate than what audiences saw on the screen.

"I kissed Bogie," Ingrid said, "but I never got to know him.

"I liked Michael Curtiz, the director of *Casablanca*. He had such talent, and I think he never had the appreciation he should have had. I don't know why. He made wonderful films, and he was a very important part of those films. He didn't seem to be liked very well personally. Again, I don't know why. I only know I liked him, and if anyone spoke against him, I defended him, but I never knew why I should be defending him at all. Well, *Casablanca* speaks for itself, and it doesn't have to shout, just whisper, but a whisper that persists over the years.

"It was Mr. Curtiz who spoke to me about the idea of typecasting. I knew it was the way, but I hadn't understood how difficult it would be to fight it. He explained I couldn't go totally against the way audiences saw me without wrecking my career. He gave me a little lecture; well, actually, it was a *big* lecture. He began with, 'Ingrid, you are beautiful.' Well, that was a good beginning. I always enjoyed hearing that.

"He went on. 'They do not want to see you play a girl with a harelip.' I could not imagine how he made such a choice, as an example. As it happened, just such a part *had* been suggested for me. I do not say 'offered,' because it didn't come close, but such a part was floating around.

"He said, 'Your audience wants to see you, to recognize you, to see you looking beautiful, wearing beautiful clothes, dresses, and accessories *they* would like to wear. They like to see you on the screen in parts in which they recognize you. In other words, you have to play Ingrid Bergman. This will not tax you too much, it will make your audience happy, and it will make a big career. Typecasting is *every*thing.'

"I said, 'No, no, no, no, no, no.'

"I was thinking how I could get around it.

"Can you believe this? When we began *Casablanca*, none of us knew where we were going. That's true. Even the writers didn't know what was going on—because they hadn't written it all yet. They hadn't even decided yet. This made for a lot of uneasiness. There were quarrels. Usually, our director was a vigorous participant in these.

"He had an ongoing argument with the Epstein brothers [Julius and Philip], who were wonderful writers. Then, [producer] Hal Wallis would argue with him. This kept us all a bit tense. We were lucky to know what our parts would be for that day. Who would live? Who would die?

"What I wanted to know was, which man was I going to choose? I felt it made a difference in how I portrayed Ilsa. I was certain no one would tell me because they decided I shouldn't know, because they had decided I would give a better performance if I didn't know. I didn't like that. I learned later that no one had let me in on it because *they* couldn't decide.

"I have been asked so many times which one I, Ingrid, would have chosen between Bogie and my war-hero husband.

"I have to speak for Ilsa, because it was Ilsa who chose. There was no other possibility. None. Ilsa did the only thing she *could* do. She believed in duty and responsibility. She could not flee her destiny. The problem was that Ilsa could never be perfectly happy, only imperfectly happy. Whichever man she chose, she would always have thoughts about the other.

"They were so unsure about the ending that they decided the only answer was to film two endings. The one they decided to do first was I say goodbye to Humphrey Bogart and fly away with my husband. In that one there is that wonderful line, as Bogie and Claude Rains walk off into the fog. Bogie says, 'Louis, I think this is the beginning of a beautiful friendship.'

"And we all knew. It had happened. It existed forever. It was so clear. There was no other possibility."

Paul Henreid was adamant about not wanting to be Victor Laszlo. Even the entreaties of Hal Wallis, whom he liked and respected, failed to convince him otherwise. The counseling of his agent, the famous Lew Wasserman, who created brilliant careers for many of his clients, among them Bette Davis, was equally unpersuasive.

Henreid was convinced that, early in his American career, if he were to accept the secondary role of Victor Laszlo, he would not go beyond that, and his career would thus be handicapped.

It was then that he sought the advice of someone he considered a great actress as well as a friend, Bette Davis.

Henreid told her about *Casablanca,* the idea of it, the story, and especially a description of his role. He said he had declined the part of Laszlo because he thought it wouldn't be a good one for his future career in Hollywood.

Without hesitation, Bette said, "You are wrong, wrong, *wrong!* It is a wildly good part for you, and you can bring a great deal to it. You can make this character so *very* interesting. I *know* you can. He is not only what you see written in the script. This part of Laszlo is much better than you think it is. Mr. [Hal] Wallis is a wonderful man, largely responsible for the success of Warner Brothers and of *my* success, so it's good for you to work with him and try to give him what he wants.

"Ilsa's character is defined by Laszlo. Ingrid Bergman is a wonderful actress. You will like working with her. And you will like working with Bogie, too. I've worked with him, and *that* I know totally."

Henreid trusted Bette's instinct and knew she had his best interest at heart. He could not go against that, but there was another consideration.

He was born Paul von Henreid in Trieste when it was a part of the Austro-Hungarian Empire. His family was titled and wealthy; but with the break up of the empire, they were forced to flee to Vienna, where young Paul decided he wanted to be an actor. When Germany annexed Austria, he fled the Nazis, first going to London, and then to Hollywood. Though he had by now dropped the "von," Henreid could not drop his strong accent, so he still suffered from being considered a German. Irving Rapper, who directed several Bette Davis films, told me that sometimes when Henreid was speaking English in normal conversation, it sounded like he was speaking German.

Lew Wasserman had explained to him that playing a non-German freedom fighter like Laszlo would be good for his image. It would also help to establish him as a patriotic working actor, as opposed to being possibly regarded as an enemy alien.

Offered a contract, and more important to him, star billing after Ingrid Bergman and Humphrey Bogart, he accepted the part. As the script was finally written, he also got Ilsa. He had been certain Bogie would win Ingrid because he was the big star.

"Mr. Wallis told me," Ingrid said, "that the moral factor was very important. It was important that Ilsa made the right choice. Mr. Wallis said it wouldn't have endured the other way. She had to leave her love for Bogart to choose the love of her husband and to help in his important work.

"It also was very important you didn't kill Claude Rains. It would have broken the hearts of too many.

"We hoped we were making a good film. We had no idea. No idea at all about what the picture was going to mean to people and for how long. I thought the writing was good, by those talented [Epstein] twin brothers. I could hardly wait to see how the film turned out. I couldn't decide which way I wanted. I decided I would be happy whichever way it happened. Both men were wonderful. How could I not be happy with either one? How could I lose? But then I was sad about whichever way it went. The way it went was right, I think, and it was right forever."

Casablanca (1942)

Casablanca, as part of unoccupied France, is a temporary safe haven for refugees from German-dominated Europe on their way to neutral Portugal. The meeting place of these desperate travelers is Rick's Café Americaine, owned and operated by Rick Blaine (Humphrey Bogart), an American expatriate whose mysterious past prevents him from returning home.

A German major, Heinrich Strasser (Conrad Veidt), is sent to Casablanca to investigate the killing of two German couriers. They were carrying letters of transit that would allow the bearers to leave for Lisbon. Perfunctorily cooperating with him is Captain Louis Renault (Claude Rains) of the Casablanca police, a self-confessed corruptible official.

The letters have been stolen by Ugarte (Peter Lorre), a petty thief, who asks Rick to hide them for him. When Ugarte is killed, Rick's place is searched in an unsuccessful attempt to find the letters.

Victor Laszlo (Paul Henreid), an anti-Nazi underground hero, arrives in Casablanca with his beautiful Norwegian wife, Ilsa (Ingrid Bergman). Ilsa is the girl who inexplicably disappeared from Rick's life in Paris on the eve of the German occupation. He has never forgotten—nor forgiven—her.

Suspecting that Rick knows where the letters of transit that will allow Laszlo to continue his work abroad are hidden, Ilsa begs him for them and then threatens him with a gun, which she cannot use because she still loves him. Ilsa left him in Paris only because she learned that her husband was still alive. She loves Rick, but understands that Laszlo needs her. Rick agrees to help Laszlo escape to Lisbon.

Rick gains Captain Renault's cooperation by telling him that he and Ilsa plan to leave, and promising Laszlo's arrest at the airport. Suspecting Laszlo, not Rick, will board the plane at the last moment, Renault phones Strasser, who rushes to the airport.

Strasser is shot and killed by Rick when he attempts to stop the flight, and Ilsa and Victor escape. When the police arrive, Renault tells them to "round up the usual suspects," after which

he and Rick leave Casablanca together to join a nearby Free
French garrison.

The letters of transit everyone needs to get out of Casablanca are a
kind of Hitchcockian MacGuffin. Everybody wants them, but nobody
knows quite what they are, only that they are highly desirable. No one
is troubled by their irrational nature. This is part of the cinematic
magic that has drawn audiences into *Casablanca*'s unreal ambience
since 1942.

"I feel about *Casablanca* that it has a life of its own," Ingrid told me.
"There is something mystical about it. It seems to have filled a need, a
need that was there before the film, a need that the film filled."

At a Film Society of Lincoln Center party for the New York Film Festival, I talked with Julius Epstein, who with his brother, Philip, and
Howard Koch, wrote the *Casablanca* screenplay. He told me that the
legendary line delivered by Rick, "Here's looking at *you*, kid," was
Humphrey Bogart's idea. "I knew the minute Bogie said it that it was
a great, great line, but an important part of the greatness of the line is
it's unique to the character who speaks it, that it comes right out of
him, that it belongs only to *him*.

"Then, Bogart's delivery was unique, never overplaying. He brought
so much to the part, when he brought himself to it, that the writer's
work was largely done for him. That voice and the delivery. Unique.
He should get credit for the line. What would that line have been
without Bogie, coming out of the mouth of some other actor, *any*
other actor? So, in the end Bogie *did* get the credit. He lives forever,
saying that line.

"And then, let me tell you something else that made the line so
great, because not everything you put into a script is what you can
write on paper.

"Think about who he was saying the line to. That face of Ingrid Bergman. There'll never be another face like that. Ingrid didn't have to speak a word. There was a look in those eyes that said it all. She had such depth. The object of Rick's love had to be worthy of it.

"That left it open for Rick to say flippantly, and not flippantly at the same time, 'Here's looking at *you*, kid.'

"See? When *I* say the line, nothing!"

I visited actress Madeleine LeBeau during the early 1990s in Rome, where she lived with her husband, writer Tullio Pinelli. I had gone to talk with Pinelli about Federico Fellini for the book I was writing, *I, Fellini*. Pinelli and LeBeau first met while she was playing the French woman who played one of Marcello Mastroiani's former mistresses in Fellini's *8½*. She had fond memories of her time in America, where she played the French girl who was Rick Blaine's former mistress in *Casablanca*. How she came to be in Hollywood at that moment was a story worthy of a *Casablanca* vignette.

In Paris during the late 1930s, LeBeau had a small part in a play in Paris in which Marcel Dalio starred. Dalio was one of the premier French actors of his time, known internationally for his performances in Julien Duvivier's *Pépé le Moko* and Jean Renoir's *La Grande Illusion*. Dalio did not have leading-man looks, but Marlene Dietrich described him as "dear, charming Marcel." He immediately noticed the beautiful seventeen-year-old actress. They were married at the beginning of World War II.

Dalio, who was Jewish, left France with his bride as the Germans were approaching Paris. It was a prescient move, since when the invaders did arrive, the Nazis used his face on posters to represent the archetypal Jewish type.

After a two-month wait in Lisbon, they embarked for Chile with visas that turned out to be forged. From Chile, they went to Mexico where they were stopped again. Finally, they reached Los Angeles. Dalio had begun studying English in Mexico.

In Hollywood, Dalio had friends who helped him to get work in films with small parts that required European types. Through this help, his young bride became a contract player at Warner Brothers and she was cast in *Casablanca*. Dalio played the croupier in the film. Before *Casablanca* finished shooting, Dalio filed for divorce on grounds of his wife's desertion.

LeBeau believed her part was going to be much bigger than it turned out. "It wasn't that I was cut out," she recalled fifty years later in her Rome apartment, "it was because they kept changing the script, and each time they changed it, I had less of a part. It wasn't personal, but I was *so* disappointed."

Her scene with the German officer was her favorite. It took four days to shoot. Steven Spielberg, so many years later, especially liked her emotional singing in the "La Marseillaise" scene.

"Now, I'm thrilled to have been part of *Casablanca*," she told me.

Near the end of the shooting of *Casablanca*, Ingrid was informed that she would, after all, be playing María in *For Whom the Bell Tolls* with Gary Cooper and directed by Sam Wood at Paramount. She was to replace actress Vera Zorina in the part.

Ingrid was thrilled when she learned that she was going to be María. She had been the original choice of the author of the book, Ernest Hemingway. She was as certain that María would be one of her greatest parts as she was that playing Ilsa in *Casablanca* would be a waste of time in her acting career.

Selznick was loaning Ingrid out to Paramount for $90,000-plus, which meant he was making a $60,000 profit on her services. Kay Brown told me that Ingrid's contract with Selznick started at $20,000 a picture and gradually increased until it reached $40,000, even when her services brought in much more money on a loan-out. At that moment, she was making $30,000 a picture. Ingrid was too happy to be playing María to give much thought to this, but later she, and especially Petter, would come to resent it, feeling Selznick collected an exorbitant amount for the selling of her services. Ingrid might not have cared, but Petter was enraged.

Danny Selznick, who saw the issue from both sides, explained it to me:

"My father created her career at a very tumultous time, when he was working on *Gone With the Wind,* and *Rebecca,* too. As she said many times, 'Why did David keep me under contract and make all that money off me?' That was her bitterness. He was paying her under a contract, and making a *huge* profit on her!

"I agreed with her that it was really outrageous, and I mentioned something about it to my father at some point when I got older. He said, 'Danny, do you have any idea how many people I had under contract, how many people I was paying that I *wasn't* able to sell to *anybody?* The money I made off Ingrid made it possible for all these other people to earn a living under contract.'

"From his point of view, yes, he did make a profit, but he spread it around. He wasn't pocketing it and building extra swimming pools. He was putting it back into the company and nurturing other talents, sending actors to plastic surgeons. He put all kinds of wonderful people under contract. The point is, he was guiding the choices Ingrid was making, and yet he was negotiating the deals, but he was also reading the scripts, sending extensive memos, etc. So, all I can say is, I think it was a fair deal.

"Whenever people talk to me about Ingrid Bergman, I always ask them to look up in *Memo from David O. Selznick* that letter he wrote her. It's a 'Dear David' letter signed, 'Love, Ingrid Bergman,' as if she wrote it. And my father put in things like 'You did this for me, you did that for me, and I'm so grateful. But in spite of that, I'm going to have to reject,' whatever it was he was offering. But in the mid-1940s she was the biggest star in the world. I don't know what he wanted her to do, but she turned it down. But what he wrote *her!* It's so funny.

"When I talked to Ingrid about it, I said, 'Wasn't that an incredible thing for him to write?' She said, 'It was,' and I don't know exactly what words she used, but they were like, 'It's shameless your father would do that,' but then she added, 'It didn't change my mind.' "

"Gary Cooper made me blush," Ingrid told me. "I have to admit I was very attracted to him. One couldn't really help being a little in love with Coop. Imagine being *paid* to do scenes with Gary Cooper?

"I was a married woman with a little girl. Nothing could be between us, but it doesn't mean a woman can't be attracted to a man the way a man who is faithful to his wife can still meet a woman to whom he is attracted. I was told that my character, María, had to seem very much in love with a hero being played by Gary Cooper. Could I do that? It was no problem at all.

"I think there is something about the atmosphere of the set, your interaction with your leading man, the special relationship with the director, it is all conducive to some attraction on the set. That can be a distraction, or a bit of sexual tension can enhance a scene.

"He was the most natural in his acting. His underplaying was more commanding than anyone could have been overplaying. Some people might have thought he didn't do anything, but it's not true. It is much more difficult to do less rather than more. He wasn't given the credit he deserved for his talent, because he underplayed, so it didn't seem he was doing anything. He was a really fine actor. I learned a great deal from him.

"I think Petter was a little jealous. Of course, absolutely nothing happened. I was married and Coop was married, and we each had a young daughter. Our daughter, Pia, knew their daughter, Maria."

Maria Cooper Janis, the daughter of Gary Cooper, stood with me at the 2006 opening of the new Le Cirque restaurant in New York City and reminisced about Ingrid Bergman, whom she remembered as the perfect mother:

"She was so nice. I would be at their house because Pia was my friend. Ingrid Bergman was the least actressy person I ever met."

In August 1942, production began on *For Whom the Bell Tolls* in the Sierra Nevada, followed by studio shooting in September. It was Ingrid's first color film, and, she believed, it would be her most memorable film. *Casablanca* had not yet opened.

For Whom the Bell Tolls was adapted by Dudley Nichols from Ernest Hemingway's novel about the Spanish Civil War. After the film was shown, she hoped that "Papa" Hemingway would be pleased with the film and, very important to her, that he would be proud of her performance. "When he didn't call, I knew it wasn't a good sign. He never mentioned my performance," Ingrid told me. "Either he hadn't noticed it because he said he 'hated' the film that had been done of his work or because he hated my performance, too."

For Whom the Bell Tolls (1943)

Robert Jordan (Gary Cooper), an American volunteer in the Spanish Civil War, is ordered to blow up a bridge during a Loyalist offensive. He must do so with a band of peasant guerrillas led by El Sordo (Joseph Calleia). Their former leader, Pablo (Akim Tamiroff), works within the group against El Sordo with his war-weary cynicism, but Pablo's strong wife, Pilar (Katina Paxinou), pulls the band together when her husband's defeatism threatens morale.

In the group is a girl named María (Ingrid Bergman), who lost her parents and was raped. She and Jordan fall in love.

When the guerillas finally fight their way to the bridge and manage to blow it up, Jordan is killed. Before he dies, he reaffirms his love for María in words to inspire her for the rest of her life.

"My haircut for María," Ingrid said, "became very popular with women because the idea of short hair and little curls seemed so simple. It looked like you wouldn't have to do anything.

"It looked easy, but it really was a terrible style for anyone to take care of. I always could handle my own hair with a few strokes of a hairbrush. Not with these short little curls which they had to keep setting in tight pin curls. They looked like they just happened. Well, they *didn't* just happen.

"Someone with a hairbrush had to follow me around constantly. I didn't have a moment between scenes because they were fussing with my hair.

"I felt so sorry for women who saw me wearing the style and thought they would like 'a María cut.' Then I felt guilty when I understood that I had created a false impression. 'The María cut' was the style most requested in beauty salons all over America.

"I have never felt good in makeup," Ingrid continued. "I think you have to start using it early in life to feel natural when you have something unnatural on your face. My mother had died, so there was no makeup in our house to play with the way little girls do. But looking at her photographs, I don't think my mother used any makeup, and she was like me.

"I always feel people looking at my face will see where the makeup ends and I begin, especially in daylight. Even light makeup feels like a mask I'm wearing to hide behind. I do not want to hide. I wish to communicate. I wish to look like myself. I don't like the feeling of looking into a mirror and seeing someone I don't recognize as myself. I never knew a person who feels more strongly about this, but I did find a horse who felt the same way. It happened when we were making *For Whom the Bell Tolls*.

"At the end of the picture, there is a moment when the guerrillas have to race across an open space to save their lives, and Gary Cooper lets everyone else go first. He is last, and everyone on the other side is set to kill him. His horse stumbles and falls on him, and breaks his leg.

"When you read this in the book, on the printed page, it's not a problem. But on the screen, the horse has to fall on the leg without breaking it. This feat requires an Academy Award–winning performance by a horse who must have the athletic skill and the intelligence to do this trick. Hollywood had incredible stunt men and stunt women, and stunt horses, but there was only one horse who had consistently done this trick, with no broken legs to show for it. Fortunately for us, he was between jobs and available. He was a lovely brown horse. I've forgotten his name, but he deserved to be in the credits.

"Unfortunately, the horse in our movie was gray. They called it dapple gray. Well, there was only one thing to do. Paint him.

"Our makeup man was instructed to do an extensive body makeup, from brown to gray. But our horse didn't like it. He was sad. He was disappointed. He was depressed. He acted as if we had rejected him, and you might say we had. We tried to talk him out of his depression and to give him a lot of attention and praise. It didn't work. We couldn't cheer him up. He was angry, but more than that, he was obviously severely embarrassed. He just stood about, hanging his head. He was feeling very sorry for himself.

"We didn't know what to do. Then, I think he got bored with just standing around feeling sorry for himself, so he did it, his best trick. We knew he had done it right when Coop was able to get up and walk around.

"We got the usual sugar lumps to reward our horse, who had saved the day, and the film, but he wasn't interested. His happiness couldn't be bought with sugar lumps.

"The makeup man took off all of the color as quickly as possible. Brown again. Then, a happy brown horse, he enjoyed his sugar lumps. He was no longer hanging his head in shame, and he seemed to immediately get over his excruciating experience with makeup. I could identify with him perfectly."

Just after *For Whom the Bell Tolls* wrapped, *Casablanca* opened, coincidentally with the Allied invasion of North Africa at Casablanca. The picture was a big success and earned eight Oscar nominations, winning for best film, best direction, by Curtiz, and best screenplay, by the Epstein brothers and Howard Koch, as well as for best editing and music. Bogart and Claude Rains were nominated, as were cinematographer Arthur Edeson and composer Max Steiner. *For Whom the Bell Tolls,* though nominated for nine Oscars, won only one, Katina Paxinou for supporting actress.

In January 1943, Petter received his medical degree from the University of Rochester, and the family moved back to California. Ingrid was asked by Selznick to stop in Minnesota on her way to do a documentary film for the Office of War Information called *Swedes in America.* At the time, it was believed that Sweden was in danger of being occupied by Germany.

Ingrid was loaned out again for another Gary Cooper film directed by Sam Wood, *Saratoga Trunk,* based on the Edna Ferber novel.

"Actresses are funny girls," George Cukor informed me. "I remember Ingrid calling me during the filming of *Saratoga Trunk.* She was giggling so much, I could hardly understand what she was saying. I said, 'Get hold of yourself, my girl. I can't understand you.' She was so tickled, she could hardly pull herself together.

" 'Oh, George,' she said. 'I was wearing my dark wig for *Saratoga*

Trunk, and Charlie Feldman,' he was her agent, you know, 'walked right by me in the commissary, and he didn't say hello.' She said hello in that funny Swedish way she had on that word, if she was excited and carried away, and not thinking.

" 'Isn't that wonderful, George? He didn't recognize me!'

"She had so much to be proud of, and *that's* what she was proud of, like a little girl playing dress-up. Ingrid never lost that innocent quality of wonder."

Saratoga Trunk (made 1943, released 1945)

Clio Dulaine (Ingrid Bergman), the illegitimate daughter of a New Orleans aristocrat, is an embarrassment socially to her father's family. They offer her a large sum of money to leave, but she will accept only if they agree to allow her part-Creole mother to be interred in the Dulaine burial plot.

Clio journeys to Saratoga Springs, a fashionable resort for the wealthy, where she encounters a Texas gambler she knew in New Orleans, Clint Maroon (Gary Cooper). He finds her amusing, especially her obvious attempts to find a rich man who will ask her to marry him. One of those is Bart van Steed (John Warburton), a railroad tycoon. He knows her background, but doesn't care.

Clint leaves to compete for control of a branch line called the Saratoga Trunk. It's a dangerous venture, and he comes back injured. Realizing she loves him, Clio rejects van Steed to marry Clint.

Warner Brothers, disappointed with the finished film, sent it overseas for American troops to see, but delayed its release in the United States until late 1945.

•　　•　　•

George Cukor had wanted Ingrid for the remake of *A Woman's Face*, but he couldn't have her, and Joan Crawford played the role. Even more, Cukor wanted Ingrid for his remake of director Thorold Dickinson's *Gaslight*, a memorable 1940 British film based on Patrick Hamilton's stage play, *Angel Street*. Ingrid loved the play. Selznick not only loaned her out for the role, but he also loaned out Joseph Cotten for the part of the hero. Ingrid was enthusiastic about working with Cukor on such a good property, but she had one misgiving.

"What worried Ingrid most," Cukor told me, "was, can you imagine, she felt she looked too healthy! Well, she *was* a robust girl. She *did* look healthy, but I refrained from telling her she might eat a little less. Dear Ingrid loved her food, especially little forbidden sweets. I always recognize a refrigerator-raider, being one myself. There were people who suggested to me that, for my own good, I might eat a little less. I never forgave them, especially since it was true."

Frequently when Cukor ate lunch with me, he would order extra desserts, and then give them to me to eat, sometimes without his even tasting them. That permitted him to enjoy them vicariously without guilt.

"Personally," Cukor said, "I thought there was no reason why a healthy girl couldn't become a terrorized victim. It seemed even *more* shocking. Like the Hitchcock villains who had to be affable enough to come through your front door, because you wouldn't let them in if they looked like ax murderers.

"One is more upset for Ingrid's character *because* she has everything and *should* be enjoying a wonderful life, but she has nothing because of the cad she has married who turns out to be an evil, greedy murderer.

"It's not easy when you see *Gaslight* to believe that young Angela Lansbury had never before appeared in a film," Cukor told me. "She is wonderfully corrupt. And she was only a teenager at the time.

"In real life, she was quite an innocent child. I rescued her from the Bullock's Wilshire department store where she had a part-time job for the Christmas season, wrapping gifts. John Van Druten, the playwright, gave me the tip. He knew that I was looking for someone to play Nancy, the maid. I knew it was a highly important part, that wonderful contrast with the romantic, pure, rather saintly Ingrid, and that too special rapport she had with the suave villain.

"She was the daughter of Moyna MacGill, who had come from England with her children as refugees because of the war.

"I did a test with her, and I was astounded. It was as if she had made dozens of films, a perfect professional.

"She had the most sullen mouth, and the quality that she was waiting for sex.

"I expected a lot of pats on the shoulder when her test was seen, but far from it. Nothing but criticism. 'Too young. Too inexperienced.' Little did they know *how* young and inexperienced! I found out later she was only fourteen.

"I didn't want her to be hurt when she didn't get the part, so I called her up, and I told her I thought she had a good future and that her test was wonderful, but she might not get the job.

"I found that what they were saying was she wasn't sexy enough. Imagine that? This was, after all, a Victorian setting.

"It was an awfully good test, so I was regretful. She was *so* good as the girl who was definitely a bad lot.

"Then, the next thing I knew, to show you how little I knew, there she was on the set. She came early, and she was where you could find her. Of course, so did Ingrid, and this was even rarer in a big star, and Ingrid made it her business never to be in the way, but always to be where you could find her.

"Ingrid was pleased by my choice. She said Angela Lansbury helped her greatly to discover and keep her own character."

"I had a hidden cookie jar in my room," Ingrid told me. "Petter was very strict with me about my eating, and I was starving. On the set and with Petter at dinner, at home, I ate a lot of cottage cheese. I especially missed the treat of a bit of something sweet at the end of the meal. I always left our table hungry. Petter, being a person of great discipline, thought it was a very good thing, my leaving the table hungry.

"After a few weeks of cookies, it turned out I had gained two pounds. Petter was so confused. He was a doctor, and he had a scientific mind. He said, 'How can it be? You have been on a diet to lose weight, and instead you have *gained* it.'"

Ingrid, who no longer blushed as deep a color, blushed only slightly. Fortunately, she felt Petter had not asked her a question and thus, she was not obliged to answer.

Had he called on her to answer directly, "Ingrid, do you know why you are gaining weight?" she would have felt compelled to tell the truth. Ingrid did not like to lie to anyone, and she particularly would never have wanted to lie to Petter.

She wondered if a small evasion, her silence, constituted a lie. It was all so upsetting, she went upstairs "and immediately I had two delicious butter cookies, which were very soothing. I felt better."

Gaslight (1944)

In Victorian times, Paula Alquist (Ingrid Bergman) fears she may be going insane. As her husband, Gregory Anton (Charles Boyer), incessantly reminds her, she has become increasingly forgetful and even hides things from herself. Expressing concern for her well-being, he confines her to the elegant house in London she had inherited from an aunt who was murdered several years before. Paula assumes that part of her madness is imagining sounds that come from shut-off parts of the house at night after the gaslights have briefly dimmed.

A Scotland Yard detective, Brian Cameron (Joseph Cotten), finds Anton's activities suspicious, and reopens the unsolved murder case. Cameron visits Paula while Anton is away and tells her that he suspects Anton killed her aunt to get her jewels, but could never locate them. He married Paula to get back into the house and continue his search. At the same time, he has been systematically trying to drive the sensitive Paula insane so he can have her committed when he does find the jewels.

Cameron sets a trap, and just as Anton finds the jewels where they had been cleverly hidden, sewn on a costume to appear as fake decoration, he is caught and bound. While the detective is summoning the police, Anton tries to persuade Paula that she should help him escape, but she mockingly acts as if he really *has* driven her insane and his life is now in the hands of a madwoman.

Paula has greater inherent strength than was originally apparent, and she and Cameron have a good future together.

"Charles Boyer," Ingrid told me, "was a splendid actor and one of the finest men I have ever worked with. I wanted so much to do the film, and I learned that there was an argument about which of us would receive top billing, who would be on the left side of the screen above the credits, and who would be on the right side, some silly thing like that. So petty.

"I didn't care at all, and Charles never said anything about it. It was probably something like his agent arguing with Selznick, who could be, who was, a very stubborn man. I would have gone down on my knees to David if it had been necessary. Fortunately it wasn't. *Gaslight* was one of my favorite films and one of the greatest experiences of my life."

Not long after *Gaslight*, Ingrid asked Joseph Cotten to go with her to a formal dinner party at the home of David and Irene Selznick. Petter had to work at the hospital that night, and Ingrid saw it as a moment of opportunity for some mischief.

Cotten had also been invited, and he was happy to escort Ingrid to the dinner until he learned what she had in mind.

Ingrid, always very persuasive with men who liked her, as nearly all men did, convinced Cotten that her prank was harmless. She asked him what sizes he wore in shirt, jacket, and trousers. Then she rented the fanciest butler's outfit and a maid's black dress with a white collar and apron, the kind that would be worn in the most elegant homes. For herself, Ingrid wanted a more up-to-date version of the dress worn by the maid, Nancy, in *Gaslight*.

Ingrid looked forward with eager anticipation to an evening that usually bored her. Each A-list dinner party at the Selznick home was a repetition of the one before. There was wonderful food, which tempted her, but she had been admonished by Petter not to partake, and Selznick had said virtually the same thing to her. She wished she could bring her knitting. She didn't like wasting time, and if she could have knitted, "there would have been something constructive to show for the time spent, a sleeve."

Cotten did not look forward to the evening. He hadn't wanted to say no to Ingrid, and he had a good sense of humor, but he wasn't certain David and Irene Selznick would find their joke so funny.

Ingrid said it was an experiment. She believed that people do not look past the uniforms of those who are serving them and do not see these people as persons at all.

They arrived and entered through the kitchen, perfectly attired for their roles, and no one asked any questions. At the party, no one ever looked up and noticed the two actors who were serving. At first, Ingrid was very serious in her demeanor, and Cotten followed her example.

As nothing happened, Ingrid grew a bit bolder. The game was growing dull. She began serving plates of appetizers with ten or fifteen pieces piled unattractively and precariously on each plate, especially to those who had declined the appetizers. When she brought the drinks, she brought one to each person who was already holding a full glass, so they were left holding two glasses and puzzled.

It was after this kind of carrying on that Irene Selznick looked up and said, "Ingrid, dear, why don't you go into my dressing room and find a dress you would like to wear for the rest of the evening. And Joe, you can get along as you are. People will think it's your tuxedo." Irene Selznick didn't show any emotion. Ingrid felt a bit let down. Cotten felt relieved.

The next day, Ingrid told Petter about her adventure. "Not to tell him," she explained to me, "would have been like lying.

"Looking at me, very stern, he said, 'Ingrid, you're going to have to change your behavior.'

"So I did. The next time I did something like that, I made certain not to tell him."

After *Gaslight,* Ingrid went for a month with a group of Hollywood actresses to entertain the troops in Alaska. Petter, who had finished his internship, tried to join the United States Army, but was advised he would be of more value to the war effort as a civilian doctor. The Lindstrom family moved into a home at 1220 Benedict Canyon Drive, which Lindstrom and Pia would occupy for many years, though not always with Ingrid. The marriage was already showing signs of strain for her.

"Perhaps it was because I was so young," Ingrid told me. "I hadn't really found myself yet and what acting meant to me—finding my many selves on-screen or onstage.

"I never cared a lot about clothes, but I very much liked to look. I never wanted to buy the most expensive, but sometimes I saw a dress I thought I would like to have, and I asked Petter, because it was he who took care of all of the money.

"Each time, he would say to me, 'You don't need a new dress. You look beautiful in anything you wear!'" Ingrid accepted the compliment instead of the dress.

"One of the things I loved most about Petter when we met was having a confidant, someone to whom I could confide not only my thoughts and the occurrences of my young life, which seemed big to me, but my innermost feeling which I had never before told anyone. I was very innocent, and I had little to tell, but it all seemed dramatic and urgent to me. And Petter was a wonderful listener. He seemed to relish every word. I couldn't wait to tell him. It seemed he was anxious to hear every word I had to say.

"After we had been married some years, I would rush in eagerly, anxious to tell Petter some small drama that had occurred in my day, and I would begin gushing, and he would say. 'Wait and catch your breath.' I would pause and begin again, and he would say, 'Don't wrinkle your forehead that way when you speak. It makes for premature wrinkles.' I began again. As I spoke, he gave me a quizzical, rather negative look. 'Have you gained some weight,' he asked. 'A pound or two?' I said I didn't know, and he suggested I go to the scale, adding that I should weigh myself each day.

"Then, he asked me what it was I had been so anxious to tell. I said I couldn't remember. He said, 'Then it couldn't have been so important.'

"I did remember what I'd wanted to tell, but I no longer wanted to tell it, not to him.

"Little cracks in a marriage . . .

"Finally, I said to Petter that I thought *maybe* we should have a divorce. I remember I said 'maybe' because I was a little tentative about asking for a divorce, but I wasn't tentative about wanting it.

"It wasn't because I had found someone else. It was just that Petter and I no longer communicated. We had been apart so much, I didn't know if I had changed, or he had changed, but what had been *us* had changed.

"Petter's first reaction was to think I was joking. Far from it. It was not something I did on a whim. I had struggled with the thought for some time.

"Petter more or less shrugged it off. He did say to me, 'How can you think such a thing when we are perfectly happy?' I was as surprised as he had been. I didn't think *we* were happy, but I was pleased that Petter was happy."

Many years later, daughter Pia summed up the marriage for me: "My parents were in love, and then they weren't."

Although Ingrid had been under contract to Selznick for six years, she had appeared in only one of his pictures, *Intermezzo*. He now wished to put her into a picture directed by another of his stars, Alfred Hitchcock.

Selznick, who had a great belief in psychiatrists, wanted to do a film about psychiatry with Hitchcock starring Ingrid. He chose a book by Francis Beeding (a pseudonym for John Leslie Palmer and Hilary St. George Saunders) called *The House of Dr. Edwardes*, set in a Swiss asylum.

Selznick selected Ben Hecht, who was familiar with psychotherapy, to work with Hitchcock on a screenplay. They produced a script after doing research at mental hospitals in and around New York City.

With *The House of Dr. Edwardes* (changed to Edwards for the film), Selznick felt no compulsion to follow the novel faithfully. The original story deals with a madman who takes over an insane asylum, much as in *The Cabinet of Dr. Caligari*. Selznick was more interested in the love story than he was in the psychiatric aspects, and that love story Hitchcock and Hecht would have to bring to the screenplay. "Though David would not have characterized himself that way, he was an extreme romantic," his first wife, Irene Mayer Selznick, told me.

Although Ingrid had never before made a film with Hitchcock, she was a fan of his films and looked forward to working with him. "The magic of Hitch," Ingrid told me, "is he took you by the hand past what isn't plausible, and you don't even know it's happening."

Spellbound (1945)

Dr. Murchison (Leo G. Carroll) is being forced to retire as the head of the Green Manors, a mental hospital in Vermont. His successor is an eminent psychologist, Dr. Anthony Edwards (Gregory Peck), who is younger than expected. He immediately charms professionally cool Dr. Constance Petersen (Ingrid Bergman).

It soon becomes evident that he is not Dr. Edwards. Constance determines that he is a medical doctor whose initials are J.B. She calls him John. He is extremely disturbed by the sight of parallel lines.

John confesses to her he thinks the real Edwards is dead, and he fears he may be responsible. Dr. Murchison diagnoses him as a paranoid amnesiac, and calls the police. John leaves. Constance follows him to New York.

She will not accept that he is responsible for the disappearance of the real Edwards. She takes him to her mentor, Dr. Brulov (Michael Chekhov), for treatment. Together, they explore John's troubled dreamworld.

As he describes a surreal dreamscape, snow starts to fall outside, and he is upset by the parallel lines of sled tracks. John vaguely recalls that something significant happened to him at St. Gabriel Valley while skiing. Recalling that Edwards liked to ski, Constance decides to take John to Gabriel Valley, hoping it will help restore his memory.

They go skiing, reenacting events that might have happened at St. Gabriel. Skiing down a long slope, John relives a painful memory from his own childhood.

He remembers his younger brother sliding down a porch banister and being impaled on an iron fence with parallel bars.

John has always felt responsible for his brother's death. This image triggers the return of his memory. He understands that the accident *was* an accident, not something for which he needs to blame himself. They stop their descent in time to avoid going over a precipice.

His name is John Ballantine. From medical school, he went into the army. After a plane crash that left him traumatized, he went to Dr. Edwards for treatment. They went skiing together, and Dr. Edwards went over the precipice.

John is able to tell the police exactly where to find the body. They find Dr. Edwards with a bullet wound. John goes on trial and is convicted of murder.

Constance returns to Green Manors, where it becomes evident to her that Dr. Murchison is the real murderer. Unable to kill her when she confronts him, he kills himself.

Murchison had killed Edwards at the ski slope, and then thrown the revolver into the ravine. John was a witness, but the event triggered his amnesia. The gun is found there with Murchison's fingerprints on it. John is cleared.

Before Dr. Murchison fires the gun, Ingrid is seen in the background from his point of view. Hitchcock asked camera director George Barnes to temporarily abandon his low diffuse lighting on female stars in order to increase the camera's depth of field. He wanted both the gun and Ingrid to be in focus, so the lighting had to be increased. "Ingrid didn't need any help from the lighting," Hitchcock said.

"I knew Hitch liked working with me," Ingrid told me. "I could feel it, and I felt that way about him. He was a wonderful director, so sensitive. There were actors who said he wasn't a good actor's director, but something was wrong with them. He was so sympathetic. He never seemed bored by my concerns, professional or private. He always listened. He was very funny. He had a delicious sense of humor, and he could be a little shocking." She said that it wasn't so much *what* he said, but *when* he said it, "always at some inappropriate moment when one wasn't expecting it.

"Hitch could always talk me out of being nervous and uncertain, which I sometimes was. He could always make me giggle."

Ingrid took her work seriously. She took life seriously. She cared about understanding her characters, so she could *be* her character.

"I loved working with Hitch," she said. "He was a genius and a dear, dear man. He was very wise, too. He became one of my most wonderful friends. I felt I could tell him *almost* anything.

"For *Spellbound*, I was worried about the utterly unromantic character who was suddenly so carried away by love that she is ready to throw away everything she has studied and worked to achieve. I didn't believe an intelligent woman would act that way without thinking everything out—until I did it myself.

"I decided the best thing I could do was just to ask Hitch. I said, 'There is something about my part I felt I must ask you. Can you help me? I don't feel it. I can't find my motivation . . .'

"And Hitch said to me, 'Fake it, Ingrid. It's *only* a movie.'

"But there was something else that was troubling me. It was something that was to trouble me many times in my life. It was the feeling that it was selfish to do something I loved so much. I said to him, 'I've been feeling that what I do isn't worthwhile. Movies. Being an actress. I'm not doing enough to help people. Of all the worthwhile things you can do with your life, I feel I should be doing something more.'

"And he said to me, 'Have you ever thought about going to a hospital and emptying bedpans?'

"Wasn't that profound?" Ingrid asked me.

What was important was that Ingrid saw it as profound. Hitchcock told me the same story from his point of view, and explained why he gave Ingrid his bedpan suggestion.

"When the actors were taking themselves too seriously, I hoped the light touch would give them some perspective. I found it rather successful."

"Ingrid was warm and wonderful," Gregory Peck said of his co-star. "She was very young, and she had a fresh quality, but she had more confidence than I did. No wonder. She was beautiful, more beautiful in person than on the screen.

"I told her once that she *wasn't* very photogenic. She seemed a bit shocked. Her face was always an open book. She responded that I was the first person who had ever told her she wasn't photogenic. I explained what I meant was that no camera ever seemed to adequately capture her natural beauty. She blushed.

"She was always very encouraging to me if I felt neglected. Hitch gave Ingrid much more attention than he did anyone else, including me. Especially me. Well, I don't blame him. The most important thing she understood right away, I didn't understand. 'Hitch will tell you if you aren't doing it right. It's a great compliment if he *doesn't* speak to you.' I wanted to believe her. Now, I know it was true. I wish I could say, 'Thank you, Hitch,' but I don't have the number up there."

Salvador Dalí was brought in to design the surrealistic dream sequences in *Spellbound*. Peck's psychoanalytical dream was to include Ingrid as a Grecian goddess who turns into a statue, but very little of what was shot was used. Peck described for me the parts of the dream sequence that were cut:

"Selznick agreed to make my nightmare an unforgettable visual, as Hitchcock wanted. He went to Dalí with the commission. As I would be lying there, the audience would share my nightmare.

"There were four hundred human eyes which looked down at me from the heavy black drapes. Meanwhile, a giant pair of pliers, many times my size, would appear and then I was supposed to chase him or it, the pliers, up the side of a pyramid where I would find a plaster cast of Ingrid. Her plaster head would crack and streams of ants would pour out of her face. Ugh. Well, the ants ended up on the cutting room floor.

"When I asked Hitch about why I was having a greatly curtailed nightmare, he said, 'Actually, the ants' contract was canceled, and we never filmed that part. We couldn't get enough trained ants, and Central Casting said all of their fleas were already gainfully employed. Aside from that,' he added, 'David [Selznick] decided it would make audiences laugh.'"

Ingrid wasn't quite certain how she felt about the plaster cast of her, with streams of ants running across her face. Hitchcock told her it would tickle. She said, "But Hitch, it's *only* a movie."

Ingrid liked to knit. As a young girl, she knitted her own sweaters. "There's so much sitting-around time making movies. It helps to see a sweater growing. I have no control over how the film is going, but the yarn is in my hands.

"Hitch asked me if I was making a sweater for him. I answered truthfully that I was not, but since I had almost finished the sweater I was knitting, I could begin one for him almost immediately. I hadn't thought he would wear one of my sweaters.

"He said he would wear it as his 'Spellbinding sweater,' and he would wear it next to his heart. He said, 'I will also wear it against my stomach, and that will require too many balls of yarn. But since we shall do many films together, there will be time, and I shall go on a diet. So please wait, and it will only require half as much sweater.'"

At the end of his terrifying vision of the world as it would have been without him had he never been born, George Bailey, Frank Capra's hero of *It's a Wonderful Life,* passes a movie theater. Advertised on its marquee is *The Bells of St. Mary's,* thus signifying for George that he has returned from the hellish future of Pottersville to the comfortable present of Bedford Falls.

Director Leo McCarey wanted to borrow Ingrid for *The Bells of St. Mary's,* a sequel to his popular success, *Going My Way,* but Selznick had no interest, and he sent her a memo.

When I spoke with her, she recalled perfectly his reasons, which she said at the time seemed to her "well thought out, even if later David proved perfect—perfectly wrong.

"He warned me that *Going My Way* was such a major hit that a sequel could never be such a success, and he didn't like sequels. He said I would just be a stooge for Bing Crosby's singing, and Leo McCarey had not offered a complete script that could be properly judged."

Despite the reasoning, Ingrid was tempted by the opportunity *The Bells of St. Mary's* offered her to work with Leo McCarey. "I was always most interested in working with the best directors, and the word was he was that."

I told her that when I was writing about Groucho Marx, Groucho told me that McCarey was the best director he and his brothers ever worked with, "and a nice guy, too."

Ingrid said, "Joe Steele, my public relations representative and friend, encouraged me to meet McCarey, because even if nothing came of it, I would know him. But I didn't want to meet Mr. McCarey under false pretenses, and I knew David wouldn't like it if he knew. I didn't like doing anything behind David's back.

"I was too tempted. I did meet that wonderful man, and I couldn't believe how full of ideas he was. You couldn't *not* like him. If you didn't like him, there was something wrong with you.

"I was determined I had to persuade David, and I did. Well, I thought I did. I learned later that RKO made David a tremendous offer, and David negotiated even more. I was paid my regular salary, and he got several times that, so I suppose that was more persuasive for him than my entreaties.

"Some people under contract to him said David was really in the white slave trade, but I never agreed with that. I owed David a lot for the way he had gambled on me. I repaid him. I feel I more than repaid him."

When Ingrid left Selznick at the end of her contract, she knew something she would never miss was receiving a Selznick memo. Speaking with me much later, she admitted she had been wrong. In later years, she missed those memos and would have appreciated one.

Ingrid was amused and touched when she heard that Selznick had proposed marriage to Irene Mayer, the daughter of Louis B. Mayer, in a memo. Both Selznick and Irene remained Ingrid's steadfast friends through all the turbulent years that would follow.

The night before the first day that Ingrid reported for work on *The Bells of St. Mary's,* the Academy Awards for 1944 were presented at Hollywood's Grauman's Chinese Theatre. Bing Crosby received the Oscar as best actor for *Going My Way,* Leo McCarey received the award for best director for that film, and Ingrid as best actress for *Gaslight.* (The next year, McCarey was also nominated for an Oscar for best picture, *The Bells of St. Mary's,* which he both produced and directed.)

The Bells of St. Mary's (1945)

Hardworking, dedicated Sister Benedict (Ingrid Bergman) is in charge of a run-down parochial school that has been threatened for a long time with demolition. Her problems are complicated by the arrival of a new parish priest, Father O'Malley (Bing Crosby), who is as easygoing as she is rigid.

Eventually, they work out their differences. In their own

ways, they make it possible for two problem students to stay in school, and Sister Benedict is even able to persuade a greedy developer, Mr. Bogardus (Henry Travers), to build a new parish school bearing his name, instead of an industrial plant.

Sister Benedict's unexpected illness forces her to leave the school. Before she leaves, Father O'Malley leads the faculty and students in making her feel that what she has accomplished has not gone unappreciated.

At the end of the film, Leo McCarey called out, "Print. It's a wrap."

Ingrid stood there for a moment, hesitating.

"I've had an idea," she said. "Could we do it again?"

McCarey said, "It's perfect, Ingrid. But, of course, if you want to try something . . ."

In the scene, Father O'Malley informs Sister Benedict that she has a touch of tuberculosis. This makes her happy, since it means she has to leave her place as a nun because she is sick, not because she has failed in her work, her greatest fear. Ingrid added some new business.

In her joy and exuberance upon learning the news of her illness, Sister Benedict throws her arms around Father O'Malley's neck and kisses him passionately on the lips.

A priest on the set leaped to his feet, protesting, "You can't use *that!*"

No one was more startled than Bing Crosby, who was still very much in his part of Father O'Malley.

Ingrid and McCarey, who shared the same sense of humor, laughed uproariously at her joke. No one enjoyed the joke more than Ingrid, unless it was McCarey.

Ingrid Bergman and Bing Crosby were chosen because of their huge box office potential. Crosby was the reason for the film, repeating his immensely popular role as Father O'Malley in *Going My Way*. Ingrid was at that time, producers said, "box office magic."

Ingrid remembered a really good thing about playing a nun. She could eat all the ice cream she wanted. Nobody worried about her gaining weight because nobody *knew* if she gained any. All that showed of her, wearing the nun's habit, was her face.

"I was like a child with money, and in the country of the greatest ice cream. Later I was to live in the land of gelati, which could be very good, but somehow Italian ice cream never caught my fancy the way the American did.

"I even dreamed about ice cream. Those were good dreams, those ice cream dreams, but they were not as enjoyable as the real thing."

Ingrid not only discovered American ice cream, but she came "to know intimately sundaes and banana splits. A hot fudge sundae was an unbelievable delight, and you could add banana and more ice cream and hot chocolate by ordering a banana split. In New York City, where I liked the ice cream best, I could eat four ice creams in a day." She frequently ordered a second dish. Then she said she had to leave and go to another place because she was too embarrassed to order a third and even a fourth portion.

"After we lived in Beverly Hills and our separation because of war was ended, my career had become unbelievably successful, so it seemed Petter and I should live happily ever afterward.

"But Petter began to scold me. It was a kind of nagging which I absolutely could count on. 'Hold in your stomach.'

"Petter loved to exercise. I didn't. He believed in regularity for the exercises, one half hour always at exactly the same time. I found exercising tedious and boring. I loved to swim and dance and walk, but even the thought of exercising just for exercise's sake left me feeling tired before I began.

" 'Have you done your half hour of slimming exercises? Don't bend your knees. Don't wrinkle your forehead. It will become permanent and you will have a line there. What did you have for lunch?'

"I would not have lied to Petter, but I had nothing to lie about. Cottage cheese and fruit. It was easy to remember, because it's what I had almost every day for lunch when I was working. It was something I had enjoyed when I first arrived in California, but I was never allowed enough, even of *that*. I was always hungry, not because I had such a ravenous appetite, but because I was supposed always to be starving. It was a difference of only five pounds, if I could have had five more pounds. I could have eaten with pleasure, whatever I wanted. To weigh five pounds less, it was torture on the rack.

"However, I felt no need to volunteer anything, about the few butter cookies I had enjoyed in between lunch and dinner. Petter couldn't really imagine anyone being so lacking in discipline as to ever desire treats between meals. He wasn't tempted. Forbidden cookies and ice cream, especially with chocolate sauce, between meals were abhorrent to him. Even as I faced the Grand Cookie Inquisitor armed with the bathroom scale, my mind was on the cookie jar upstairs, well hidden, I hoped.

"I knew that Petter was only thinking of my own best interests. I certainly thought so at the time. Later, it occurred to me that he might have been thinking of his own best interests, too.

"As a child, I had lived in a home with perfect harmony. My father loved harmony, in life as in music. I don't ever remember being criticized. I was admired, loved, praised by my father. He loved what I did, and I always did my best, because pleasing my father was the greatest pleasure I could have.

"Petter chided me, and I grew tired of so many chides. He said what he was telling me was so I wouldn't get a big head. Well, I thought that was a funny image, indeed, me with a big head. The first time he said it, it made me giggle. That made him furious. He felt I was laughing at him. So, when he said it again, I didn't giggle. It wasn't funny anymore, and I didn't feel like giggling anymore.

"He chastised me, he said, so I wouldn't 'go Hollywood.' He didn't explain what 'going Hollywood' meant to him. I could only imagine.

"Petter had always seemed to enjoy California and to be very social, though I always had the feeling he didn't really have his heart there in Hollywood and he didn't really like so many of the people, except the Hitchcocks, Alfred, Alma, and their young daughter, Pat. He loved them and had a good time with them. He said they were 'real people.' And he thought Hitch was a genius, a true genius, a person of value, as good as a doctor.

"The criticism of me caused me to lose confidence with other people, which was bad for my career, and to lose confidence with him, which was bad for our relationship, our marriage.

"All that criticism was very hard on romance and passion. I began to feel that he saw me as a property to be protected. Petter's interest, when he had finished all his studies to be a doctor, a specialist, was in having another baby, hopefully a boy. Meanwhile, I began to worry that, in bed, he was checking to see if I had put on a few ounces."

Over the years, Ingrid and her diary had grown apart. She gradually confided less of her innermost feelings than she had done in Stockholm and in her first years in Hollywood.

As she had more exciting events to tell her diary, she told it less. She no longer took time at night to pour her heart into "Dear Book." She found herself not taking time and not *making* time.

One day, Ingrid looked at her diary and was shocked to find she had been writing words, not feelings, abbreviated thoughts, and she had been "guarded, careful."

"I was no longer open. My diary must have been bored by me. Had *I* changed? Somehow, I no longer felt the same bond with my diary. It wasn't that I told lies to my diary. That would have been really terrible. It was more that I was evasive. What you *don't* tell is a lie, too.

"Earlier, I had put on paper thoughts I didn't even know I was thinking, but it was no longer like that.

"As my life was filled with events, my diary had become just an agenda."

Years later, her daughter Isabella told me that she thought her mother had stopped writing freely in her diary because "she had become so famous and was afraid of its being stolen."

Ingrid went to Paris, arriving June 6, 1945, just at the end of the war in Europe, to entertain the U.S. troops. She recited passages from Maxwell Anderson's *Joan of Lorraine,* a play she hoped to do on Broadway. She joined a group that included Jack Benny, Martha Tilton, and Larry Adler. Since hers was the first group to arrive as the war ended, Ingrid was surprised to see Marlene Dietrich leaving the Ritz Hotel. Dietrich greeted Ingrid:

"You are late."

Dietrich had actually been there while the war was still on. The headquarters for the press and the entertainment group was the Ritz. Ingrid hadn't been in Paris for eight years.

Sitting in her room, Ingrid was wondering about dinner when she saw a note slipped under her door. Opening it, she found it was from two men staying at the hotel. They had recognized her and wished to invite her to dinner. The note said they would have sent her flowers, but they had only enough money to buy either the flowers or a lovely dinner, and they preferred to eat dinner with her. She preferred it, too.

The note was signed by Irwin Shaw and Robert Capa, who identified themselves as press. Actually, Shaw was a playwright who later would become a noted novelist. Capa was a war photographer, perhaps the most famous of his time. He would play an important role in Ingrid's life.

Ingrid, who was always ready to eat, especially in Paris, had been contemplating her dinner possibilities: to go alone downstairs to the restaurant, or to eat alone in her room. Neither was what she wanted that night in Paris.

Ingrid, Shaw, and Capa went to a modest restaurant for a delicious dinner. There was good conversation and laughter from the first moment, and Ingrid found them to be wonderful company. Later, as she thought about that night, Ingrid knew she felt drawn to Capa.

She never thought of him as Robert, but as Capa. He fascinated her. She was thirty. He was thirty-one.

"I was very insecure about performing for the troops," Ingrid said. "It wasn't exactly what I did. I didn't sing or dance, but I was so anxious to do anything I could. In addition to some pieces from *Joan of Lorraine*, which I was preparing, I did a skit with Jack Benny, poking fun at *Gaslight*. *Joan of Lorraine* wasn't what the soldiers were hoping for, and probably not *Gaslight*, either, but they were very warm and so appreciative.

"Jack Benny and our little troupe went on to Berlin. When I arrived, Capa, who had left Paris, was already there in Berlin.

"Berlin was in terrible condition. Horrible. Destruction everywhere. The buildings were all broken. There were bathtubs in the middle of the street. People were living in the streets in front of the wreckage of their homes. They gave you the address where their apartment had been, and they were living there, at where their apartments had been, only they were living in the street.

"It was a great help for me to have Capa there. He radiated tremendous inner strength. It helped me to have a shoulder to lean on, a man's shoulder. I had read about the horrors of the war, but being there was different. I could feel it deep in my soul.

"Everyone, except for me, went to see a concentration camp. They said it was important to see it. Capa felt I should go, and I felt very guilty about not going; but I thought if I saw it, it would be in my mind all the time and that I would never be able to work again. I was afraid

I would never be able to get it out of my head and it would drive me mad."

Actress Sylvia Miles was also in Berlin at the end of the war. "I didn't want to see the concentration camp," she told me, "but my first husband pushed and pushed until I went. I've never gotten over the horrors I saw there. I still have nightmares about it."

Ingrid, being half German herself, found it difficult to believe that the German people were responsible for such atrocities. "They said Germany had done this to itself, but there were innocent people, children not born when Hitler came to power, people who never voted for him nor supported him, people who didn't know what would happen. I knew there were good people in Germany. There were people there who had been kind to me. It was impossible to understand what had happened."

Capa told Ingrid, "You have to be wary of me. I don't seem to be lucky for people—especially for me."

Born in Hungary, Capa had gone to Germany in 1932. After he skied away from the Nazis to safety across the Alps, he chose Paris as his new home, and then went as a photographer to cover the Spanish Civil War.

Capa spoke five languages, but he told Ingrid that he thought and dreamed in pictures.

With the Nazis in France, he escaped to America. He went to work for *Collier's* magazine and to England to cover the war there. To accompany an airborne division, he parachuted over Sicily with no previous jump experience.

In 1944, as a war photographer, Capa landed in the first wave on Omaha Beach. His photographs of the Omaha landing were among the most famous of World War II, and Capa became celebrated for them.

"Capa believed he would live a short life," Ingrid told me, "and he never hesitated to take every risk, thus increasing the likelihood that his belief would come true.

"He was really a very lucky person. He had to be, but if you push luck long enough, one day, even the best luck runs out, I think. Some people have more than others, but no one's luck can be infinite.

"It seemed to me that Capa had to gamble until he lost.

"I remember once he told me it was good for him to lose all his savings gambling, so he would have to work harder. I didn't know if it was true what he said, or if he was just saying it to stop me from saying anything about his gambling and losing all his money.

"Capa filled a need I had been feeling, before I even met him. I suppose I had begun to long for someone before he came along, and he filled the part of the person I had been imagining, to fill that need.

"He was brave, *too* brave, intelligent, funny, a romantic.

"As a young man escaping the arriving Nazis, I think he got into the habit of risking his life, the excitement of it, the adrenaline rush. It seems to me, looking back, that after he escaped the Nazis, it was as if he felt he only had his life on loan."

Early in the relationship, which quickly developed into a love affair, Capa told Ingrid he could not marry her because he already was married—married to the work he loved.

"He told me," Ingrid remembered, "that he could not leave me all alone, especially if we had a child. To go into danger, he said he *had* to be free to do what he did. I respected him for it, but I worried that his last photograph would be of someone aiming a gun at him.

"He would go. He would return. He would go. I would worry. I wasn't made for that kind of anxiety. I understand I would have dragged him down. My fear would have done that. It might have made *him* fearful.

"People said he had something special other people didn't have. I think it wasn't something he had, but something he *didn't* have. He lacked—fear."

It was Ingrid's hope that Capa would come to California and be a set photographer, and he could do portraits. His photographs could illustrate his articles. Once, on a visit to see Ingrid, he tried being a set photographer for *Arch of Triumph*, but only to earn a little money, always being short of money.

Capa was not willing to change his life, nor did he think he could. It would have required the kind of compromise on his part that Ingrid's father made in order to be able to marry Ingrid's mother.

If Capa could have resigned himself to living in Hollywood, to doing portraits, to being a set photographer, to having a photographic studio, and they had lived together, Ingrid wondered if she would have felt the same way about him.

"At the time, I don't remember consciously thinking about it, but later I wondered if Capa being a photographer and loving photography the way he did made in my mind some association between him and my father. Certainly there was no other resemblance."

Ingrid recalled Capa arriving in Sun Valley in 1947. She and Petter were there on a skiing holiday. Ingrid felt that Petter noticed something unspoken about her easy rapport with Capa, and she felt that he did not like what he saw.

Capa was a fine skier, but Petter was a *great* skier. They were both naturally athletic. Both were serious competitors. Ingrid, who admitted she was never a very good skier, immediately twisted her ankle, and had to remain in the ski lodge most of the time.

Capa, who was passionate about gambling, quickly left the slopes for the casino. Unluckily for him, he won the first time. He had with him his total savings, which amounted to about $2,000. Petter, watching the people gamble, observed Capa recklessly losing money and told Ingrid. He never enjoyed seeing money being thrown away, even though he didn't particularly like Capa. Petter told Ingrid that Capa should be stopped.

Ingrid left her hotel room and limped painfully on her twisted ankle to the casino. She tried to persuade Capa to stop, but Capa told her he would play till he won a lot of money or until he lost all he had. Capa was determined to win or to lose everything. He told her he preferred to win, but instead he lost all of his money. "He was a gambler," Ingrid said. "He always played till he lost. I came to understand that, if not to be able to accept it."

Seven years later, in 1954, Capa went to Vietnam to cover the French colonial war for *Life* magazine. He was with soldiers and some other foreign correspondents as part of a French armored column about to go deeper into enemy territory.

During a rather long pause in the gunfire and fighting. Capa got out of the jeep with his camera and walked ahead of the group, looking for something to photograph. There had been a lot of enemy fire, and even during a lull, everyone knew the enemy was near. Why did Capa go forward alone? There was much speculation, but Ingrid felt she knew the answer:

"Time passed differently for Capa. It passed slowly when there wasn't risk. I believe he got bored."

There was an explosion. The soldiers found Capa lying in the road. He had stepped on a land mine. He was forty years old.

Robert Capa received a posthumous Croix de Guerre.

"Capa was one of the people I cared most about in the world in all my life," Ingrid told me. "So many years after, his memory is still vivid, and the pain never went totally away. It's crowded out some of the time by all of the good memories, as well as other sad memories that come one's way, but it never goes totally away.

"Capa awakened a sexual side in me I didn't know was there," Ingrid said. "He helped me to be *me*. He was not inhibited. He was tender, and loving. It was obvious he had had very much experience with women. I didn't mind that, but I hoped he would find me unique. I hoped he would not lose his respect for me.

"Capa was lost completely when he made love, as he must have been when he took his war pictures. I learned what it was to forget everything.

"With Capa I discovered a strange thing. He never felt guilty while making love, but he seemed to feel guilty before and afterward. It seemed he felt guilty all the time, except when he was making love. I never knew what he felt guilty about. I think it was about being alive. He had seen so many people die, and he was alive, so that may have made him feel guilty about being alive when so many others weren't.

"Once after we made love, he talked about his wife, who had died assisting him in a battle zone. At the time, it hurt my feelings that he talked with me about her at that moment. Later, I came to feel it was an act of trust, not meant to hurt me, but because he felt so close to me that he did not have to watch what he said. Actually, Capa had never married his young companion, Gerda. German Jewish of Yugoslavian descent, she was taught photography by Capa. In Spain, she was killed by a tank.

"Looking back," Ingrid continued, "I am certain he did not ruin my marriage. The best of our marriage, Petter and me, was over, and I think, if anything, Capa kept it going longer.

"He did not want to marry me because he did not want to give up his dangerous work as a war photographer. He loved what he did, the way I loved acting, but what he did was a matter of life and death.

"He was a romantic. He did not think he needed to save for his old age, because he didn't think he would have one. Long after Petter and I were divorced, he stepped on that land mine.

"Capa had made me doubt the value of what I was doing. He cautioned me about falling into the trap of doing what was easy and well paid, and brought glory. He told me if I did so, I wouldn't feel fulfilled. He said I should open my eyes to the truth of things. His words unsettled me.

"The time I spent with Capa did not add up to so many hours in my life, but they had an out-of-proportion effect. He articulated what I was feeling vaguely, a sort of dissatisfaction. I didn't just want to take from life, but to be of value, to put something back into life. I wanted to do something to be worthy of my good fortune. Acting was my joy, so it didn't seem possible that doing what brought me the greatest joy in life was enough."

Selznick wanted to follow the enormous success of *Spellbound* with another Hitchcock film starring Ingrid. From Selznick's story department came a 1921 magazine short story called "The Song of the Dragon," about a woman who has been carefully coached to participate in a confidence scheme in which she might marry the victim. It became the basis for *Notorious*. Again, Ben Hecht wrote the screenplay with Hitchcock's collaboration, which always meant the usually uncredited participation of Alma Reville Hitchcock in the background.

"I loved to visit the Hitchcocks," Ingrid told me. "Hitch's wife, Alma, was one of the best cooks in the world. I always had second helpings of everything, especially dessert. I would have had third helpings if Petter had permitted. Usually, he gave me terrible looks if I had a second helping, which caused me to lose my appetite, or *some* of it. I wouldn't have been able to get away with second helpings, except Petter was so busy eating his own second helpings that he wasn't noticing me.

"I told Alma, who was a dear little person, that I thought she was the world's best cook. She offered to share her recipes with me. It was a generous offer, but I told her I couldn't cook. She said she would teach me.

"I never had time, and I didn't really like to cook, but sometimes I regretted not learning to make just a few of those dishes.

"Hitch and Alma had a lovely daughter, Patricia, who jitterbugged with Petter. He loved to jitterbug and told me it was the best exercise. He was so meticulous. He always brought three extra shirts to their house for when he perspired so from the vigorous activity."

Pat Hitchcock told me, "Ingrid and her husband used to visit us at our Ranch up in Santa Cruz, and Ingrid and I would go riding, And Peter, her husband, would run. He was a great runner. He liked to do that.

"Then, down here in Los Angeles, I would take their daughter Pia out when she was a little girl, and we would go for walks along the golf course. I knew Pia until she moved to New York, when she got married.

"I was very fond of Ingrid. She was a very good friend. And so was her husband, Peter. He was a great friend of ours."

Notorious (1946)

FBI agent T. R. Devlin (Cary Grant) has been sent to Miami Beach to recruit Alicia Huberman (Ingrid Bergman). Since her father has just been convicted as a German spy, it is believed she will make a convincing undercover agent. There is no question of her loyalty to the United States, only of her morals. She agrees, and they fly to Rio de Janeiro together. Before Alicia is assigned, she and Devlin have an affair.

Her assignment involves resuming a romance with a German agent in Rio, Alexander Sebastian (Claude Rains). She is to infiltrate the circle of scientists, diplomats, and spies who congregate at his mansion. Devlin is disappointed when she accepts, but makes no objection.

Sebastian, who is still in love with Alicia, asks her to marry him. She reports this to Devlin, who still makes no objection, though his disappointment has turned to anger. His superiors are delighted to have an agent placed so strategically, and she accepts Sebastian's marriage proposal.

Against the wishes of his mother (Leopoldine Konstantin), Sebastian marries Alicia. She is introduced to his inner circle of friends, and becomes acquainted with the secrets of the mansion, all but those of the wine cellar. Sebastian has the key.

Devlin tells Alicia to have him invited to an upcoming social event at Sebastian's mansion. She is to steal the key from Sebastian's key ring before the party, and return it afterward.

At the party, Devlin and Alicia go down into the cellar, where they find some bottles of sand, not wine. When Sebastian discovers them together in the wine cellar, they pretend to be having a tryst initiated by Devlin, and he believes them.

After the party, he realizes the key has been returned to his ring, and he suspects Alicia of being a spy. Knowing what will happen to her son if the group of conspirators learn he has married an American agent, his mother plots to poison Alicia slowly with arsenic.

Even though he has asked to be reassigned far away from her, Devlin becomes worried about Alicia, who seems sicklier each time he sees her. When he visits her at the mansion, she is in bed, and he realizes what is happening.

He carries her out of the house, while Sebastian, his mother, and the group of Germans look on. Sebastian begs them to take him with them, but Devlin leaves him to his fate.

The sand, when analyzed, turns out to be uranium ore.

Selznick was unhappy with the "MacGuffin" they finally decided on, uranium ore, which seemed to him absurd. He sold the property to RKO a few months before the first atomic bomb, using uranium, was dropped on Hiroshima.

A celebrated scene in *Notorious* is the long kiss between Ingrid and Cary Grant. Hitchcock defeated the Production Code limitation on the time a kiss could last—only a few seconds—by breaking up their long kiss into many short ones, as they talk.

Hitchcock now had one year left on his Selznick contract, and one more film. He was already making plans for the pictures he would be filming with British producer Sidney Bernstein. Ingrid and Grant had told Hitchcock they would love to make a film for him at his new production company, Transatlantic Pictures. Only Ingrid was free to be able to take advantage of this opportunity after her contract with Selznick expired. Grant was previously committed at that particular time.

"When our contract was finished," Hitchcock told me, "I knew I wouldn't miss those memos. Those memos were the essence of the man. Selznick wore his mind on his sleeve."

Ingrid was never enthusiastic about doing *Arch of Triumph*. She didn't feel right about her part, but she loved the idea of working with Charles Boyer again. "I had the feeling that Charles may have been needing work and money. But he was such a gentleman, and he would never have said a word about it.

"It was a fine cast directed by Lewis Milestone and written by [Erich Maria] Remarque, but I just couldn't like my character, and unless I could get into her shoes, I didn't feel I'd be believable. In the end, the money people, who didn't have enough of it, cut the film so it didn't make much sense. I had felt unsure, and I don't think my performance helped the film. Reviewers and audiences didn't like it all that much, either."

Arch of Triumph (1946, released 1948)

In Paris just before World War II, Austrian refugee Dr. Ravic (Charles Boyer) falls in love with Joan Madou (Ingrid Bergman), a Parisian lost soul, after he saves her from suicide. He rearranges her life for her, but when he must journey to the Riviera, she reverts to her former aimless existence.

When Ravic returns to Paris, he kills a Nazi, Haake (Charles Laughton), who tortured him in Vienna and killed his fiancée. He returns to Joan and asks her to leave her current lover, millionaire playboy Alex (Stephen Bekassy), and come back to him. She refuses, and in a momentary rage, he shoots her and then tries desperately to save her. As she dies, she says, "Ti amo," as war is beginning.

"Don't tip the box," Ingrid remembered hearing as she and Charles Boyer began a love scene. "Not very romantic," she said. In one scene, she and Boyer were supposed to move toward each other for a romantic encounter. "I thought it would be more effective," Ingrid said, "if we could *run* toward each other for our passionate embrace, but that wasn't possible. Charles was standing on a box, and he would have had to take his box with him. What we had to be most careful about was that he didn't fall off, and more difficult, that we didn't start giggling and not be able to stop.

"I was taller than Boyer, but he was such a great actor that as he played his part, he grew taller.

"Charles brought his little son, Michael, who had been born during *Gaslight,* to visit the *Arch of Triumph* set. Michael was the most beautiful child, and looked just like his father. I was so happy for Charles and his wife, who were sublimely happy with their little boy.

"It was many years later that I heard the story of the terrible tragedy. When the very handsome young man was twenty-one, for that important birthday, his father gave him a key. It was a key to an apartment of his own.

"What I heard was the young man fell madly in love with a girl who didn't return his feelings. Tragically, there was a gun, and Michael shot himself.

"Heartbroken, Charles and his wife moved to Geneva. When she was diagnosed with a brain tumor, they returned to America. She died, and a few days later, he took his own life."

•   •   •

On October 1, 1946, Ingrid arrived in New York City to start rehearsing *Joan of Lorraine,* the Joan of Arc play written for her by Maxwell Anderson. She took up residence at the Hampshire House on Central Park South. The play, directed by Margo Jones, opened at the Alvin Theatre on November 18, 1946.

In the cast was Kevin McCarthy. I talked with him about Ingrid and *Joan of Lorraine,* in 2006, just after watching him on television in the 1956 classic *Invasion of the Body Snatchers.*

"I remember going to the first rehearsal of *Joan,* and there she was: The Great Figure.

"But it was just like we were all actors together. She seemed like a normal person, not like a star. She had a very great command of the personality that she was and of the character that she played. You use your imagination, and the grand life becomes the ordinary life for the people who are living it.

"She was a terrific gal, natural and unassuming. She *was* the star, and I was playing the Bastard of Orleans. I was an actor she wouldn't have any particular knowledge of probably, but I said, 'You want to come over and have dinner with me and my wife?' 'Sure,' she says, and she came up for dinner at our apartment on East 56th Street.

"On opening night, I remember—you know, the things you do on opening night for good luck—she said, 'Will you kick me in the backside?' She kicked me and I kicked her. And it worked. The play ran for about six months. That's a pretty good run."

The play ran until May 10, 1947, and Ingrid won the Antoinette Perry award for her performance. Toward the end of its run, Victor Fleming, Ingrid's director from *Dr. Jekyll and Mr. Hyde,* approached her proposing a *Joan of Lorraine* film to be produced by Walter Wanger. Maxwell Anderson's stage play would furnish only Ingrid's character, although the playwright would be one of the screenplay adaptors. Onstage, *Joan of Lorraine* is about an actress's approach to playing a larger-than-life subject, and then being completely taken over by the character itself. Ingrid had intended making another Hitchcock film after her Broadway run, but it had been delayed.

Filming of *Joan of Arc*, as it was now called, began September 15, 1947, at the old Hal Roach Studios in Culver City. The budget was $4.6 million.

Joan of Arc (1948)

In fifteenth-century France, Joan, a peasant girl in Lorraine (Ingrid Bergman), hears voices that tell her to lead France to a victory over the invading English.

Impressed, provincial officials send her to the court of Charles VII (José Ferrer) at Chinon. After trying to trick her, he becomes convinced. He appoints her to lead French armies against the English, and inspired by her they win victory after victory.

Charles turns out to be a poor ruler, and in spite of her popularity with the people, Joan becomes disillusioned. She is captured by the English and put to trial as a heretic. Found guilty, she is condemned to be burned at the stake.

Joan of Arc was nominated for seven Oscars, including Ingrid as best actress. It won for the color cinematography of Joseph Valentine, Winton Hoch, and William Skall, and the costume design of Dorothy Jeakens and Karinska.

On the first Halloween after Ingrid returned to California from her New York run of *Joan of Lorraine,* she paid a visit to the Hitchcocks, which Alma Hitchcock told me was unforgettable. Hitchcock was home in bed with a terrible cold. When Ingrid called him, he was cross and unhappy. He found being in bed with a cold "very boring," and as Alma said, "Hitch could never abide being bored."

A few hours later, Ingrid was on her way to the Hitchcock home in Bel Air, but it was not an easily recognizable Ingrid Bergman. Her beautiful complexion was green. Her soft light hair was completely covered by a matted black wig that looked like horsehair, because it was. Her protruding fanglike teeth had great gaps between them. A studio makeup person had assisted her with the makeup. She had asked him to do a "make-down" instead of a make-up. They had also helped her in the costume department where she selected a sweeping black cloak and a matching witch's hat to complete her ensemble.

Ingrid described her face as "seasick green, exquisitely revolting." She asked the makeup man, "Do I look horrible enough?" He reassured her that she did, but she asked him to hook her nose a little more.

In the car, she had to take off her witch's hat, which was too high, but it was back on her head as she rang the buzzer of the Hitchcock home. The door was opened by Alma, who told me she was startled by the black apparition waving its green hands, dancing about and making bloodcurdling shrieking sounds.

Ingrid put a finger to her lips and whispered, "Shhh!" then said in her familiar Swedish accent, "It's me, Ingrid. I want to surprise Hitch."

Years later, Alma recalled for me leading Ingrid to the bedroom.

"Hitch was wrapped in covers, his eyes closed, appearing to be dozing. Ingrid began a cackling laugh, her yellowed, broken teeth and fangs adding to her ghastly appearance.

"Hitch calmly opened his eyes and said in a very even tone, 'Ingrid, wherever did you get that terrible dress? It doesn't do *anything* for you.'"

Alma then described a petulant Ingrid responding, "Oh, Hitch! You spoiled it all. It's all right for *you* to frighten everyone; but then you won't let anyone frighten *you*, not even a little."

"My husband and Ingrid had a very special bond, mutual admiration and a love of practical jokes," Alma said, and impractical ones, too.

"They were two of a kind, those two. Of all the beautiful actresses my husband worked with, Ingrid was the one he had the greatest rapport with."

When Ingrid's seven-year contract with Selznick ended, people told her that Selznick had made a fortune on her pictures, both on those he produced and on those produced by others who bought her services from him. Alfred Hitchcock was among those who were resentful about what he considered being "held in slavery," because of the seven-year contract he had signed with Selznick.

Ingrid and Hitch had a great friendship and disagreed on few issues, but she did not share his resentment of Selznick. She defended the producer, saying that David had put a lot of money into her career that he could have lost if she failed. "I earned more money with him than I would have ever earned in Sweden, and because of him, I made some great films and did some work I'm proud of. I had a wonderful career in America and had the experience of working with so many fine, talented people, and I became known throughout the world. To have worked with Hitch and to have made *Spellbound* and *Notorious* . . ."

The work, not the money, was always more important to her. This is not to say that the work was not important to Hitchcock, but he minded the control he felt Selznick had over his films and his life.

When her seven-year contract was completed, Ingrid did not renew. Petter was adamant that she did not need Selznick. He felt that Selznick was only "taking phone calls" from those who wanted Ingrid's services. He believed that he could guide her career and that, in terms of money, he could certainly do much better for her, for them.

Ingrid would not argue with Petter because she hated any argument, and he always won anyway. She, however had mixed feelings.

She respected Petter's ability to drive a hard bargain, but she also feared it. She worried that Petter might drive away a better part, a better film while being concerned with the money.

• • •

"There are a few days which make all the difference in one's life," Ingrid told me. "Usually when they are happening, you don't notice that something is happening that will change your life. A wedding, having a child, those things, yes. But those days like the one I went to see *Rome: Open City* at a Los Angeles theater are unique.

"It was 1949 and I was having a wonderful career doing what I loved, acting, but something was missing. I didn't feel fulfilled. And I was ashamed of feeling that way and would not have told anyone except Petter, and even with Petter, I was hesitant to say anything.

"One afternoon, I went into a theater with my husband to see an Italian film by a director I had never heard of. The sun was shining when I went in, and I hoped I would be entertained by something interesting. It was *more* than interesting.

"I came out of the theater another person than the one I was when I went in. I didn't want the film to end. I wanted to go *into* it.

"When the film was over, I looked at the credits again. One name stood out, the director, Roberto Rossellini. It was also *written* by Roberto Rossellini. He had also produced it, even written the music. He was a genius.

"I was fascinated by the man and the way he had caught life.

"I knew I just had to meet this man. He could do anything, and I wanted to work with him. It was some years later, after my life had changed totally, after my life was no longer in Hollywood, but in Italy that I learned that in my haste and excitement, I had misread one of the credits.

"The music *was* by a Rossellini, but not by Roberto Rossellini. It was by his younger brother, Renzo Rossellini."

A grown-up Isabella Rossellini remembered her mother telling her, "Seeing *Open City*—and the consequences of it—was the most important event of my life."

A few months after Ingrid had seen *Rome: Open City,* she was in New York to do a radio show. She saw that at a tiny movie theater on Broadway there was a film playing by that man, Rossellini. She had no difficulty buying a ticket. There were only a few people inside the theater, and one of them was sleeping.

The film was *Paisan,* and Ingrid was stunned. If this man Rossellini could make two films like this, what else had he done? What else *could* he do? What could *Ingrid* do acting in a film made by such a genius? She knew she *had* to make contact with this man.

In Hollywood, Ingrid had asked people about Rossellini, but he seemed to be unknown. She thought New York City would be different. It wasn't.

Ingrid, bubbling with enthusiasm, told her good friend Irene Selznick that she wanted to write to Rossellini, even though she didn't know Italian, and tell him how much she admired his work and how eager she was to work with him. She wrote that the only Italian she knew was her last line from *Arch of Triumph,* "Ti amo" (I love you).

Her friend saw no reason why she shouldn't write, and when she returned home, Ingrid completed her letter and showed it to Petter, who expressed his approval, although it was not something he saw as particularly important. She did not, however, know where to send the letter.

Then, one day in a restaurant, a man who was Italian asked her for an autograph. She asked him where he lived in Italy. He answered, "Rome."

"Do you know Roberto Rossellini?"

"Everybody in Rome knows Roberto Rossellini."

Ingrid was elated, and she asked for Rossellini's address.

He didn't know the address, but said she could reach Rossellini at Minerva, his producer. She just had to write to Minerva Film Studios, Rome.

What Ingrid didn't know was that Rossellini's relationship with Minerva had ended badly, as his business relationships often did. There were lawyers and lawsuits, and Rossellini wasn't speaking to his former associates, and they weren't speaking to him.

The mail to Italy was slow, but her letter arrived in time to be in a fire that had burned down Minerva Film Studios. Miraculously, the letter was found in the ashes, and Rossellini was called.

His response when he heard who was calling was to hang up. The call came through again. Rossellini hung up again. The people at Minerva gave up and *sent* the letter to him.

The name Ingrid Bergman was not familiar to him. People tried to explain, but all of the Hollywood films that had established her reputation had been made during the war and had not been seen in Europe except by the U.S. military. In Europe, if she was known at all, it was for her prewar Swedish films. Then, suddenly, Rossellini remembered the first *Intermezzo* and a bombing raid during the war.

"When Roberto first received my letter," Ingrid said, "he told me later it had to be explained to him, 'Who is this Ingrid Bergman?'

"He was told I was a *very* big Hollywood star. He wasn't too impressed until they told him that I was Swedish and had been a leading Swedish actress before I went to Hollywood.

"Then, he remembered seeing *Intermezzo,* the Swedish one, and me in it.

"It's no wonder he remembered because he saw it only by chance, under very special circumstances, and he stayed and saw it three times, not because he liked it *that* much, but because of the bombs falling down outside the theater."

"Do you know that I met Ingrid on the screen before I met her personally?" Rossellini told me. "I didn't remember her name, and I did not think it was an important meeting, but I was glad I was not killed.

"I was trying to escape bombs. It was in the north, in a small town, and we were being bombed. No one knew who was bombing us.

Some said it was the Germans, others thought it was the British. But you didn't ask a bomb which language it spoke, so I rushed into the shelter of a cinema. It was a poor wooden structure which could barely stand and certainly could not withstand a bomb. I knew that, but I thought if I had to die, what better place than a movie theater watching a movie? The Swedish *Intermezzo* was playing.

"But I did not want sitting in that theater to be my *last* memory. I thought about how I much I *wanted* to do and what I *had* to do. I not only had many films I had never seen that I wanted to see, but there were so many films I wanted to *make*.

"I was a not a victim of the bombs and was able to leave undamaged. I never would have guessed that this girl who was the leading lady of this film would become the leading lady of my life.

"Ingrid was *so* natural. She brought with her a great deal of Ingrid to any part she played, and that made the part hers. She was a fine actress, but the way she made the part hers, that made her a star.

"A star cannot help being a star, and I confess that when we began making films for her, it turned out not as we had hoped, as we had expected it would. I did not make films that were right for her. I wanted her to be right for my films, but she could not reshape herself so much. Also, the films were then contrary to what her audience expected from her, and they were not what my public expected from me.

"Ingrid met me first on the screen, too. But she did not see me; she saw my work.

"I have told everyone for years that I received Ingrid's letter, about *Rome: Open City* and *Paisan,* saying that she had seen my films and wanted to work with me directing her, on my birthday. My birthday is the 8th of May. As I told Ingrid and everyone from that time on, I received her letter on my birthday. It was destiny.

"It was a good story, and it was *almost* true.

"I received her letter on May seventh. It was still a birthday present, but it wasn't such a wonderful story, so I always say I received it on the 8th. That is my revelation which you may print in your book. It was only a little lie of a few hours. That couldn't hurt. Or could it?"

Hitchcock was sent a treatment of Helen Simpson's novel, *Under Capricorn*, by Selznick's office in 1944. He saw enough promise in the story to buy the screen rights for a token price, and then he put it aside for later consideration. He and Sidney Bernstein were already making plans for their Transatlantic Pictures venture, and they would need properties to develop. It strongly appealed to Ingrid, who agreed to make the picture for Transatlantic, and who encouraged Hitchcock to do the film. Before James Bridie was brought in to write the screen-play, Hume Cronyn worked on a treatment, to which Alma Hitchcock also made contributions. Hitchcock wanted to make the film in the style of *Rope,* in long, uninterrupted takes.

"I did *Under Capricorn* because Ingrid liked it," Hitchcock told me. "From that, I learned that it was better to look at Ingrid than to listen to her.

"But I did want to work again with Ingrid, even if she did think we should go on location to Australia. She was wonderful, and I was cap-tivated by her, though that was not a good reason to listen to her ideas on what would make a good picture, especially a costume picture, or on going to Australia.

"People say to me, 'Mr. Hitchcock, why don't you make costume pictures?' I say, 'It's for a very simple reason. Nobody in a costume picture ever goes to the toilet.' That means it's impossible to get any detail into it. I don't make Westerns because I don't know how much a loaf of bread costs in a Western."

Under Capricorn (1949)
Charles Adare (Michael Wilding) arrives in Australia in 1831

with his uncle, the new governor (Cecil Parker). Unsuccessful in Ireland, Charles hopes to make his fortune in Sydney.

He is befriended by Samson Flusky (Joseph Cotten), a prosperous ex-convict. Sam's wife, Lady Henrietta, "Hattie" (Ingrid Bergman), was a friend of Charles's sister in Ireland. Sam hopes that the young man will be able to cheer up his wife, who is a mentally unstable alcoholic. Meanwhile, the attractive housekeeper, Milly (Margaret Leighton), secretly loves Sam, and encourages Hattie's drinking.

Sam had been sent to an Australian prison after he confessed to a killing that Hattie actually committed. She had followed him there and waited for his release.

Charles's efforts to rehabilitate Hattie conflict with Milly's intentions. Eventually, Sam becomes jealous, and in a rage accidentally shoots Charles. This time, Hattie accepts the blame for the shooting.

Milly, seeing her chances to win Sam slipping away, attempts to poison Hattie, who is rescued in time. When Charles recovers, he tells the authorities that the shooting was accidental.

Hattie stays with Sam, whom she really loves, and Charles leaves for Ireland because he sees no future for himself in Australia.

Jack Cardiff, the film's famed cinematographer, described for me what he termed "the daunting challenge" of shooting *Under Capricorn:*

"It could best be characterized as a chaotic situation. It was *that!* Topsy-turvy.

"They built a huge composite set of the entire mansion. It filled the largest stage at Elstree's MGM Studios. I wondered how on earth I could possibly light so many sets at once! Since the camera was going to have to track on a crane noiselessly all over the place, the whole

stage floor was carpeted. I was more involved than usual in preproduction planning. I worked more closely with the director than usual.

"Each long take had to be covered in one shot with one camera. I'll
give you an example:

"Michael Wilding enters through the front door of the mansion,
into a large circular hall with a winding stairway. He turns to his right
and walks along a narrow corridor into the servants' quarters. After
saying something, he returns to the hall, along another passage into a
large drawing room. More dialogue and more camera movement, and
then the camera follows him back to the hall. Now he goes up the
stairs and walks down a hallway to a door. He opens the door and
enters a bedroom, approaching a large bed where Ingrid Bergman is
sleeping. As he and the camera near her, the bed itself tilts toward the
camera to avoid the camera having to crane up for an overhead shot.

"We rehearsed the whole day and shot the next day. I had to light
all of the sets we'd be using in one go. The noise was indescribable. As
the electric crane rolled through the sets, whole walls opened up, furniture was whisked out of the way by frantic propmen, and then just
as frantically put back as the crane made a return trip.

"The most incredible take was when the camera ends up in a dining room with eight people sitting at a long Georgian table. Hitch
wanted a shot of the guests, looking down the table, then to track in to
a close-up of Ingrid Bergman at the far end.

"The Technicolor camera, inside its enormous blimp, was more
than four feet high. To crane above the table, over the candlesticks,
the wine and the food, it would have been necessary for the camera to
be very high up, looking down on the heads of the actors. The problem was solved by cutting the table into sections, and then fastening
everything down very firmly—food, plates, silverware, glasses, nap-
kins, salt shakers, everything.

"Each actor had a section of the table. The camera was now posi-
tioned at table level instead of six feet above it. At the beginning of the

scene, the guests are all sitting in their places enjoying a leisurely banquet. The camera moves forward, bearing down on each guest, but at the last moment, each of them falls back on a mattress while holding on to his section of the table with all the props stuck to it.

"I don't know how Ingrid kept a straight face while watching her fellow actors fall back like dominoes. It was hilarious, but it worked. I think a film of *Capricorn* being made would have been far more successful than *Under Capricorn* itself."

During the filming of *Under Capricorn*, Ingrid and Petter met with Roberto Rossellini in Paris to discuss a possible Bergman-Rossellini film, and they agreed it would be a good idea.

In January 1949, Rossellini flew to New York City to accept the New York Film Critics Award for best foreign film, *Paisan*. Afterward, he intended taking a train to Los Angeles to discuss *Against the Storm,* as *Stromboli* was first titled, with Ingrid and with potential Hollywood backers. At the same time, he had in mind making a film called *Air of Rome,* starring Anna Magnani, which was to be about Italian immigrants in New York.

"When I won the big prize and was told I was to go to New York to receive it, my first response was to be happy," Rossellini told me. "My second response was to be unhappy. My third response was to have mixed feelings. That last response is the story of my life.

"No matter what the scoffers say about getting awards, in our hearts we are all glad. Even the producers, who don't have hearts, are glad in their wallets.

"However, this was a prestigious award, one of the most, so it would not only be heartwarming for me, but it would be important, I hoped, for getting money for my next film. It showed that I was internationally accepted, and that would help future distribution of my films. Also, as a big bonus, I would have the opportunity to go on to

California and visit Ingrid Bergman. I decided that for Miss Bergman, I would have to fly.

"I did not like to fly. It seemed unsafe, not like the security I felt when I was driving a racing car.

"In the car *I* was in control. In the plane, I was not in control of my own destiny. I had to depend on a pilot and a co-pilot who I did not even know. I had to put my life into their hands. How did I know how qualified they were for the responsibility?

"If I could have flown the plane myself, I would have felt in control, but I would not have liked being responsible for anyone's life but my own.

"I was given the air ticket, and there was not time or money to go any other way. I imagined the headlines about the death of Rossellini in a crash into the Atlantic. Of course, only in Italy would there be headlines, and maybe even there I would not merit a front-page headline. It would depend on the competing news that day. An important soccer match or a visiting Hollywood starlet would easily push me to a single column at the bottom of an inside page. If it said, 'Rossellini Dies in Crash,' people might think it was a review for my film.

"But I survived. I received the award, and I took the train to meet Miss Bergman. When I met her, she was more beautiful than I could have imagined, the most beautiful woman I had ever seen. Without makeup. She was more beautiful in life than on-screen. She glowed. The camera could never fully capture *that* glow.

"Her smile lit up southern California, which was already a bright, sunny place. Too bright. I never liked the brightness of that sun. It revealed every pore on everyone's face, except Ingrid's. The skin on her face was perfect. She wasn't like other people there. She wasn't like anybody anywhere.

"Her husband had come with her, but I didn't notice him at the time. I don't think anyone ever looked at him when Ingrid was there to look at. Men could only look at Ingrid, but I noticed that women stared at her, too. They may have been comparing themselves to her. The comparison would have to be unfavorable because Ingrid had no competition. She was unique.

"Her husband was called Doctor, but since so many men call themselves Dottore in Italy, I didn't really think about it."

Ingrid's impression of Rossellini was just as favorable.

"From the moment I first met Roberto," Ingrid told me, "I was fascinated by him with my ears rather than with my eyes. He was a nice-looking man, very masculine, with a lot of life in his eyes.

"But it was what he said rather than what I saw that caused me to want to know him better, to spend more time with him, and to be directed by him."

Rossellini went to the Beverly Hills Hotel, which he couldn't afford, but he felt was necessary for his image. It was also the way he enjoyed living, even if no one knew about it. Italian regulations limited the amount of money he was permitted to take out of Italy. The even greater limitation was that he didn't *have* any money to take out of Italy.

Ingrid and Petter understood the hotel was far too expensive for Rossellini, so they invited him to stay at their guesthouse on Benedict Canyon. They told him that it would be far more convenient for trying to find financing for a Rossellini film that would star Ingrid.

During the time Rossellini was staying in the Lindstrom guesthouse, Petter was spending a great deal of time working at the hospital. Ingrid drove Rossellini around to show him southern California and to introduce him to people he should know in Hollywood. Rossellini was much in demand as a dinner guest, if not as a director. A high priority was the dinner at the weekend beach house of Billy and Audrey Wilder. Wilder was a fan of *Rome: Open City* and *Paisan,* and Rossellini was an admirer of Wilder.

Wilder spoke German, English, and some French. His wife, Audrey, spoke only English. Ingrid spoke Swedish, English, German, and a little French. Rossellini spoke Italian and some French. Wilder described it as a *Gemütlichkeit* dinner, "Comfortable, and no one got ptomaine poisoning from Audrey's cooking." Everyone knew Audrey's reputation for being the best cook in southern California because her husband had been the number one publicist in the creating of that reputation. Audrey Wilder had learned to cook after they married, endeavoring to please Wilder's sophisticated taste buds.

Petter was not at all concerned about Ingrid's spending so much time with Rossellini. He had his patients to think about, and it would not have occurred to him to feel threatened or jealous.

Petter had perfect confidence. He was tall and, the world had assured him, handsome. He had natural athletic prowess and he also worked at physical fitness. He was a believer in proper diet, exercise, muscle-building, hiking, was an outstanding skier, and every woman who danced with him proclaimed him the best dancer with whom she ever had danced. Just recently, he had become a superb jitterbugger. His mental accomplishments and his credentials as a doctor were notable. Ingrid could have no reason to look elsewhere, since she already had a perfect and a faithful husband.

Also, Petter could not help but notice, without paying any special attention, that Rossellini was shorter than Ingrid, balding and had too large a waist.

Samuel Goldwyn had been speaking with Ingrid about making a film. He was fond of her as an actress and as a person. He told her that he would make *almost* any film she wanted. Ingrid went to Goldwyn and asked him if he would meet with her and Rossellini.

"We met," Ingrid told me, "and Sam and Roberto seemed to get along, even without a language in common. Roberto had managed to learn enough English for communication, and there was a press conference to tell everyone that we were going to make a film. There were many questions. Too many. Sam couldn't answer any of them, so he made up a story, which wasn't at all the film Roberto was going to make, just not to be embarrassed in front of the press."

Ingrid then did something that forever hurt her relationship with Goldwyn. In an unplanned, completely spontaneous moment, Ingrid, knowing that Rossellini could not present his story in English, rose and blurted out the plot, which was totally different from what Goldwyn had just described. "I speak first and think about it later," she said to me more than once.

After that, Goldwyn was skeptical. As soon as the press left, he asked to see another Rossellini film.

Unfortunately for Rossellini he had brought one, *Germany: Year Zero*. It was the third film in the trilogy that also included *Rome: Open City* and *Paisan*.

Goldwyn had a dinner party, and after dinner, *Germany: Year Zero* was shown. When it was over, no one said anything and no one applauded, not even the perfunctory polite applause that always followed even the most boring or disliked film, in deference to the host, who had offered his home, who had given the audience dinner, and who also gave many of them employment.

A few days later, Goldwyn called with dozens of objections, but what mattered was he said he definitely would not put any money into a film by Rossellini.

"I was crushed," Ingrid remembered, "but Petter had an idea. It was a very practical possibility, but I didn't like it."

Petter knew that Howard Hughes wanted to make a movie with Ingrid, and Hughes had bought RKO. Ingrid knew Hughes, though she had never liked him from the first moment they met. She didn't have any strong reason for feeling the way she did, aside from sensing that he particularly liked her and might want to add her to his collection of conquests. She attributed her negative feeling toward him to her woman's intuition and to what she had heard and read about him. She felt uneasy with a man who apparently thrived on feminine conquests.

It was in New York City that Cary Grant introduced the flamboyant millionaire to Ingrid after considerable urging by his good friend Hughes. Grant told me it was one thing he never understood, "Ingrid being so dead-set against Hughes."

Ingrid loved Cary, and found it impossible to say no to him, but she really didn't want to have dinner with Hughes that night. She accepted, however, and Grant, Hughes, and Irene Selznick had dinner and went dancing at El Morocco.

Hughes was respectfully proper and polite, and they talked. He had been a perfect gentleman. Ingrid always remembered what Hughes said to her at the end of the evening about his loneliness, telling her that he didn't have friends. Ingrid had a good time, but when Grant called again on Hughes's behalf, she declined.

She did accept on one occasion when she and Cary couldn't get reservations to get back to California, and Hughes, who owned TWA, offered to fly them there. When Hughes bought RKO, he called Ingrid to tell her that he had just bought the studio—for her.

Ingrid replied that she was an actress and didn't know what to do with a studio, but what she really wanted was a good part, a good script, a good director.

After Goldwyn's rejection, Ingrid called Hughes, who was staying in a bungalow at the Beverly Hills Hotel, very close to Ingrid's home. Hughes arrived in less than fifteen minutes, still wearing his tennis clothes.

Ingrid introduced him to Rossellini, but Hughes didn't pay attention to the Italian director, only to her. Hughes didn't even want to hear the plot of the film being offered. He just said he would do it, and asked how much they needed.

He had only one question, not of Rossellini, of whose presence he seemed virtually unaware, but of Ingrid.

Hughes wanted to know if she would be beautiful in the film with a wonderful wardrobe. When he learned that this was not what the Italian director had in mind, he was disappointed but said they would do the film anyway. Then, the next film at RKO would be the one with Ingrid of which he dreamed, wearing wonderful clothes, with great accessories. Hughes said accessories were extremely important. None of the three, nor of the four when they were joined by Dr. Lindstrom, knew what the future held. The RKO film Howard Hughes imagined producing for Ingrid would never happen. Hughes's money sent Ingrid to Italy, not for a few months as all expected, but for seven years. Hughes would never see her again.

When Hughes agreed to put up the money for the film that was to become *Stromboli*, Ingrid Bergman was lost to Hollywood as an actress, lost to him as a friend, lost to Hitchcock as potentially the star of another film as great as *Notorious*, lost to Lindstrom as a wife, and lost to America as an icon of wholesomeness and purity.

"Life is really made up of small things," Ingrid told me, "or things that seem small at the time."

Shortly before Christmas 1949, Ingrid took Pia to a toy shop. Pia's Christmas gift already had been planned, a bicycle. In the toy shop, however, Ingrid and Pia encountered a huge stuffed cow wearing a white apron, standing there in the corner. Pia knew her own mind, and it quickly became clear she wanted the stuffed cow, called Elsie, more than a bicycle or anything else.

"She was willing to sacrifice the bicycle for Elsie," Ingrid said, "because there were many bicycles and only one Elsie."

Ingrid, who never liked making decisions, great or small, went home to Petter and told him about Elsie. She wanted to buy Pia the gift Pia loved, but when Petter heard that the stuffed cow cost $75, he was appalled. His "No!" was loud, clear, adamant.

He considered a large cow doll with an apron to be an absurd waste of money. Such an object could serve no purpose. "It will just stand in a corner," he said. "The bicycle is practical and useful."

Ingrid was accustomed to accepting Petter's authority in most instances, perhaps in all, but it was with a certain sadness that she missed the acquisition of Elsie because she knew their daughter would be disappointed. As Ingrid generally did, she was prepared to abide by her husband's decision. It was the way a Swedish wife was supposed to behave.

She would be the one who had to tell Pia, who was always such a good girl. Especially *because* she was such a good girl, Ingrid didn't like to deny her wish.

Ingrid would have loved to see the look of Christmas joy on Pia's face when she saw Elsie, although Ingrid knew it probably wouldn't have been a surprise because she wouldn't have been able to keep the secret for long. Whenever they went to the toy store, Ingrid observed where her daughter's glance went first, and her own, as well.

Elsie remained there in the corner during the great rush of holiday buying. After Christmas and the New Year, the rejected cow was still there. Elsie, it seemed to Ingrid, looked forlorn.

Pia got a bicycle, a very nice one, and Petter had, of course, been right, but . . .

Ingrid worried that someone would buy Elsie, and Pia would be unhappy. No one did.

About this time, Roberto Rossellini arrived in Los Angeles. Knowing about Rossellini's shortage of cash because of Italian currency laws, Lindstrom insisted that Rossellini borrow $300 and Rossellini accepted the loan.

Rossellini wanted to visit a toy store. He planned to bring his son, Renzo, in Italy, a cowboy outfit with boots and a cowboy hat and, for good measure, an Indian feather headdress. His son could be both a cowboy and an Indian, though not at the same time.

Ingrid took Rossellini to the local toy store where Elsie still stood in the corner. Rossellini saw Elsie.

According to Ingrid, as soon as he saw the large cow with her apron, he announced that he was going to buy that wonderful doll, no matter what the price. "I want to buy it for Pia. She will love it."

"Money was not a consideration for Rossellini except when he didn't have it. 'No matter what it costs, Pia has to have it,' he said. Roberto's well-worn, fine Italian leather wallet was full of money, the $300 he had borrowed from Petter."

While Ingrid was weighing all the possibilities as to what to do, which she usually did, Rossellini blithely made the purchase.

It was a perfectly good-spirited act on the part of Rossellini. He was repaying the Lindstroms' hospitality by wanting to make their daughter happy, but *how* did he know it should be Elsie? True, Elsie had high visibility in the store, but it wasn't enough to explain it. There seemed to be more at work than that. Ingrid believed it was a special sign.

Ingrid told me that when she left for Italy, she thought she would only be gone for a few months. She said what she most wanted me to write when I wrote about her was that when she left Benedict Canyon that day for Italy, she had no idea that she was leaving for longer.

Ingrid left behind her favorite dresses, which were at the dry cleaner's, the paintings by her father, the photographs from her childhood, and the reel of motion picture film showing her as a child with her mother. She took only $300 with her.

Above all, she left Pia behind. Ingrid repeated that she had no idea that she was leaving for more than a few months in Italy, and the person in the world she most wanted to understand that and believe it was Pia.

Three

⚜

INGRID AND ITALY

As Ingrid's plane approached Rome, a drama was unfolding, precipitated by her imminent arrival. It involved a bowl of spaghetti and the tempestuous several-year affair of Anna Magnani and Rossellini. Magnani had starred in Rossellini's *Rome: Open City* and his two-part *L'Amore.*

The excitement was fading for Rossellini, who had tired of Magnani's emotional eruptions. Even if the affair had run its course, it was not like Magnani to accept someone else choosing the moment to end it. Also, Magnani wanted to star in future Rossellini films, of which the next was to be his first American film, *Air of Rome.*

It was Isabella Rossellini who told me about the story of Magnani and the bowl of spaghetti:

Rossellini was spending a weekend with Magnani in Amalfi. He had told the concierge he was expecting word from Los Angeles and that when it came, he wanted total discretion. He did *not* want the communication to be given to him when he was with Magnani. He emphasized the importance of absolute secrecy in front of the fiery Magnani.

Later, as Rossellini and Magnani went toward the dining room, they passed the concierge. When he thought Magnani wasn't looking, the concierge winked slyly at the director, showing that they were men together with a man's secret.

Rossellini could only hope that his suspicious companion had missed the wink. As they were seated at their table and began to enjoy their dinner, it appeared to a relieved Rossellini that the wink and all it implied had gone unnoticed. He could relax and enjoy the meal.

Magnani was tossing the spaghetti, vigorously, but not *too* vigorously. She knew just how Roberto liked it. She added the olive oil and tomato sauce, not too much, certainly not too little. She arranged the *parmigiano*. She smiled, proud of her creation. She knew it was just right.

Then she lifted the bowl, leaned forward and poured it over Rossellini's head. She didn't say a word, the only time in her relationship with him that he could remember her without words.

It was said that this was the end of the Rossellini-Magnani affair, though it was obvious that it must have ended well before the wasted pasta.

Isabella said the bowl-of-spaghetti story became part of anecdotal history, much repeated by those who were in the restaurant, as well as by those who were not. It was a story that Rossellini loved. It showed how passionately Magnani felt about him, how much she cared.

It was only much later that he told the story to Ingrid, long after Magnani and Rossellini were no longer lovers and, rather, it was Ingrid and Rossellini who had become lovers.

"A romantic relationship with Roberto was the last thing I had in mind," Ingrid told me. "I was keen to be in one of his films, but I wondered in what language would I speak?"

Ingrid didn't know any Italian except *ti amo,* and Rossellini knew no Swedish and wasn't comfortable in what English he knew. Their only language in common was French.

•   •   •

"I had never seen anyone so beautiful," Federico Fellini told me. "For us in Italy, it was as if the Virgin Mary had just descended upon us from Disneyland.

"I would like to have made a film with Ingrid. I don't know exactly what, but I would have been inspired if I'd had any hope. I knew it was hopeless because Roberto was very possessive of his prize, his great jewel, and he wasn't going to let anyone have Ingrid for a film, and especially not an Italian film, and especially me. Our great friendship had turned into a certain rivalry.

"One tried not to stare at Ingrid, but you couldn't help but notice her incredible complexion. She didn't have any pores."

Ingrid was stunned by the dazzling reception awaiting her in Rome on March 20, 1949, the reception by crowds of paparazzi (before Fellini was to give them their name in *La Dolce Vita*) and fans. She had never experienced anything like it before. It was a little thrilling, and a little frightening, but Rossellini whisked her away in his red sports car, driving very fast. He had been there early waiting for her, as was expected by her. She told me if she had known that it would be perhaps the only time he would be punctual, she would have appreciated it more. For Ingrid, punctuality was a way of life, for Rossellini, a step in the courtship of the woman he found the most beautiful in the world. They went to Rome's Excelsior Hotel, where another crowd was waiting, of people and paparazzi.

"There were people laughing and shouting as though their dearest lost relation had arrived. I knew immediately that I would love these warm, demonstrative Italian people who were so ready to take a stranger into their hearts."

Rossellini kept a small apartment at the hotel, and Ingrid was to have one of their grandest suites. Waiting in Rossellini's apartment were many of the most acclaimed film people of Italy. Ingrid was so dazzled, nervous, and emotional at the time that many years later, she remembered it all as something of a blur.

"As we were entering, Roberto was angry about the paparazzi and especially the photographers who came so close that they were touching us. Roberto tried to hit them with his fists. He tried to smash their cameras. I always remember when, in his rage, he tore the jacket of a photographer.

"Roberto was a fighter. I had not seen this angry side of him before.

"But, when we arrived upstairs at the party, just a trip in the elevator, his anger turned off completely, as if he had never felt it. He was among friends, and I saw that they perceived him as a god and treated him as one."

There was one person she noticed more than all of the others, a big man with a soft voice who attracted her, especially after Roberto told her that it was this man who had done all the drawings that were pinned on the walls. They were caricatures of Ingrid, Rossellini, apart and together, and some others whom Ingrid didn't recognize, but she liked what the artist referred to as his "funny little drawings."

Rossellini said to her, "I want you to meet someone who will be one of the great names in the history of Italian films, my friend, Federico Fellini."

Ingrid was also drawn to a tiny woman whom she found quite engaging. She learned she was Federico's wife, Giulietta Masina. They would become friends.

Many years later, Ingrid told me that one of her regrets was that she hadn't taken as souvenirs some of the wonderful Fellini drawings.

A few days later, Rossellini took Ingrid away from Rome, "not," as she remembered, "on his white charger, but in his red sports car," and he proceeded to show her some of the most historic and beautiful places in Italy.

"As we were in the car one day, I said to Roberto that I didn't know if he remembered tearing the jacket of the photographer. The man had looked so unhappy, as though it was his only jacket.

"Roberto said, 'It probably was, so the next morning, I had a new one sent to him.'

"My eyes filled with tears. Roberto was a totally good person. I knew I loved him for his professional brilliance, and for his personal brilliance, for his vitality and his endless energy, his great warmth, but there were sides to him I didn't even know yet. He had compassion. He was sentimental and caring."

Danny Selznick described Rossellini as "so charismatic."

"My God! The energy! You seldom meet somebody who has that. Rossellini had an earthy energy. He walked into a room and there was an explosion of energy. My father had fabulous energy. He was famous for it. But he didn't have that testosterone exploding."

On April 3, Ingrid wrote a letter to Petter telling him of her feelings for Roberto and asking for forgiveness. The next day, she set out with Rossellini for the island of Stromboli in the Tyrrhenian Sea.

Driving to Stromboli, Roberto wanted to share his Italy with Ingrid. He was courting her, using Italy from Amalfi, Capri, Naples, all the way to Calabria by car, as a perfect setting. Roberto introduced her to everyone he knew, and that was a great many people, almost everyone, it seemed to Ingrid.

"Roberto was the greatest tour guide, a scholar about Italy who knew everything. There wasn't anything I could ask him that he didn't know.

"Later, I learned there were a few things he hadn't really known when I asked, but he was never at a loss, and he just made up the answers. He wanted to impress me, and he did. I had fallen in love with Rossellini when I fell in love with the work, and then the man didn't disappoint me."

Rossellini was a professional driver, having raced Ferraris. He went faster than Ingrid would have preferred, but he gripped the wheel like a racing car driver. He knew the road and, at that time after World War II, there weren't many cars. There were quite a few horses and donkeys.

Though they stopped at the best hotels, it was not the standard of luxury to which Ingrid was accustomed. At the hotel in Stromboli, there were silk sheets with real lace trim and hand embroidery, but no private bathrooms.

When Ingrid arrived at the hotel, crowds had gathered to greet her and Rossellini. Ingrid warmly returned the greetings, and then she went to her large and airy bedroom. After about ten minutes, she wished to go the bathroom. She opened her door, but she was still in full view of the crowd outside, so she closed her door.

After ten minutes, she opened the door again and peeped out. The crowd had not diminished. It seemed to have grown.

Ingrid was observed, and there was applause. She quickly closed the door.

She waited another thirty minutes, not wishing any more applause, considering the nature of the occasion. She decided she would not, *could not,* be deterred this time.

Boldly, she opened the door. There it was. Resounding applause accompanied her all the way to the washroom door.

Once more, when she exited, the applause accompanied her back to her bedroom door.

"Only in Italy," she told me so many years later.

Ingrid had to write what was the most difficult letter of her life. She didn't know exactly what to say or how to say it, but she knew she had to make it clear to Petter that she wanted a divorce.

During the Italian trip with Roberto, Ingrid had realized that when she returned to California, she did not want to remain married to Petter.

She wanted a divorce, not in the vague way she once had wanted it, but in a very specific, thought-out way.

Ingrid felt she had to be totally honest with Petter. Of all people in the world, she had to be honest with *him*.

During the trip from Rome to Amalfi, she had fallen in love with Roberto Rossellini. She didn't know at exactly what moment it had happened or when she knew it, but know it she did. And she was not only in love with him, she loved his milieu and wanted to be a part of it. It was what she had been missing in Hollywood.

She wrote all this to Petter hoping he would understand, but knowing he wouldn't.

Ingrid had been struck by how natural the actors seemed in *Paisan* and *Rome: Open City*. Rossellini explained how he achieved this quality:

"I cast for *Paisan* by stationing my camera and cameraman in the middle of wherever the scene was to take place, on a street corner, in a park, wherever. Then, passersby would stop to see what was happening. As a crowd gathered, Federico [Fellini], and I would walk among them, choosing our actors. If I liked the way someone looked, I cast him in the scene, adapting to whatever he was like as a person rather than asking him to adapt to my imagined character.

"I wasn't bound by a script because my script only had suggestions of what the character might say or do. Then, for the next scene, I might have to change the plot to accommodate something the person said or did unexpectedly, which you never could have thought of. But this kind of actor was usually good only once. As soon as he felt successful playing himself, he thought he was an actor and tried to play somebody else, which he was not capable of doing."

Rossellini's son Renzo told me, "All of my father's pictures, whatever they *seem* to be about, are really metaphors for something else. He would start out with a big idea about the real world and then try to concentrate it into a film that would hold our attention for an hour or two, and perhaps afterwards affect our thinking about that big idea. *Stromboli* is not really a film about a woman who can't adjust to married life. It's a film about Europe trying to adjust to peace after the war."

As Roberto Rossellini had explained it to me, "This is simply a movie about a character who cannot stop thinking she is at war, even after the war is over and the skills she developed during wartime are no longer needed or relevant. She is so cynical, a cynicism justified during wartime, that she cannot shed her hard shell until all seems lost, and then, for the first time, she cries for pity. It is a problem of war that it does not prepare us for peace."

Stromboli (1950)

Karin (Ingrid Bergman), a Czech refugee after World War II, marries Antonio (Mario Vitale), an Italian ex-soldier she has just met because she is desperate to get out of a displaced persons camp. He takes her to his small, primitive fishing village on the island of Stromboli where she is unhappy and lonely, shunned by the local people except the lighthouse keeper (Mario Sponza).

Her husband, suspecting she is having an affair with him, beats her and then confines her to their home. Knowing she is pregnant and not wanting to live anymore, Karin leaves for the volcano where she intends to commit suicide in the lava flow.

Exhausted, she is overcome by the fumes of the volcano and collapses. Awakening in the ashes, she feels changed and starts back to the village to make what she can of her life.

"I stood out like a sore thumb in *Stromboli*," Ingrid told me. "There were many things which hurt the film besides me, but I feel I had a big negative responsibility in the way the film was. In the business of making films, what we, Roberto and I, regarded as our personal life had become the property of everyone who paid a film admission and everyone who didn't. *Stromboli* already had bad connotations and a stigma before anyone ever saw it. It was a famous picture no one saw. It was the film that was associated with my downfall, my being a fallen woman. It seems I had spoiled my image, broken it, when I hadn't even understood I had one.

"I think I was too well known as an actress to disappear into the part on the screen. Roberto liked to use unknown people, nonprofessionals in almost all of the parts.

"He didn't like rehearsing too much because he really didn't want acting. He disliked actors. He thought of them as kind of phony people, very vain, who just wanted to look their best even when they were supposed to look their worst. And he didn't want 'a performance,' he wanted *reality*. That's why he didn't give the actors their dialogue in advance, because they might repeat it to themselves and look in the mirror to see what effect they were having. He gave it to them at the last minute, and then he made only one or two takes, and not any more. He didn't want anything that was mechanical.

"Many people had difficulties with this, but as he mostly worked with people that were not actors, it didn't matter. As you know, Italians are very free and exhibitionistic. They could make up their own dialogue and they had a very good time doing it. As you can tell by the pictures, they looked very real, indeed, because they were not acting at all. They were just playing themselves and that's exactly what Roberto wanted.

"But for a professional actress like myself, it was very, very difficult. We were not at all used to this. We were used to *acting*. But I tried as much as I could to come into the mood of these amateurs.

"It was very, very difficult, though, because I could never know when they had finished the dialogue they were making up and when my cue came up. I'm afraid that on my face there was always a worried expression because I was too concerned about their performance and therefore I couldn't always think of my own. Sometimes it was very funny.

"There was one scene I remember so well in *Stromboli.* I was playing with some amateurs from the island. They didn't know English and I didn't know Italian, so I was speaking my lines in English, because afterwards it was all going to be dubbed, as they did in Italy in those days. Of course the amateurs never knew when to come in with their dialogue, so Roberto had put a string around their big toes, and he would pull the string when one should speak; and then he pulled the other one, so when he pulled them they spoke their dialogue. He had them on strings, like puppets, which of course made me laugh and cry at the same time. Then *I* was the one who was blamed because the scene was spoiled!

"I was worried that my Hollywood years might have led to my having learned stylized ways. After having seen his realistic films, the ten years I had spent in Hollywood seemed very artificial. Roberto wanted me to be natural, but I found I had to act more to be his idea of natural than I ever had acted before. Directors, producers, people had called my quality 'natural,' but Roberto's idea of natural was not *my* naturalness. He said I was not to look beautiful. It is what is called a left-handed compliment. He wanted me to save my looks for at home. He said my problem was my face was too beautiful. Well, I always knew *that* couldn't last forever, but I considered it fortunate to have it for a while.

"I have always wanted as an actress to change as much as I could, to do always different things, different parts. I wanted to be an actress, not a face. Of course, there are parts everyone is limited to by your physical type, but I wanted to be full of surprises. I wanted to surprise my audience and to surprise myself.

"As it turned out, my audience didn't *want* to be so surprised, at least not by me. They seemed to want most from me my Hitchcock image from *Notorious.* For me, as an actress, I felt I couldn't know if I offered always the same image, but it was worse to disappoint. I never wanted to disappoint people.

"The rule seems to be that they, the audience, which we speak of in the singular, is really plural and has brought its expectations to the movie theater.

"I think *Stromboli* would have been better off with a little peasant girl Roberto found somewhere who did not bring baggage with her. Maybe that would have pleased his audience. I didn't. And his films weren't what *my* audience wanted to see me in, either!"

Ingrid emphatically denied that Rossellini's films with her were inspired by her and by their life together.

"He definitely did not draw on my own life. If you will examine *Stromboli* from the beginning, it was about something that he had seen in Italy. When he went to the refugee camps that were in Italy after the war, he saw this kind of woman who will do anything to get out of there. He had spoken to one of them, and she said, 'I'll marry *anybody*. Later, I can get rid of him, but I'll be out of here.'

"I am asked often, personally and professionally, do I have regrets about going to Italy to meet Roberto. I can answer no. Not now. But yes, I had some along the way.

"There were moments of such pain. The greatest pain for me is bringing pain to others. I didn't want to hurt Petter, who had been such a good husband to me. Where would my life in acting be without him? I don't know if I would have found myself if I hadn't found Petter, if he hadn't found *me.* But it was hurting our child that was most terrible.

"I thought our films, Roberto's and mine, were better than people said. Many of the people who said they weren't good and spread that word hadn't seen them. That is terrible when you put a part of your life into something and it doesn't please people, and they say you have created an ugly child. If they buy tickets and didn't get their money's worth, well, then they have paid for the right to express negative opinions.

"*Stromboli* was a picture which became most famous for our scandal rather than for itself. Maybe in another time, in the future, audiences will look at *Stromboli* and see it and the others that followed it in another way. I hope so, for Roberto's sake. I thought, when our marriage ended, 'Roberto isn't stuck with me anymore.'

"I didn't fit in to what he wanted to do. I couldn't help it. I wasn't the right type for his films. I wasn't exactly the right type for his private life either, but by the time both of us understood that, we had three lovely children. I believe I would have stayed married forever, or at least until our children grew up, but Roberto left for India and brought back his new family.

"It would have been much better if only Roberto had permitted me to act in the films of the other wonderful directors who wanted to have me in their films. I would have learned so much, and he would not have been forced to misshape his pictures around me. But even for his friend, Federico [Fellini], he didn't want me to do a film."

When on August 2, 1949, Ingrid left Stromboli, she was grateful. In four months, she had given up her position in Hollywood as the number one star. She had disappointed and alienated many people around the world, particularly her husband, Petter, whom she had known since she was a girl in Sweden, her only child, Pia, and her husband's family in Sweden.

She was shocked by the letter from Joseph Breen, the vice president and director of the Production Code. This group was dedicated to judging American films to insure that moral standards were upheld. She was asked by Breen to deny the "rumors" that she was about to divorce her husband, leave her child, and marry Roberto Rossellini.

She was reproached by members of the Lutheran Church in Swe-

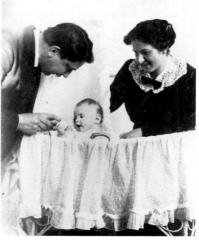

Friedel Adler with her husband, Justus Bergman, about 1909. They were newly married. *(Collection of Isabella Rossellini)*

Justus and Friedel with baby Ingrid in early 1916. Ingrid could not remember her mother, who died only two years later. *(Collection of Isabella Rossellini)*

Justus and Ingrid in 1920.*(Collection of Isabella Rossellini)*

Justus Bergman believed that among all the children's portraits he took, one of those children would become famous. He didn't realize that his own little Ingrid would be the one. (*Collection of Isabella Rossellini*)

Ingrid, wearing her father's hat, overcoat, shoes, and spectacles, holding the afternoon Stockholm newspaper, dated May 7, 1922. She is seven years old. (*Collection of Isabella Rossellini*)

The twenty-one-year-old Ingrid waiting on location near Stockholm during the filming of *Intermezzo* (1936), the Swedish film that led to David O. Selznick's bringing her to Hollywood. *(Potsdam Museum Archive)*

BELOW: Ingrid accompanies Leslie Howard in *Intermezzo: A Love Story* (1939). Ingrid studied singing and piano and was an accomplished musician. *(Museum of Modern Art)*

Because of Ingrid's great popularity, *Rage in Heaven* (1941), which had gone unnoticed when it was first released, was reissued, with many people regarding it as a new film in 1945. In the film, Ingrid is married to psychotically jealous Robert Montgomery. *(Museum of Modern Art)*

Ingrid appeared with Spencer Tracy in *Dr. Jekyll and Mr. Hyde* (1941) playing against type. *(Museum of Modern Art)*

RIGHT: "Here's looking at *you*, kid," the famous *Casablanca* (1942) line, which writer Julius Epstein told the author was actually suggested by Humphrey Bogart. *(Museum of Modern Art)*

Paul Henreid and Ingrid prepare to board the plane to Lisbon as Claude Rains, influenced by the pistol in Humphrey Bogart's pocket, orders Louis Mercier to let them go. Originally, two different endings were to be shot, but everyone knew this was the right one when they saw it. *[British Film Institute]*

Gaslight (1944), directed by George Cukor, was the first of three films in which Ingrid co-starred with Charles Boyer. Ingrid won her first Oscar as best actress for her performance. *(Museum of Modern Art)*

BELOW: Ingrid was positive her performance in *For Whom the Bell Tolls* (1943) would be remembered long after *Casablanca* was forgotten. She is shown with Gary Cooper, whom her character, María, loves, and Katina Paxinou. *(Museum of Modern Art)*

Ingrid, as a half-Creole girl who is a victim of racial prejudice, in Edna Ferber's *Saratoga Trunk* (1945), with Gary Cooper, who is prejudiced only in her favor. *(Museum of Modern Art)*

BELOW: As a psychiatrist, Ingrid is trying to discover the true identity of the man she loves, an amnesiac, played by Gregory Peck, in Alfred Hitchcock's *Spellbound* (1945). *(Museum of Modern Art)*

Salvador Dalí showing a dubious Ingrid the gown she will wear in his concept of a Freudian dream in *Spellbound*. *(Museum of Modern Art)*

Bing Crosby and Ingrid, as well as director Leo McCarey, won Oscars just before starting *The Bells of St. Mary's*. (*Museum of Modern Art*)

BELOW: Alfred Hitchcock, Ingrid, and Cary Grant relaxing between scenes in *Notorious* (1946). Grant was a leader in lobbying for Ingrid's return to Hollywood when it seemed everyone had turned against her, and then in welcoming her back to Hollywood. (*Museum of Modern Art*)

In *Notorious*, Alfred Hitchcock sidestepped the Production Code's limit on how long a kiss may be held by breaking the one between Cary Grant and Ingrid into many short segments. (*British Film Institute*)

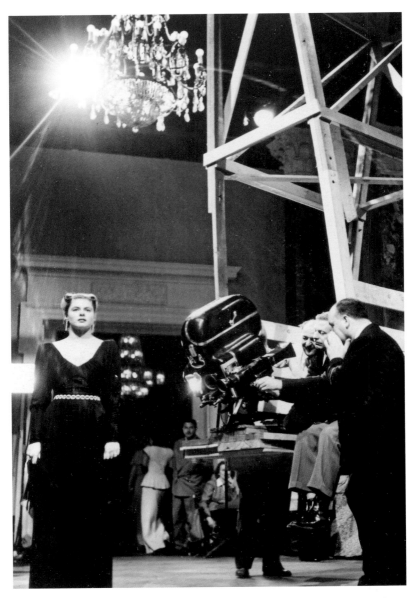

For the shot that starts with an overview of the entire ballroom and goes to a key in Ingrid's hand in *Notorious,* Hitchcock had this huge wooden elevator constructed and used a special lens. *(British Film Institute)*

Ingrid out of armor in *Joan of Lorraine* (1948), one of her numerous appearances as Joan of Arc. (*British Film Institute*)

Ingrid stands with Michael Wilding, while Joseph Cotten looks on in the background. *Under Capricorn* was one of Ingrid's most difficult films because of director Alfred Hitchcock's continuous ten-minute takes. (*British Film Institute*)

Hitchcock makes himself useful to Ingrid on the *Under Capricorn* set between shots. (*British Film Institute*)

Roberto Rossellini (left) and the twenty-six-year-old Federico Fellini (right), while they were shooting *Paisan* in 1946. The unidentified monk (center), a nonprofessional actor, appeared in one of the segments of the film. (*Studio Longardi*)

Stromboli (1950) marked not only Ingrid's first non-Hollywood film in a decade, but her first Roberto Rossellini film. It became the symbol of the scandal that changed her name and career. Here she is with Mario Vitale. (*Potsdam Museum Archive*)

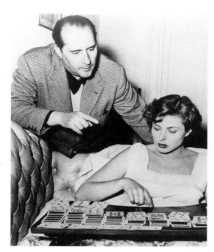

Some solitaire! Rossellini can't resist directing the star of his films and his life even in a game of solitaire in 1952. (*Potsdam Museum Archive*)

Ingrid with her son, Robin, who was usually called "Robertino," in 1957. (*Studio Longardi*)

The happy Rossellini family, 1956. Clockwise from left: Ingrid, Robertino, Roberto, Isotta Ingrid, and Isabella. (*Collection of Isabella Rossellini*)

Helen Hayes was chosen for the part of the dowager Empress Marie in *Anastasia* (1956) because someone confused her with Helen Haye, the British actress who had created the part onstage. Ingrid won her second Oscar as best actress. (*British Film Institute*)

Jean Marais plays a general soliciting career advice, and something more, from Polish royal pretender Ingrid in Jean Renoir's *Paris Does Strange Things* (1957). (*Museum of Modern Art, Criterion Collection*)

ABOVE: Robert Donat, Curt Jürgens, and Ingrid in *The Inn of the Sixth Happiness* (1958). Shortly after the picture wrapped, an ill Donat died at the age of fifty-three. (*British Film Institute*)

Sir Ralph Richardson and Ingrid in a British television adaptation of *Hedda Gabler* (1963). She had just appeared in a French language version of the Ibsen drama in Paris. (*British Film Institute*)

Isabella and Ingrid in London, 1969. The photograph was taken to dispel rumors in the press that scoliosis had left Isabella crippled and deformed. "Mama usually did her own hair," Isabella told the author, "but for this picture, she went to the hair-dresser." (*Collection of Isabella Rossellini*)

Goldie Hawn, then a popular TV personality, made her film debut with Ingrid in *Cactus Flower* (1969). (*Museum of Modern Art*)

Liza Minnelli hoped she would learn something new about the art of acting from Ingrid in *A Matter of Time* (1976), directed by her father, Vincente Minnelli. She did. (*British Film Institute*)

Isabella Rossellini remembered Martin Scorsese asking Fellini if he knew a romantic, private place in Italy where he and Isabella could be married. Fellini said, "Yes. Stromboli." (*Studio Longardi*)

Isabella was cast in *A Matter of Time* because of her resemblance to her mother. As she's dying, Ingrid's character imagines the nurse tending her, Isabella, is herself as a young woman. (*Collection of Isabella Rossellini*)

Ingrid smiles radiantly at the audience in Hollywood honoring Orson Welles at the American Film Institute tribute gala on February 9, 1975. (*American Film Institute*)

It was Liv Ullmann's idea to wear glasses in Ingmar Bergman's *Autumn Sonata* (1978) and Ingrid and Liv's idea to "play against" dialogue they didn't think suited their characters. (*Museum of Modern Art*)

Ingrid wore no makeup to play Golda Meir, only a gray wig, in *A Woman Called Golda* (1982). She preferred to stress the spirit of the character, rather than trying to impersonate Meir. (*Museum of Modern Art*)

den and by the priests of the Roman Catholic Church, especially in America, and there were letters from people who thought she should be burned at the stake, not as Joan of Arc, but as a witch.

"There were terrible letters that came to me, each envelope filled with hate. Some of the letters said I would burn in hell for eternity. Some said I was an agent of the devil and that my little boy was the child of the devil. Others said my baby would be born dead or he would be a hunchback. They wrote about every kind of terrible deformity that would affect my baby. People wrote to me addressing me as 'whore' and 'slut.' I could not believe that so many people hated me.

"Whatever people thought of my private life, it seemed to me it was *my* private life, and I hadn't done anything to them. I was in shock. Letters came from all over, but more of them were from America. America is a big country, so there were more people to write letters of every kind.

"Roberto asked me why did I look at them, since they upset me so much. He said it was like reading reviews of reviewers of your films who always hate your work. Of what use?

"I said it was because that was the only way I could find the letters from friends who were encouraging and supporting me."

Ingrid was Hollywood's first lady, the number one actress in box office for three years, when she left Hollywood. She told me that perhaps she had given it up so easily because success had come to her so easily.

"I had adjusted to being popular and I enjoyed it, professionally and personally. Good things are easy to adjust to.

"I could not adjust so easily to life on *Stromboli*. I didn't like our always being late with the film, and the constant warnings from the producers. We were always late and always falling more behind. We had bad luck with the weather, but what made me feel so desperate

was when we started filming and Roberto told me he had no thought
of finishing on schedule. 'Impossible,' he said. He hadn't even
planned on finishing on time.

"This was very shocking for me. My word meant so much to me,
and I could not imagine giving it without meaning it. I always worried
about the producers who had put their money into what we were
doing, and I felt we had a responsibility toward them and their invest-
ment.

"Roberto was the opposite of me. He said to me, 'They are producers, so it doesn't matter.' He saw the producers as his natural enemy.
Well, if it wasn't true at the beginning, it was at the end."

When, during the filming of *Stromboli,* news reports of a rumored
affair between Ingrid and Rossellini shocked the world, the word
Stromboli became a trigger for laughter, innuendo, and the inspiration for countless salacious jokes.

No denials were forthcoming. Then, after it could no longer be
ignored, the unthinkable, the unspeakable happened. On December
13, 1949, the rumors were confirmed. Ingrid admitted that she was
having Rossellini's baby. She was more than seven months pregnant.

Ingrid was still married to Petter, and Roberto was still married to
his wife, Marcella. Both, especially Ingrid, were having difficulty
obtaining divorces. What started out as a sensational news story
became one of the major scandals of the twentieth century. The tem-
pest that followed was comparable to the scandal decades later when
Princess Diana and Prince Charles separated and subsequently
divorced. Ingrid had been Hollywood royalty.

Roberto Rossellini was born into a wealthy family on May 8, 1906, the
eldest of four children. It was not old money, but it was just as spend-
able. His father, Giuseppe, was an architect who had built several
Rome theaters.

The family fortune, however, was made by an uncle who, having no children of his own, took Roberto's father into his home. The uncle arranged for Roberto's father to marry his mistress's beautiful niece, Elettra, who was only seventeen when her first child, Roberto, was born.

"His father actually built many important cinemas in Italy," Isabella told me. "That's why my father went to the movie theaters so much. He took all his friends with him. He had a lot of friends anyway, but then he added every boy who liked to go to the movies, and every boy liked to go free. Before the time when Father was born, his family was quite wealthy, and the family business was thriving. Some people said Father died after spending all the money that was put aside, but it was *his* father who began doing that."

"Our money had come so quickly," Roberto Rossellini told me, "all in one generation, to my grandfather who wasn't really my grandfather. He was my granduncle Angelo. Maybe we spent it so fast because we didn't have faith it would last. We were right."

The Rossellinis kept what they called "an open table." Roberto's young mother didn't know most of the people who came in to partake of the delicious food and wine that was the family's signature of limitless hospitality. Rossellini remembered that when he was a boy, the open table was always there. When he spoke with me sixty years later, he said that though he never gave it a thought as a boy and took it for granted, he had come to believe the open table was an important influence in his life and a factor in shaping his personality, an unquestioning spirit of generosity. "I've tried to take the open table with me," he said.

Ingrid's childhood had been shaped by the loss of those nearest and most loved by her; Roberto Rossellini's life was shaped by a multitude of illnesses.

These illnesses ranged from serious to life-threatening. As a child, he survived malaria, cholera, and appendicitis. The most serious illness of all was when, at thirteen, he contracted influenza during the epidemic of 1918–1920. Millions died worldwide.

For three months, Roberto hovered between life and death. Part of one of his lungs was removed. His mother promised God that if Roberto were spared, she would wear black for the rest of her life. Roberto *was* spared, and Elettra, from age thirty-one on, began wearing black, which fortunately was her favorite color. Gradually, she added mauve, of which she was also very fond.

Restored to health and on a hiking trip, Roberto was lost for a few days and then discovered badly frozen. This led to a damaged kidney and recurrent attacks of pleurisy. In spite of these disabilities, he remained physically active.

"In my late teens," Rossellini told me, "I did a lot of dangerous things. There were people who said I did them because I was trying to kill myself.

"Exactly the opposite. It was because I loved life so much that I did them. Motorcycles, cars, sex. I wanted to feel life at its greatest intensity."

It was feared that young Roberto would never reach manhood, but adversity seemed to have strengthened rather than weakened him, showing a will to survive that would stay with him all his life.

Because of all his childhood physical crises, the young Rossellini had spent much of his life in bed. Sometimes he went to bed for a few days to "restore" himself. There he was loved, spoiled, indulged, and he felt secure.

"I came to like my bed so much, it led to a lifelong habit of spending a great deal of time there, not just as a place to restore myself, but as a workplace. When my colleagues came to work on a script, I remained in bed. Why not?"

"In those days," Italian director Michelangelo Antonioni told me, "Roberto lived in a big, empty old house he'd somehow found in wartime Rome. He was always in bed, because that was the only piece of furniture he had, and we worked on his bed with him in it.

"I immediately liked Rossellini as a man, even though he talked too much without letting others say anything. I was impatient, but I soon found out he had quite a lot to say because he always knew where he was going, even if *you* didn't. It was all said with the drama of an immense personality. Sometimes I felt he spent so much time in bed because he was saving up all his energy to talk. He had to make deposits and refill his energy bank."

Federico Fellini agreed. "The most important piece of furniture, the only piece of furniture that counted for him was the bed, and he was incredibly fussy about every aspect of it. The mattress, not too soft and not too firm, of course, the Egyptian cotton sheets, the goose down pillows, many of them, and the soft white duvet.

"When I went to work on [Rossellini's] *Un Pilota Ritorna* [*A Pilot Returns*, 1942], we worked in his bedroom. There weren't any chairs in the room, but colleagues were welcome to sit on the bed. There were a few chairs and a table in another room, so if we needed some chairs, we borrowed a few from the dining room and dragged them into the bedroom."

Sometimes as an adult, Rossellini went to bed for a few days. "I've had some of my best ideas there. I found the bedroom my most creative room, with no joke intended.

"I hated being sick in bed, but I knew I had to learn to like it, or I would go crazy. Like everything I did, I went too far. I learned to love it.

"My mind is always working, and that requires a great expenditure of energy," he told me. "I have never known how to rest my mind, but I learned through so much childhood sickness how to restore my body.

"Above all, there in bed, I learned I had to gain control of my mind. I had to make peace with my own mind. I could never turn off my mind. It can be very tiring, and I need to rest much of the time because thinking depletes me and uses my energy.

"There in bed, my mind could travel, so I had to learn how to send it out on adventures because that is what life is about, after all, adventures. At least that is what, very early, I decided my life would be about, physical and mental adventure.

"It doesn't matter so much whether your life is long or short. What matters is how it seems to you as you are living it. Or that's the way it seemed to me when I was very young.

"Finally, my illnesses and accidents came to an end, and I could leave my bed, but I decided I liked my bed better than any other place, except perhaps the driver's seat in a Ferrari racing car.

"Since I was a very physical person with tremendous energy and liked to be in motion, being in bed was very difficult for me," Rossellini told me. "I could never sit still. I had a foot that tapped by itself. The only place I could sit still, and even not completely there, was in the cinema. There, I could stay and see the same film two or three times, though I did shift position many times.

"I liked to sit down low in the seat, with my legs straight out. If someone was sent by my family to find me, because I was late getting home for a meal, they went back empty-handed because they didn't see my head above the chair. It looked like an empty seat. The only one who could find me was my younger brother, Renzo, who was usually with me. But if they sent him, he knew he had to start from the front row and go up the aisle looking for my feet."

Ingrid didn't know any of this when she married him. All of these narrow escapes may well have changed Rossellini's attitude toward life and contributed to his low interest in thinking a great deal about the future, quite the opposite of her own view of life.

"Women loved Rossellini," Fellini told me. "I tried to understand why, because I was interested in being loved by women. I didn't understand then what this fascination he had was, but now I *think* I do. It was because he was fascinated by *them.* Women like a man who is interested in them. He would think it was he who was spinning a web, then *he* would be caught in it. Love affairs and films. Films and love affairs were his life."

Daughter Isabella said, "Father wanted very much to be a gentleman. He always had a perfumed handkerchief in his pocket to offer the ladies, in case they cried, and several did.

"Father always followed the speed signs. I think the traffic rules were also part of being a gentleman. It was also because as a Ferrari driver, he understood fully the dangers of the road. He wanted us children to be aware of the responsibility of driving. I guess I was *too* aware, because I never did learn to drive.

"My father wasn't eccentric. He didn't come across as you would imagine an eccentric today. You know, someone who dresses in a funny way. He was always perfectly dressed. Very traditionally. Conservative. And he could turn on and off his charm. If he decided to charm you, there was no way to escape. That was how he got so much money for his work from banks when he didn't have good enough collateral, even any collateral at all."

Rossellini married Marcella De Marchis on September 26, 1936. They had two sons, Romano and Renzo.

When Romano died suddenly at the age of nine, his younger brother was devastated. Renzo described him as "my kind, sensitive, intelligent brother who showed me everything."

Romano had undergone an emergency appendectomy. He developed an infection and drugs were not available because of the war.

"It was a time of terrible grief for my parents," Renzo said. "They cried so much. I know it changed my father. He was never the same."

At the funeral, someone trying to be kind and consoling said to five-year-old Renzo, indicating a large figure of Christ, "Your brother is with Jesus."

Renzo, telling me about his memory of the moment, said, "A kid responds differently, in his own way.

"There was a figure there of Jesus. I pummeled it. I hit it as hard as I could, crying. And I screamed at Jesus, 'Give him back! Give him back!'

"No one in our family ever got over my brother's death. I always call my mother very early on his birthday or on the anniversary of his death.

"They put Romano in the family tomb in the cemetery.

"My father went to the cemetery every day for hours. It was near the train station. The main train station was one of the major targets for bombs. Most of the bombs hit the cemetery. The bones were all uncovered. It was not corpses and skeletons, but bones. There were bones everywhere. It was like that for a long time. Bones kept turning up.

"I was a kid there among the bones.

"My father and mother were there so many hours that they set up a pole for a telephone booth for my father at the cemetery, so he could conduct his business there every day."

Fellini described working on the two Rossellini films that impressed Ingrid so much:

"*Rome: Open City* was written in a week. There was no heat, and I worked in the kitchen by the cooking stove. I was credited for writing and as assistant director. I deserved it, but everyone doesn't give what you deserve. Robertino [as Fellini called Rossellini] was never stingy with anything.

"He said he had backing from a rich countess. Women really loved him.

"We made *Rome: Open City* and *Paisan* just after the liberation of Italy by the U.S. military forces. We did *Open City* for less than $20,000, so you can imagine what kind of salaries we had. I, personally, have no idea what I was paid back then. The money was of absolutely no interest to me as long as I could survive. I was doing what I wanted to do with people I wanted to work with.

"It had a documentary style, some of which was a deliberate roughness. The style was called neorealism. It developed out of necessity, because of film shortages and shortages of virtually everything in Italy at that time. There was fluttering electricity, *when* there *was* electricity. It was melodrama perceived as truth because events like the ones that happened in the film had just shortly before been happening right before everyone's eyes in the streets.

"Neorealism was the normal way in Italy in 1945. There was no possibility of anything else. With Cinecittà in shambles, one had to shoot at the real location, with natural light, if you were lucky enough to have film. It was an art form invented by necessity. A neorealist was in reality any practical person who wanted to work.

"*Paisan* is an episodic tale of the American advance into Italy during World War II. It represented a very important moment in my life. I had the chance to continue my association with Rossellini, who certainly influenced my life. I learned a lot about filmmaking, and I saw Italy, places I'd never seen before. I met Italians I had never known. I saw the ruins and disasters of World War II, and the war seemed more immediate for me than when it was happening. These images became part of me.

"Roberto was a very intelligent man and a highly intuitive person. He could look deep into the hearts of people and understand what it was they *really* wanted. Then, he offered it. I think he was sincere at the moment and that was what made him so believable. Then, he had a short memory. But I suppose later there are some who would say that about Fellini, that I had a short memory."

Ingrid told me, "People couldn't help but believe in Roberto because he believed so totally in himself."

· · ·

On February 2, 1949, Renato Roberto Giusto Giuseppe was born to Ingrid Bergman and Roberto Rossellini. He immediately became known as Robertino, or as Robin. Italian law required that his first name not be the name of a living relative. The name Robin was the combination of Roberto and Ingrid. This small baby had produced a very big scandal.

"The paparazzi tried to bribe the nuns in the hospital, if you can imagine that," Ingrid told me, "to get a photograph of me or my newborn son, preferably of me holding him. The paparazzi know no limits. One journalist had his wife check in as a patient. They pleaded to have the door left open just a crack, so they could get that photograph."

I was reminded of Federico Fellini, who was responsible for the term "paparazzi" to describe invasive press photographers. After his death, so many years later, a paparazzo bribed his way into the Rome hospital and photographed Fellini's dead body. Only one tabloid was willing to buy the photograph, and then there was a shocked reaction against their printing it. People boycotted the tabloid.

Rossellini and Ingrid did not even tell the nuns when they were leaving the hospital. He told her to be ready to make their escape in the middle of the night. He arrived for her and the baby at 4 A.M. To no avail, the nuns pleaded with them and tried to stop them, but stopping Rossellini from leaving with Ingrid and his son would have taken more force than the nuns had at their disposal.

Ingrid and the baby got into Rossellini's sports car. There was another car there. A friend of Roberto's was waiting. He followed their car in his. Then, he swerved and blocked the road so the press couldn't follow.

Isabella, Robertino's younger sister, remembered when she was a little girl, five years later, "We had to keep our blinds closed, and curtains and drapes drawn, because the paparazzi wanted to shoot into our windows. We would have had their lenses right in our house. We grew up with paparazzi constantly following us."

When Ingrid and Roberto's first child was born, the birth certificate said that the father was "Roberto Rossellini" with the "mother temporarily unknown." Under Italian law, Ingrid, who was still legally married to Dr. Petter Lindstrom, could not be listed as Robertino's mother. By Italian law, her legal husband would have been presumed to be the father. Lindstrom would have had the right to take possession of the baby. A further complication was that Rossellini himself was still married.

Stromboli was released in America by RKO on February 15, 1950. Howard Hughes, who owned RKO, had been dissatisfied with the slow pace of the original film and ordered it severely cut, for which Rossellini never forgave him. Considering the extent of the international scandal and tumult that had preceded it, the film itself was a disappointment even to critics sympathetic to Rossellini and audiences eager to see an Ingrid Bergman movie. Ingrid's part in the film was a terrible disappointment to everyone. Of those who were disappointed, perhaps the *most* disappointed person of all, professionally and personally, was Howard Hughes.

Senator Edwin C. Johnson of Colorado denounced Ingrid Bergman on the floor of the U.S. Senate on March 14, 1950. He suggested a bill that would protect America from the threat of such "moral turpitude" as "aliens" like Ingrid posed. When Ingrid was denounced on the floor of the U.S. Senate, she could not have imagined such a thing was in the realm of possibility. Even years afterward, she said it was difficult to believe it had happened to her, that she had been capable of creating a scandal of such monumental proportions.

Ingrid was now considered unbankable in Hollywood, and her future career was in jeopardy.

"Petter was bitterly angry," Ingrid said. "He kept using the word 'cuckolded' with those close to him to describe what had happened to him. Of course, never in the presence of our little Pia."

Ingrid was cut off from her daughter Pia, who at twelve was old enough to understand what was being said and written, and to hear from her classmates how her mother had deserted her father and her, and run off with an Italian film director with whom she was having a baby out of wedlock. "I never wanted to be my mother's judge," Pia told me.

"Petter was unrelentingly unforgiving," Ingrid said. "He felt mortified in front of his medical colleagues and, indeed, before the whole world, including his conservative family in Sweden. And I could understand his point of view."

Even the condemnation of *Stromboli* on the U.S. Senate floor didn't help the film at the box office. Rossellini defended its financial failure, saying he had been forced by the distributors to cut the film to where it was incomprehensible, and then it was cut even more by RKO. This was not unique for films imported into the United States during the 1950s. Fellini's *Il Bidone* was cut exactly in half, and a long scene crucial to the understanding of his *Nights of Cabiria* was restored only in the mid-1990s.

Stromboli satisfied neither those who were expecting Italian neorealism nor those who wanted to see an Ingrid Bergman Hollywood-style movie, nor even those who were looking for an exploitation shock film in keeping with the scandal. "The most shocking revelation in *Stromboli* is that human beings will do *anything* to survive," Rossellini said.

Isabella, who had recently seen a rare, relatively uncut version of her father's film at the British Film Institute in 2005, said that she believed that twenty-first-century audiences will approach *Stromboli* and her father's other post-neorealism films differently. She believed the uncut version was much closer to her father's intention.

"I often feel that when people are going to see one of my father's films, if I could just speak to them before they see the film, they would understand it. I think audiences today are more sophisticated and able to appreciate Dad's work. I would say, 'This is not the typical film that grabs you so you're sitting on the edge of your seats. You have to give it a little bit of time, then you're going to be completely *in* the film. But you have to slow down your pace.'

"His neorealistic films are easier to get because they're about the war and great tragedies. Intrinsically there is pathos and melodrama just because they are about something very emotional. But when he did the films with my mum, he was dealing with emotions that exist in a society like ours at peace, where things don't seem dramatic, and yet there is a turmoil inside, a longing, or a sense of the transcendental inside the persons. They are the feelings that we never express.

"I think my mom was disappointed by the work she did with my dad. I don't think she understood it completely. I don't know exactly why. Maybe it was because part of her Hollywood background depended on a certain amount of melodrama. One can become accustomed to depending on melodrama. If you look at *Stromboli,* I think the only melodramatic scene, one that has a certain amount of pathos, is the fishing scene. Even so, at the end of the film, you are left with the sense not of how they live, because it's beyond being a documentary, but also how they *felt*. That's why my father's films don't need to depend on melodrama. Maybe Mama thought there were just too few people interested in this approach to filmmaking. She was accustomed to big audiences, and she enjoyed having them enjoy what she enjoyed."

On May 24, 1950, Mexican divorces having been secured, Roberto Rossellini and Ingrid Bergman were married by proxy in Juárez, Mexico, with two men standing in for them. Roberto and Ingrid went to a church in Rome with a few friends, among them, Fellini.

Petter received his official U.S. divorce from Ingrid in Los Angeles on November 1, 1950. Ingrid would be allowed to see to Pia in London during the child's next vacation, and then she would have to come to California if she wanted to see her daughter. Petter was the guardian of Pia's share of the money Ingrid had set aside for her. Petter and Pia would live in the Benedict Canyon house, which had been bought with Ingrid's film earnings. The divorce went uncontested by Ingrid, who was anxious to have it for the sake of her baby son. The grounds were cruelty and desertion.

Ingrid spoke with me of what she called "the Big Scandal."

"Everything had been such high drama," Ingrid said, "like a bad movie, everything at the same high emotional state, so there was no relief.

"I had been feeling very guilty about what I had done.

"I had no conception of the role I played in people's lives. I didn't know they thought of me after they left the cinema, except as the character I played. I thought private life and public life were separate, perhaps not for a political leader, but for an actress.

"I thought I would not be able to act anymore. That was terrible because acting is my life. And I paid a terrible, *terrible* price in unhappiness when Petter would not let me see Pia unless I went to California, and Roberto would not allow this. I seemed to represent some kind of evil corrupting force and the absolute symbol of feminine shame. Ilsa could be forgiven in *Casablanca,* Alicia could be forgiven in *Notorious,* but Ingrid in Rome could not."

Vicki Rossellini, Renzo Rossellini's wife, an executive vice president at Twentieth Century Fox, told me that Rossellini had been deeply concerned about the surviving son of his first marriage liking the beautiful future stepmother he had brought home.

He took Renzo to Ingrid's hotel suite to meet her. Renzo liked her even more than he ever told his father. Of course, he kept his feelings a secret from his mother, who loved his father and had been deeply hurt by her husband's desire for a divorce so he could marry Ingrid Bergman.

"Ingrid made it so easy and natural the first time we met," Renzo recalled, "and after that, it was always that way. I was so nervous, I could hardly breathe, and she was so much more beautiful than I could have imagined, and I had a pretty good imagination.

"She began speaking with me, not as people, especially women, talk to a child, but as a person, one-to-one. I forgot I was nervous, because she was able to put anyone at ease, even me.

"She was so graceful, she made *me* feel graceful. We had a wonderful conversation. I knew it at the time, but I guess I was still pretty nervous, because after it was over, I couldn't remember it, so I suppose I was more nervous than I realized. It was clear that she wasn't going to try to be a mother. She understood I *had* my mother, but she was going to be my friend, I felt.

"She couldn't speak much Italian, and she had a funny accent, but I loved it. Right away, it seemed like I always knew her. I could easily understand why my father loved this angel, and I was glad she was going to be a part of my life.

"I remember she had this great laugh. Even so long after she died, I still can hear her wonderful laugh."

Ingrid wanted to bring a gift that a little boy would love, so before going to Italy, she turned to Gary Cooper to select a gift for Roberto's young son. Cooper chose an elaborate cowboy outfit. Rossellini had already brought one back to Italy, but it seemed a second one wouldn't be too many.

After their first meeting, Ingrid sent Renzo a photograph of herself, on which she wrote, "From your kindly stepmother." It was treasured by Renzo until, years later, the picture was burned in a fire that destroyed his Malibu home.

Ingrid described for me how her next Rossellini film, *Europa '51,* came into being:

"While he was doing *St. Francis of the Flowers,* Roberto was talking to me about it. He wondered if Christ came back, how would we treat him? Roberto's mind never stopped contemplating and creating.

"By that time, we were married, and he was looking for stories for me so we could work together. He said, 'I am going to make a film about St. Francis, but he's going to be a woman and she's going to be you.' That's why he wrote *Europa '51*. He called it *Europa '51*, because that's how he always thought up his titles. It was 1951 and we were in Europe. He asked, How would we behave in '51 if a woman gave up a rich husband, a rich life, all her rich friends, everything, and just went out into the street to help the poor?"

> *Europa '51 (The Greatest Love, 1951)*
> When the son of a wealthy American couple living in Rome commits suicide because he feels his mother doesn't love him, the mother, Irene Girard (Ingrid Bergman), goes out on the street as a modern St. Francis, dispensing money and help to anyone who seems to be in need. Her husband, George (Alexander Knox), tolerates her behavior as mildly eccentric until she starts helping criminals. Then, he commits her to a mental institution.

When she and Rossellini were about to do something important to them in their professional or personal lives, Ingrid would make "a little cross on his forehead" with her finger.

"It didn't help our films, however," she said.

"Roberto was, in a way, very religious. It wasn't formal religion. He wasn't a man who went to church or to confession, or anything like that. But he had a deep kind of feeling that there was something more to life than we know. As you know, *Stromboli* ended only with this woman looking at the sky. There was no end, which the public objected to. Of course she would realize that there was a duty that she had to go back and have the child and live with her husband; but at the same time you don't know this, and you have to guess it and fill in that ending. But it is always that ending.

"The same ending with *Voyage in Italy*. As you remember, the two people, the married couple, drift apart because they are never alone. They are always with friends, and they are going places and they both have different lives. They come to understand that their own marriage is not so good when they are together on their own.

"Miracles that happen in little villages always intrigued Roberto very much. He was fascinated by the faith, the carrying of the Madonna, the crying, the spectacle of it all and the fact that miracles actually happen. Roberto believed in miracles. People got out of wheelchairs and walked and suddenly people who had been blind could see. I mean this is what everyone *wants* to believe. That is what they do in the small villages of Italy. He put that part into the movie. There is a major confusion and people start to scream 'Miracle, miracle,' and they run around. We get separated and we call for each other and we find each other and fall into each other's arms. We realize that we do love each other, so I believe the marriage is going to be good."

Rossellini confirmed for me what Ingrid had said about *Europa '51*. "It was while I was filming *The Flowers* that the idea came to me. What if someone like St. Francis appeared on earth today. Would he be treated any better than a lunatic? I don't think so. But this was in 1951 and it was quite a different world. Let me retell you a story told me by a friend of mine, a famous neurologist.

"A successful cloth merchant had gotten involved in the black market during the war. He thought nothing of it until one morning he awakened with a very bad conscience. It was so bad, in fact, he couldn't function anymore until he had turned himself into the police as a criminal. The police, themselves, were probably more involved in the black market than he, but they had no serious moral problem about it. They assumed he was mad and sent him to a psychiatric hospital.

"My friend examined him and found him quite sane, but since he was not acting like any average man, there was something absolutely wrong here. He had to be classified as either an exceptional person, an eccentric genius, a saint, or a lunatic. When I heard this story, I saw this man's dilemma as the situation in which Europe found itself in 1951. How could this have happened to such an advanced, intelligent civilization? I transformed a modern St. Francis into a woman because I was searching for a good part for Ingrid. And I think she liked the idea because she saw it in some ways as a modern Joan of Arc. This is a significant coincidence, because I would like to have filmed it in France, but couldn't."

Fellini's wife, Giulietta Masina, was also in the picture. One day, at lunch in New York at Le Cirque, she told me that she had never been an envious person. She said that her friend Ingrid was the only person she ever envied, not professionally, but personally—because of her wonderful children, the young Rossellinis.

Giulietta had desperately wanted children. After losing one baby in a miscarriage, she and Federico had another child, a boy whom they named Federico. He lived only a few weeks, and Giulietta was told she could have no more children. Not to be able to have a family was the sorrow of her life.

Toward the end of shooting, Ingrid found out that she was going to have another baby. She said that she was glad her first baby was a boy. Rossellini had never stopped grieving for his firstborn son, Romano.

She hoped the next baby would be a girl because she knew her husband wanted a daughter. When Ingrid returned from the doctor with the news there were *four* hands and *four* feet, which meant twins, Rossellini was more than twice as happy, Ingrid remembered.

"He was immensely proud of his accomplishment, and he told everyone that *he* did it, two at a time. I faced it with joy, but with just a little trepidation. I so wanted to give Roberto the daughter I knew he wanted, and I had not found having Pia and Robertino to be difficult experiences, easy in fact, but I had never tried two at a time, and I wasn't certain I knew how to do it.

"I had been told to expect my babies to come early because that's what twins do; however, mine didn't act like twins are supposed to. When they didn't come early, I expected them on time, but nothing happened. Maybe they were late because they had Roberto's gene for lateness. They were very late. The doctor told me laughing, 'They like it where they are!'

"I was worried. I was terribly uncomfortable. I couldn't eat. I couldn't walk. I couldn't wear anything except a big old robe that looked like a tent and I looked like an elephant. I couldn't go any-where, and worse yet, I didn't *want* to go anywhere. I went to the hos-pital.

"I spent the tenth month in the hospital. They suggested that labor be induced. Roberto opposed that because he said we would never know their proper horoscope. Then, they were born, first beautiful lit-tle Isabella, the name I had chosen. We knew we were having a daughter. We didn't know about the second baby, whether it was a boy or a girl.

"It was a girl. Each weighed seven pounds. They were beautiful. It was all worth it."

Isabella Fiorella Elettra Giovanna and Isotta Ingrid Frieda Giu-liana were born on June 18, 1952.

"They were such beautiful little girls, fat little babies. They didn't look exactly alike, being fraternal twins, and I had no problem to know them apart. Their personalities were so different. Ingrid, as we called her, was very pacific and restful, and she slept a great deal of the time. Isabella seemed never to sleep. She was always watching and curious with her eyes following you in the room. Her eyes looked straight into mine like they were looking to see into my soul, and she seemed to be thinking. I didn't tell anyone, even Roberto, because I didn't want people believing I was crazy, but her brow seemed to be working, and sometimes I believed I could hear her thinking, not *what* she was thinking, but *that* she was thinking."

"My dad loved children," Isabella said. "He would have liked more. He always took us with him. He couldn't get enough of us children. He loved even the children of our employees. In Italy, women moved from the countryside, and at the time we were young, all the house-keepers were from Italy. They would leave their children with the grandmother in the country, and the young girls would come to work in the city as maids. My father never accepted that. He always had the children stay with their mothers, and we always grew up with all our employees that stayed forever with us. The husband came, too. My father wanted everybody together, and not to break up anyone's fam-ily. It was something peculiar then because nobody else did it. I think he came from an older tradition of wealth and the grand style, which he applied to everyone in his universe.

"The way I see it, being Ingrid Bergman's daughter and resembling her is like being born with a great athletic body or beautiful blue eyes, or a high intelligence," Isabella told me. "It's an asset. It certainly is. But it's not the solution to your whole life; it's just an asset. You still have to do things, and be lucky, too.

"I have no memories of my parents living together as my parents. I might have vague images, but I'm not certain when it's a real memory. Probably not. It might be something I was told.

"Over the years, I was with them together, of course, but not as our family, except when I was too young to remember. Then, it was only after my mother had left that I remember the times together.

"I did know them separately. Seldom together, so I don't have many memories of them together. I remember sometimes, maybe for one of our birthdays, eating a cake together. I remember some cakes. For me, the two are separate memories."

• • • •

In 1952, Ingrid and Rossellini participated in a film called *We, the Women*. It was in five parts, each directed by a famous Italian director and featuring an internationally known actress. The other directors were Alfredo Guarini, Gianni Franciolini, Luigi Zampa, and Luchino Visconti. The other actresses were Anna Amendola, Emma Danieli, Alida Valli, Isa Miranda, and Anna Magnani. The Bergman-Rossellini part was the third segment.

> *Siamo Donne* (*We, the Women*, 1953)
> Episode 3, "The Chicken"
> As herself, Ingrid Bergman takes great pleasure in growing roses. A next-door neighbor has a chicken who takes equal pleasure in eating roses. The story is about how the two antagonists battle each other.

The Bergman-Rossellini segment was shot on a fall afternoon in 1952 at their Santa Marinella country home. It was improvised with their three children participating as actors. Rossellini said it was commedia dell'arte. Ingrid remembered it as "more of a home movie."

Afterward, Rossellini left for Naples, where he was to direct a production of Verdi's *Otello* at the San Carlo Opera. There, he was offered the opportunity to do something more, a project of his own choosing. He chose the oratorio *Jeanne d'Arc au Bûcher* (Joan of Arc at the Stake) not only because he had just been speaking with Arthur Honegger and Paul Claudel, who had created the oratorio, but because it featured a spoken narration that would be ideal for Ingrid. Ingrid, in fact, had two recordings of it, one of them spoken by Vera Zorina, the actress she had replaced in *For Whom the Bell Tolls*.

"Paul Claudel and Arthur Honegger were still alive and knew we were doing it," Ingrid said. They both died in 1955, and I was heart-broken. They were great men, and I was privileged to meet them."

"I first staged it in Naples, and then at La Scala in Milan," Rossellini said. "It was successful, so we went to London with it, and then to the Opéra in Paris, to Spain, and Sweden. We were going to tour South America with it. Ingrid learned her part in five languages."

A film was made that is a literal record of the dramatic oratorio as Ingrid, directed by Rossellini, performed it around Europe. The text by Paul Claudel was based on the Joan of Arc story. Arthur Honegger set it to music in 1935, and it was first performed in 1938. Ingrid's role is that of the narrator.

Ingrid herself was moved by the memorable performance at La Scala after having just premiered the production at the Teatro San Carlo in Naples.

"I thought constantly of my father," she told me. "He *so* loved opera. He would have been so proud."

"Ingrid kept doing those versions of Joan of Arc," Danny Selznick told me, "*Joan of Lorraine,* and *Jeanne d'Arc au Bûcher* of Claudel and Honegger. Roberto and then later Lars [Schmidt] continued to produce plays and films where Ingrid was Joan of Arc, although the original Joan of Arc was obviously an *extremely* simple girl, and not a great beauty. But Ingrid had that inner spirituality which you could identify with Joan.

"I remember in Rome, she was telling me she was doing Joan again. And I said, 'Ingrid, I can't *believe* you're still doing Joan of Arc!' Like the movie wasn't enough, Walter Wanger's movie. And she laughed. She said, 'I don't know. I have a fixation, I guess.'"

"For me to put it on film," Rossellini said, "was as much to keep a record of a wonderful theatrical event as to approach film in a different way. I didn't want to impose cinematic techniques on an already perfect work, yet I wanted to take advantage of any film resources I could without being obtrusive. This has led some critics to complain that as a film it is static. You will notice I said *some* critics, because so few have ever seen it."

The oratorio, if not the film, was well received wherever it played, except in Stockholm. There, the critics took the opportunity to express their feelings, not about the music nor the performance, but about Ingrid and the scandal. At the suggestion of Edvin Adolphson, who had cast her and directed her in her first film, she answered those critics at a benefit matinee for a recent polio epidemic. "They accused me of being a publicity-seeker," she told me, "but I had to remind them that *they* were the ones exploiting my life to sell newspapers." It was even more dramatically effective done just after Ingrid had been speaking for the persecuted Joan of Arc.

Ingrid's visit to Sweden brought her some joys she hadn't anticipated. Her childhood piano teacher came to a performance, as did her schoolmates and some of those who had attended drama school with her, all of whom brought with them good memories.

The most wonderful surprise for her were the ladies who came and said they were her mother's friends. They had known Ingrid when she was a baby or young child. Some of them had strolled with her mother with their babies. All of them had liked her mother very much. It was wonderful for Ingrid to see how her mother had fit in and been happy among friends.

She knew about her parents' wonderful relationship because her father had talked about it with her, and she had read the letters between her parents, but she never understood how well her mother had lived in a world of friends and neighbors in Stockholm, in the world of her father.

These lovely ladies brought her mother to life for her and gave her new memories. She thought how her mother would have appreciated those old friends bringing images of her back to her daughter. She knew her mother would have been grateful to them.

Back in Rome with her children, Ingrid thought about the mother she had never known and what they might have done together had Friedel lived longer. Then she thought about what she could do together with her own daughters.

"I wanted to give my little girls a happy memory," she told me.

She decided that making Swedish gingersnaps with their Swedish mother would be perfect. It would introduce them not only to baking, but to their Swedish heritage.

The girls enjoyed baking the cookies, but not eating the cookies. Everything that could go wrong had. The cookies were burnt, not edible, and didn't produce the desired introduction to Swedish culture that Ingrid had in mind.

Ingrid's effort, however, did produce a memorable shared experience. "It's funny how the memory of Mama making gingersnaps with my sister, Ingridina, and me has stayed with me to this day, I can almost taste those burnt gingersnaps," Isabella told me.

Ingrid sometimes wondered if she should have offered more advice to her children. "It wasn't my way," she told me. "It wasn't the way of my perfect Swedish childhood. I didn't enjoy those summers with my strict German grandmother's rules for everything, down to how you put your socks into your shoes. I went the other way, with few rules and not much advice.

"The advice I remember giving my daughters was, 'I think you have to beat a pillow so hard you can almost hear it cry.' Of course, the pillows had to be taken outside so the dust doesn't circulate inside the house. Pillows need fresh air as we all do."

Ingrid never was one to offer advice to others. She was more likely to ask *their* advice, and then follow it, or not. "It's so presumptuous to offer unsolicited advice, and I am no oracle of wisdom."

Though she had never liked to cook, Ingrid genuinely liked to clean. She enjoyed not only the result, but the actual work, which used her abundant energy. "Mama was always so vigorous," Isotta Ingrid told me. "She had that tremendous energy."

Isabella remembered when her mother's third husband, Lars Schmidt, bought a theater in Paris, Ingrid was so appalled by how dirty it was that she set about physically cleaning it herself. Isabella felt what her mother taught her about cleaning was valuable, and she still orders the same brushes from Sweden that Ingrid liked to use to clean glasses. What Isabella enjoyed most about cleaning with her mother was the shared activity. It established "a cleaning bond" between them.

Federico Fellini explained how Ingrid's generosity was instrumental in both his career and that of Anthony Quinn:

"It was Giulietta who introduced me to Anthony Quinn. She had a part in a picture with him, and she presented the idea of *La Strada* to him.

"Rossellini and Ingrid Bergman wanted to persuade Tony Quinn to do my film, so Ingrid invited him to a wonderful dinner and afterwards they screened *I Vitelloni,* so he could see my work. The dinner or my film must have impressed him. Robertino was very persuasive and he always got what he wanted, but he told me the dinner and showing my film was Ingrid's idea. At the time, I believed he might just be saying that, but later I thought about it, and I remembered that Ingrid liked Giulietta very much."

Anthony Quinn told me, "I was in love with Ingrid from the first moment I met her. What man wouldn't be? She was radiant.

"She was in Italy, Rome, when I met her, married to Rossellini. How I envied that man, being married to the most beautiful woman in the world—and the nicest. It was her idea to introduce me to Federico Fellini. He was looking for someone for *La Strada.* Playing Zampanò, the strongman, changed my life.

"Ingrid was a warm Swede who married a cold Italian looking for warmth, and the Italian man is rumored to be that way, warm. Well, some are, and some aren't. Rossellini could turn it on when he wanted to.

"Ingrid got trapped through her own nature, looking for that warmth. Then, after the children, her sense of responsibility took over.

"She was a wonderful actress, but Rossellini used her only in his pictures, not letting her work with Federico [Fellini] and other directors. He was a know-it-all.

"Ingrid suffered a great deal, for very real reasons, and because she was made that way."

After ten years in Hollywood, Ingrid had found the Italian cinema of Roberto Rossellini "very different."

"It simply was the difference between day and night," she told me. "In Hollywood, I was accustomed to the scripts being prepared meticulously, well in advance. Every detail was set down, every shot, every angle, every camera movement was written down on paper, and they had artists who painted what should be on the screen, including furniture, streets, trees, mountains, and whether it was a close-up, long shot, wide angle, over-the-shoulder, everything in perfect detail. There was some flexibility allowed, of course. A few directors were free to make changes. They had that power, but mostly the script was absolutely set when we actors arrived.

"Hitchcock was very strict, and Leo McCarey liked to improvise, but he always stayed within the limits set by the script. And going from Sweden to Hollywood, I did not find it so different. In the Hollywood studios—and in Sweden, too, for that matter—it was like a railroad station. They were afraid that without a timetable, there could be a wreck.

"With Roberto, it was more like a battlefield where only the general knows what his soldiers are supposed to do. There was *nothing* set, except in his mind, and that was, as I used to say, just a skeleton of a plan. He made pictures just like a writer picks up his pen and starts writing a story on paper, except he did it with his camera on film.

"Roberto invented the dialogue every day. So it was important that every day was one of his good days, and that he did not have a headache. Roberto knew more or less what he wanted, but he didn't yet know exactly the words. Very often he would tell an actor, 'Here is the scene. You are walking down the street and you run into so-and-so. What would you say to her?' When he told me to do this, I said, 'I don't know *what* to say.' Then he said, 'Well, then, just make up something. I want this piece of dialogue to come to you naturally, like the scene is really happening to you, so you can say anything that you would naturally say.'

"Well, of course, I *didn't* know what to say. That made me very tongue-tied and shy. I was not a writer, and I believed that's what writers do. You wouldn't expect the writer to say your lines for you, would you? So I was too stunned and frightened to even speak naturally in a normal situation, because actors usually are not writers, and I certainly couldn't invent very much under those circumstances. He would sometimes write down my dialogue, exactly what he wanted, in Italian. I still couldn't speak Italian, so he would explain it to me in French, and then his assistant, who could speak some English, but not very well, used to translate what he had written into English.

"Even if he had an English writer on the set, he wrote everything down himself because it was very difficult for him to take anybody else's word that it was right. He had an instinctive feeling for how he wanted to arrive at a certain pitch of emotion, and he had to do it in his own way.

"It was sometimes very difficult for me since I had been trained for ten years in Hollywood, with the same thing before in Sweden. Their way was to be very thorough and totally prepared. I had been trained to believe that this was the right way. No, the *only* way.

"I remember when poor George Sanders came to do *Journey to Italy* with us. He couldn't adjust to this method, or I should say, lack of method. He just broke down. I couldn't believe it. I have never seen anything like this big, strong man, so sure of himself as an actor, crying like a child. I had to make myself strong and not cry myself to be able to help him, so he could believe. But I cried a few tears on the inside, too.

"He said, 'I just can't go on. I can't do this commedia dell'arte stuff, and invent my lines at the last minute.'

"Roberto never really liked to rehearse. He wanted that absolute sense of improvisation, and it made George Sanders very, *very* unhappy. Unfortunately, it showed up in the film, his unhappiness. My unhappiness, too.

"The unhappiest part of it was, the audience was unhappy. Then, Roberto was unhappy."

Viaggio in Italia (Journey to Italy, 1954)
Alexander (George Sanders) and Katherine (Ingrid Bergman) Joyce, a well-to-do English couple, inherit a house in Italy. Bored with each other and close to divorce after an uneventful ten-year marriage, they decide to break their tedious routine by making a trip to Italy. The change has a temporarily salubrious effect on them, but soon Alexander is involved with a prostitute (Anna Proclemer) and Katherine is as unhappy as ever. In spite of all this, there is still something between them that keeps them together.

Just as they are about to separate, they attend a religious festival and experience a spiritual reunion. Afterward, they decide to stay married because there is so much in their individual lives that they share.

"When this film came out in France," Rossellini told me, "exhibitors tried to change it into a commercial film because, after all, didn't it star two Hollywood figures? But their mutilations had one substantial benefit for me. I received a letter from François Truffaut commiserating with me and saying he loved the film. That's how we met.

"This is a film about the perceived difference between Anglo-Saxons and Latins. I wanted to show northern people that we are not monkeys in a zoo, as they sometimes seem to regard us.

"The couple who come to Italy in the film are legally, but not emotionally, married. They are incorporated, and they don't understand that their unsuccessful marriage is part of their successful business. There is no affection between them. They think that one day they woke up to find such things gone along with their passion. The real reason is, this aspect of marriage was never there to begin with, and that's what they discover when they come to Italy and see a different kind of life, and love."

"Mum became the inspiration for Father," Isabella explained. "I think that Father was so moved that such a big actress wanted to work with him. She became his muse. Somebody who apparently had everything—fame, beauty, success—still she felt an unhappiness, a longing to do something deeper or to analyze what was an 'anguishment' we have, an existential 'anguishment,' so when you see *Journey to Italy*, I think my mother is, herself, the muse of the film.

"But I don't think my mother saw it that way. You know, she kept on saying, 'How boring is this lady who has everything, and she still complains!' And instead I think that Father saw that Mother had everything, and still complained. And that's what became what he was aiming at.

"Personally, in their life together, I think, my mum completely adored my father, I mean, found him charming, amusing, intelligent, infinitely generous. And I think that my mum seems to be very daring when you look at her career, how she left Sweden, so young, to go to Hollywood, and nine years later, going to Italy."

• • •

Fellini told me that Ingrid often talked with him about the great advantages a director had working for a Hollywood studio. " 'They could give you *anything*,' she told me. She talked about the 'miracles' they could achieve for a director and what I, Federico, might be able to do, making a film for a world stage, to be seen everywhere, as American films were. If I made some Hollywood pictures, everyone in the world would know my work. She offered to help me make the connection, because even though she said she herself was no longer in the good graces of many in Hollywood, still she had friends. She particularly loved 'Mr. Cukor.' George would help, she knew, if she asked. She said that in Hollywood I would not have 'the limitations' of working in Italy."

Fellini told her, as he told me later, "Limitations are the best thing. Without knowing you have limitations, you can't even begin.

"You can do anything you want, anywhere, spend any amount of money. Nothing would more surely stop me. Where could I begin? How could I make an end to it?"

Fellini was most surprised to learn from Ingrid that she suffered from stage fright, not only before she went onstage, but before she went on the set for a film, especially the first day of shooting. "I was surprised because she always seemed so calm and good-natured, and in control. She did not seem to be a person who worried, like me.

"When I went to a film set to begin a new picture, I always felt sick and I was desperate that no one should know! If the director is not calm, confident, without worry, then how can those he is directing believe in him? But I did confess to Ingrid that I had the same problem and that it was even worse for a director to feel insecure.

"She smiled and said, 'That's the way Roberto feels.'"

Fellini was surprised, because he had always believed Rossellini had perfect confidence.

"Roberto could never have worked for a studio in Hollywood," Ingrid told me. "It wasn't that he didn't have the discipline. It was that he didn't *want* the discipline. He believed in himself and he could never have accepted all of the opinions and orders from others. He had to work from inspiration and he was inspired a great deal of the time. But, oh, when he wasn't! . . . He might just disappear from the set with some feeble excuse, or even no excuse at all. It was quite upsetting to everyone, but some could adjust to his moods. I tried. I suppose I never did completely.

"In the beginning, I thought Roberto and I were very much alike, soul mates. Well, perhaps we *were* soul mates, but we weren't very much alike. What we were alike in was how much each of us cared about our work, but our work, as it turned out, wasn't soul mates. Our attraction was more of opposites than of likes.

"I remember the first time he left the set, because he said he had a terrible headache. I was so worried."

Sometimes Rossellini would go to bed for a few days because of a headache. Ingrid was incredulous when she first experienced one of Roberto's headaches. There were some who doubted the headaches were real, thinking them only an attempt to get attention, but Ingrid was not among those. To this, Ingrid answered, "No need. Robert always *had* everyone's attention. He had no need for a headache to accomplish this. His headaches were real. In any case, they were real to Roberto, and that is, after all, what matters.

"The headaches came when he couldn't get the inspiration. As you can imagine, he had to work on his own without any close supervision. Only Roberto supervised Roberto.

"The way Roberto and I liked to work was, you could say, I *would* say, the simple difference between day and night.

"He was the opposite of Hitch, who saw the film in his head before he made it. He wanted to know it all before he began a film. We were his chessmen, so we couldn't venture from our board, even our squares, but as long as we kept our places, we could have a lot of range. Our expressions belonged to us. In Hollywood, they liked to have everything on paper. They preferred to have a script set long in advance, and we actors would get that.

"Hitch had no respect for the kind of director who created and planned on the set. He said that wasn't what a director did. That was what a writer did. Hitch never said a word against Roberto, but I know he wouldn't have approved of Roberto's method. With Roberto, it wasn't the players who improvised, it was the director.

"All of this naturally made it more difficult for Roberto to raise money. His directing style meant producers had to trust him totally, not only to make a good picture, but to bring back their money.

"Roberto did not think much about money unless it wasn't there, for a film or for pasta. Of course, we always had money for pasta.

"I can recommend the best diet there is in the world for a woman who wants to lose weight or keep her weight. She should go to Italy.

"A big plate of pasta. Meat or fish added. Fruit.

"They say it is best not to eat between meals. Europeans do not eat between meals. I loved ice cream in Sweden, but not the way I loved it in America. The greatest danger for me is ice cream, especially American ice cream, and the most terrible thing is with hot chocolate sauce—cold ice cream and hot chocolate sauce. I could get fat thinking about it."

While touring with *Joan of Arc at the Stake* in 1954, Rossellini found the time and money to make a picture in Germany with Ingrid.

Angst (*Fear*, 1955)

The wife (Ingrid Bergman) of an older industrialist (Mathias Wiemann) is having a casual affair with a younger man (Kurt Kreuger). The woman's former lover (Renate Mannhardt) appears and begins blackmailing her. She pays, but when she learns that it is her husband who is behind the blackmailer, she feels humiliated and lost. Her husband saves her from suicide, and they are reunited.

"This is my most structured film," Rossellini told me. "It has a beginning, middle, and an end, which is not characteristic of my films, of me, or of life. Straightforward love stories have no interest for me. They are too predictable. I used this conventional structure because it was based on a Stefan Zweig novel *(Der Angst)* which is structured that way. The novel is about confession, and I wanted to portray a metaphor of Germany in the postwar period, when honest soul-searching was so important. So, it is a film about the purifying power of confession. Audiences went expecting to see an Ingrid Bergman film, and they were disappointed."

Fear was Ingrid's last Rossellini film and the second film she had made in Germany, the first having been *Die vier Gesellen,* fifteen years earlier at UFA in Berlin. This one was shot in Munich in 1954, in German, as Rossellini said was his preference for a German subject. Later, however, it was dubbed into Italian, and that was the version most often shown.

While making *Fear,* Ingrid was reunited with her aunt Elsa Adler, Aunt Mutti, who had survived the war. Isabella remembered meeting *Gross Mutti,* Grandma, as Ingrid called her aunt in front of the children. Aunt Mutti later moved to Copenhagen.

Rossellini's apologies for accepting *Fear* cloaked his need to make money. *Joan of Arc at the Stake* had provided some rescue from poverty, but Rossellini's taste for luxury went far beyond what a touring oratorio and a low-budget German film could satisfy. There would have been no money problem at all if he had allowed Ingrid to accept some of the parts she was being offered. She was still a bankable property in Europe, if not in the United States. Rossellini was not in demand. He was considering an offer to go to India to make a documentary film.

"Roberto asked me why I wanted to work with other directors, too. This was after we had made five films nobody went to see. I had told him many times that I wanted to learn from working with other directors. This always led to a row. I think he would have preferred me to say I wanted to *sleep* with other directors. Perhaps he would have been more likely to say yes.

"If I had said, 'I want to go to bed with Federico [Fellini],' he wouldn't have liked it. If I had said I would like to make a film with Federico, he would have *hated* it! My making a film for another director, after we were married, would have been adultery. Worse.

"I never liked to argue, and Roberto did, so I was always the loser, because it made me feel terrible, while he seemed to thrive on the adrenaline it produced.

"But finally I felt I had to speak what I had been thinking. I could not help but tell him why I wanted to work with some other directors. I said, 'I would like to make a successful movie, that people want to see.

"'And I would like to buy the children new shoes.'

"He didn't say anything at all. He looked hurt. He had never done that, so I felt very badly."

"While we were growing up," Isabella told me, "periodically, our furniture would be taken away to pay Father's debts. We bought our furniture at the flea market, knowing that in the not-too-distant future it would be going, taken for debts. Because of Mama and us children, they were not totally hardhearted. When they took the beds and the headboards, they left us the mattresses.

"Mother, who could be very practical as well as sentimental, had made a lamp shade out of a black hat from *St. Joan.* They took that, too. They just snatched it away. She loved that hat, and losing it made her very sad. I saw my mother's face. It meant so much to her.

"At the time, I thought she let them take it because she was too proud to beg for it. Later, I thought she probably didn't think to save it at the moment it was taken, because she was so upset.

"The worst thing was, it didn't look like anything to anyone, so it was probably thrown away, because no one else would have known what it was."

All her life, Ingrid couldn't bear to be in debt. As a little girl, when she went to the bakery to buy a butter cookie and the chocolate-covered butter cookie cost extra, she took the plain cookie for which she had enough, or she went home to get the additional *ore*. She didn't like owing money, even for twenty minutes, though her credit at the bakery would have been very good.

Ingrid suggested to Roberto that they live within their means, because having debts so troubled her. That meant a small apartment, no servants. She said she would shop and cook . . .

As she spoke, she saw how downcast Roberto had become.

"Life like that wouldn't be worth living," he said sadly.

Ingrid understood. For her husband, it could only be the grand life as he had known it from the time he was born.

According to Fellini, Rossellini felt an artist shouldn't speak about money. "He didn't think he should even *think* about it. Money for him was to be used for buying time and life, and for the satisfaction of whims, the luxuries which he felt were not really luxuries, because, he said, one person's luxuries are another's needs."

"I was not perfectly happy with Roberto," Ingrid said, "but it wasn't even. It was up and down. I had rapturous happiness. I shed an ocean of tears. He wasn't ever boring.

"I had never thought a great deal about money, but Roberto thought less about it. With Roberto, I was deeply troubled about money for the first time in my life, and that made it impossible for me to be happy.

"I was prepared to be poor. Or I thought I was. I was prepared to live in a modest way and to cook and clean, although I'd never really learned to cook. I could clean a house very well. I even enjoyed it, especially if I didn't *have* to and could do it at a moment when I was free. Sometimes I could use up a surplus of energy that way, instead of fretting.

"But I did have a terrible dislike of debt. I could never bear to be in debt."

Ingrid told bedtime stories to Robertino, and one night, when he was about four, Ingrid asked her young son to tell *her* a bedtime story.

"There was a poor, poor, poor child," he said, "who was only about five years old. He had no money for food or clothes. He had no place to live, so he decided to leave town and try his luck somewhere else.

"So, he goes to the garage, gets into his Rolls-Royce, and drives away . . ."

When I asked Ingrid if she had any explanation for what Robertino's story meant, she answered, "He's Roberto Rossellini's son."

Jean Renoir visited Santa Marinella during the summer of 1955 with a screenplay for Ingrid to read. It was a period piece called *Elena et les Hommes* (Elena and the Men), a comedy that would star Ingrid. She was delighted with the idea and with the prospect of working with Renoir. She was also thrilled to have a full script, making it seem far better than it probably was. That November, Ingrid and her children took up residence in Paris to shoot the film simultaneously in French and English.

Elena et les Hommes (*Paris Does Strange Things*, 1956)

Polish princess-in-exile Elena (Ingrid Bergman) manages to survive in belle epoque Paris through her association with men of ambition and means. She likes to inspire these men to achieve their goals, but then loses interest in them, and looks for another.

Her latest subject is General Rollan (Jean Marais), whom she is trying to convince that he should take control of the French government by a coup d'état.

Elena's confidant is Count Henri (Mel Ferrer), who aids her in her intrigues, both in and out of the boudoir, though he sometimes takes malicious pleasure in blocking her absurd schemes. Tired of only being an escort to the beautiful but penurious princess, he proposes something more between them. Tired of her exciting but meaningless existence, she accepts.

When it became known that Ingrid was again working with other directors, her American agent at that time and good friend, Kay Brown, who had moved to International Creative Management in New York, found the perfect comeback role for her: Anastasia. Director Anatole Litvak instantly approved her, but Twentieth Century Fox had misgivings. In a poll they had conducted to determine her acceptability among American moviegoers, she had registered negatively, but Litvak was determined to have her. He also wanted the English actress Helen Haye, who had played the dowager onstage, and is best known for her appearances in Alfred Hitchcock's pre-Hollywood British films. He got instead, quite by accident, the American actress Helen Hayes, who didn't know the play, but performed in the film to general acclaim. The confusion in names worked to the advantage of Helen Hayes, but to the disadvantage of Helen Haye, who lost the opportunity to play what would have been her most famous screen role. She died shortly afterward.

Anastasia (1956)

An exiled White Russian general, Bounine (Yul Brynner), encounters a disheveled young woman (Ingrid Bergman) aimlessly wandering the streets of Paris. She bears a resemblance to the Princess Anastasia, the only member of the Romanoffs believed to have escaped being murdered by the communists. Whether she is the real Anastasia or not is unimportant to Bounine and his group of conspirators. They want her to be accepted as Anastasia so that they can collect the large bank account rumored to have been deposited abroad by Czar Nicholas II.

As they groom her to play the part, she remembers things that only Anastasia could know, and they come to believe they have found the real princess. After passing the test by persons who, it seems, could not be deceived by an impostor, she is presented to the Dowager Empress (Helen Hayes), the Russian royal family's grandmother, who finally pronounces her the authentic Princess Anastasia.

The Empress feels it would be expedient for Anastasia to marry fellow royal exile Prince Paul (Ivan Desny), but Anastasia loves Bounine, and she chooses personal happiness over royal position.

Even though Ingrid's performance in *Anastasia* won the New York Film Critics Award for best actress and the picture was well received by movie audiences, Ingrid remained a controversial figure in America. Her appearance on the popular Ed Sullivan TV program was considered and then canceled when many viewers responded negatively.

She was performing onstage in Paris while the Academy Award ceremonies were simultaneously taking place in Los Angeles. In Hollywood, Cary Grant was waiting in the audience to rush up to the stage in the event Ingrid's name was announced. It was, indeed, and Grant accepted her Oscar for best actress.

Ingrid learned the news in her Paris bathtub, announced by young Robertino, who was carrying his portable radio and listening to the French broadcast of the Oscars.

Ingrid cried tears of joy into her bathwater.

• • •

While Ingrid was in London filming *Anastasia,* the children stayed with Rossellini in Rome. Offers to direct a stage play and a film for Twentieth Century Fox, *Sea Wife* with Richard Burton and Joan Collins, had not worked out, and Rossellini was becoming increasingly depressed by his apparent inability to fulfill the promise of *Open City* and *Paisan.* His daughter Isabella felt that he was a victim of changing times.

"Father made his own world, but I don't know if it was his own world or if it was the world of people who grew up in time of wars. I think the times made the difference. This was the world of people who saw everything; the monarchy come down, the dictatorship come down, who saw wealth destroyed, their money destroyed, times when anything was possible. What's the use of saving your money if it's going to be worthless?

"And every rule was changed. Everything that had been there for centuries, even the monarchy. That meant anything could happen. I think my father didn't have any rules, though he was not an anarchist. He didn't have any rules because he lived between the two wars, so the only thing that was true was human contact, human understanding of one another. About the rest he didn't care.

"I think that when you're in the war with all the fear and the hunger, life is so changed. Mostly the fear. Father always told me that during the war, fear had a taste. 'It had a taste in my mouth,' he said. 'I would be so afraid, I would taste it.'

"Still, I think he found it intriguing, how the people survived and how they adjusted to normalcy after all that. I think Father was able to communicate this on film."

In mid-1956, Ingrid was offered the lead in a French stage production of Robert Anderson's successful Broadway play *Tea and Sympathy* at the Théâtre de Paris. The producer asked Rossellini to direct. Robert Anderson went to Rome to persuade them.

Rossellini was unimpressed. He did not like the play and declined for both of them. Ingrid disagreed and accepted for herself. She liked the play as much as her husband disliked it.

She was right. The play was sold out for nine months, and Robert Anderson became one of Ingrid's best friends. Rossellini, meanwhile, went ahead with his plans to make a film in India.

Rossellini had been talking about going to India, telling friends he wanted to make a film there for so long no one took him seriously anymore. Fellini said he had heard so much about it that he decided "either Rossellini was never really going, or if he went, he was never coming back. Or both."

Rossellini was in Paris for Ingrid's opening night in *Tea and Sympathy*. If there was ever anything he was certain of in his entire life, it was that this play had absolutely no chance for success. He predicted that it would close the next day. He was not pleased that Ingrid had gone into it, against his advice, and was about to make a fool of herself.

When the play ended, the ovation for Ingrid was as great as any ever known in the French theater. As she was taking her bows, Ingrid saw Roberto, who had been standing in the wings, leaving the theater.

"He would be around if I failed," she said, "to catch me if I fell, because he was that kind of friend. He didn't know what to do with my success. And Roberto could never have admitted he was wrong."

When Rossellini left the theater that night, he knew that Ingrid would be busy for a long time on the Paris stage. The play obviously was going to have a long run.

Rossellini finalized his plans, and the next day Ingrid said goodbye to him as he left for India. She knew she would not be seeing him for a long time. It turned out to be almost a year.

Rossellini wrote letters to the children, but they were not very informative. Mostly, there was a lot of news about the weather in India, which didn't interest them, but they were glad for any word from their beloved father and the idea that it came from India amused them. They just wished he would hurry home to Italy, to Paris, to where they could be with him.

Rossellini was going to be in India for many months when Ingrid received her salary check for *Tea and Sympathy*. It was the first money she had earned and held in her hand since she had earned some kronor as a film extra in Stockholm. *Tea and Sympathy* was the same as then. She loved what she was doing so much, she could hardly believe she was being paid for it.

She was a Swedish citizen with an Italian husband, working in France, and she didn't have a French bank account or any other in her own name. She had to learn how to open an account and deposit her checks.

In Italy, Rossellini had taken care of their money, "if you could call what he did taking care of it," Ingrid commented. "Roberto took care of our taxes, mostly by not paying any. There wasn't much to pay tax on because our expenses always exceeded our earnings. Roberto may never have paid at all because he never *had* anything to pay on, or with, and probably it was against his principles."

In Sweden and in Hollywood, Petter had taken care of everything. "He was so meticulous in everything, he probably paid *too* much tax."

Ingrid's third husband, Lars Schmidt, totally handled Ingrid's business affairs, even after they were divorced.

"I came from a time when women didn't think so much about careers, and expected to marry and have a man take care of them.

"I hoped my daughters would do better than I in preparing themselves to know how to take care of their money. I am determined to leave them sufficient money to help, but because I have four children, I will not have enough money to give them financial independence for life.

"They are free to use whatever I give them in any way they wish, even foolishly. But I hope that it will provide them with two things: I want them to know that each one has a home, a place to be where and when they choose." She said that she also wanted each one to have "a parachute, in case they fall, to have the money to pick them up."

Swedish theatrical producer Lars Schmidt, based in Paris, was producing *Cat on a Hot Tin Roof* there. He was especially proud of having brought the play to Paris because he was a great admirer of Tennessee Williams.

Ingrid and Robert Anderson attended a performance of *Cat*. During the intermission, Schmidt poured champagne for them, and there was a brief introduction.

Kay Brown, Ingrid's agent, was also Schmidt's agent in America. I spoke with Brown years later when she was finishing her career at the International Creative Management agency in New York.

She had thought Ingrid and Schmidt, both Swedish, in Paris, in the theater, and staying at the same hotel, the Raphael, should meet.

They went to dinner together and had two languages in common, Swedish and theater. He remembered that they had met before when he had poured champagne for her. She said, "I thought you were the waiter!"

Then, Schmidt left to travel, and when he returned a few months later, he called her and invited her to lunch. She said no, because she had to be with her children.

He took someone else to lunch, and when they arrived at the restaurant, Schmidt saw a smiling Ingrid at lunch with a man he recognized as Robert Anderson.

At the end of lunch, he walked over to Ingrid's table and, speaking in Swedish, said, "Is this your son?"

Ingrid laughed. After that, they began seeing each other.

I spoke with Robert Anderson at the Beverly House in Beverly Hills,

California. He was there with his second wife, actress Teresa Wright.

He told me that he had been invited to the opening night of his play in Paris but he had declined. His first wife was dying, and he wouldn't leave her.

His wife died, and Ingrid encouraged him to come. He told me that he had felt completely desolate, as if his own life had ended.

"Ingrid wanted me to come to Paris and lose myself in the life of the theater. I went to Paris and found Ingrid the most compassionate person I have every known.

"At that moment, she saved my life. She was never too busy to save a lonely soul."

"Roberto and I had success problems and money problems," Ingrid told me. "A little success, I think, would have helped our marriage. Roberto didn't show much that it bothered him, but it had to strike at his self-esteem. He was a man of great pride.

"Roberto *never* compromised. Never. He usually wouldn't budge. If there was an argument, you knew he would have to win, and he would never change his mind—unless he changed it all the way. On occasion, he would totally reverse his position, but no compromise."

As the marriage broke up, there remained a bond between Ingrid and Rossellini because she never lost her respect for his achievement. For her, *Rome: Open City* never faded. That film and *Paisan* had insured his immortality.

"Marriage," she told me, "should produce deep friendship. I have always believed that. Even if the marriage doesn't last, the friendship should.

"Besides, you can never really divorce the father of your children.

"Roberto, and Petter, too, are forever a part of my life.

"Roberto and I started out with such high hopes. Perhaps that was a problem, too. There was farther to fall.

"I felt, at a certain time, when Roberto went to India that he was escaping me, the sight of me, which had come to represent the broken dreams, the professional ones, and the personal ones, too. Looking at me reminded him of our failures."

As Ingrid had learned more Italian, she and Roberto had less and less to say to each other. She sometimes wondered if they had understood each other better before they could understand each other's language, when they only had his French and her smattering of French.

"Mama spoke Italian very well with an accent and some mistakes," Isabella told me. "She always pronounced *telèfono* in the American way, but adding an 'o' to the end of it, so it sounded like 'telephone-o.'

"She would say, translating into Italian, 'It's raining cats and dogs.' Now, in Italian, we don't have that idiom. So, when mother would say it, everyone would look puzzled, and then they would look out of the window, wondering what they would see. Everybody was looking out the window! Like a surrealist painting. She would make little mistakes like that, but she was very fluent in Italian, and in Swedish and English. I think German, she forgot. And French, she always had a hard time, though she lived in France for a long time. I think she spoke mostly with Lars in Swedish, and her friends were all mostly English. She did theater in French, but she didn't speak so much French in her real life.

"My mother always respected my father's work. My father didn't always respect her work as much. He believed she had spent too much time doing 'pure entertainment.' Some professional success together, she felt, would have been good for their marriage."

"I thought about leaving Roberto," Ingrid said. "We no longer had real communication. But I felt I couldn't leave him after I'd ruined him."

Beyond that, there were the children. Roberto and she had three very young children, and she could not get a divorce because she was afraid of hurting them. If Ingrid wanted a divorce from Roberto

Rossellini in Catholic Italy, she might lose custody of her three young Rossellinis. Having lost Pia, it was too terrible to imagine having had four children and really not having any of them.

"Having created such a scandal to get married, how could I create another by leaving Roberto? Impossible.

"We were stuck like the Duke and Duchess of Windsor. After what we had gone through to get married, it wasn't easy to admit to the world that it wasn't a perfect success."

After about nine months, Ingrid began hearing gossip from India. Roberto was having an affair with a married woman, the wife of a producer. She was a screenwriter, Sonali Das Gupta, who had been working with Roberto. Apparently, there was a tremendous scandal about it in India, and the young woman had to remain locked away from her husband's relatives, who wanted to take possession of her, either to return her to her husband, or to punish her.

Roberto called to tell Ingrid that what she was hearing wasn't true. Actually, she hadn't heard *that* much, but she knew, knowing Roberto, that whatever the gossip was, it was true, especially when he tried to reassure her that it wasn't. An agitated Roberto called her again from India. Knowing what phone calls to and from India cost then, Ingrid understood that Roberto must be desperate. Ingrid was extremely concerned. He explained that he was having some difficulties with a producer, nothing new in the life of Rossellini.

He wasn't being allowed to leave India. From his voice, Ingrid knew that his predicament was serious. She said to him, "You sound like it's life or death."

"Worse," he said. "They won't let me take my film out with me. You know people who might help me . . ."

Ingrid immediately called her good friend, actress Ann Todd. Todd knew the sister of Jawaharlal Nehru, India's prime minister. A meeting was arranged for Ingrid with Nehru, who was in London. She was thrilled by Nehru, the man. Nothing was promised.

Then, almost immediately, Rossellini was allowed to leave and, above all, to take his film with him. Sonali arrived in Paris a few days before he did.

Before she was to see Roberto, Ingrid received a call.

Sonali asked if she could meet Ingrid. Ingrid agreed and went right over to see her. Sonali was holding a baby boy. Ingrid realized that her husband had not been gone long enough to be the father of this baby. The young Indian writer had left her husband and an older little boy in India, and she was expecting a child of Roberto's.

Ingrid thought, "Poor thing!"

At home with Roberto, Ingrid noticed he seemed more distracted than attracted, and her words just slipped out.

"Roberto, would you like a divorce?"

He received the question very much as some years before Petter had responded to, or rather, not responded to, her question.

Ingrid decided it was important enough to repeat: " 'Roberto, would you like a divorce?'

"He didn't appear to have heard me, but I knew he had.

"I waited.

"He said, 'Yes.'

"So, that was it. That is what it had come to. I looked at Roberto. He didn't look unhappy at all. It seemed my words had not broken his heart.

"Even more surprising to me, I hadn't broken *my* heart. I didn't feel as terrible as I thought I would. I didn't feel terrible at all. I suppose I could say, I felt relieved.

"My guess is that Roberto felt that, too. I had been *too* much. I had been too much of a burden, a responsibility, for him.

"Of course, it wasn't going to be as simple as it seemed at that moment, and even at that moment it didn't seem simple for very long."

There were a few "little requests" Rossellini had in mind. The first was that the children would never go to America, "the land of Howard Hughes," and that they would never fly TWA, his company.

Ingrid's out-loud laugh was mirthful. "How will I stop them when they are fifty?"

"That was Roberto," Ingrid told me. "Roberto would never change. Roberto would always be Roberto."

"Roberto said he would accept that this applied only until they were eighteen, because after that, it would be difficult to control them, but if she brought them up properly, they wouldn't want to ever go to America.

"Then he added that the children could only live in Italy, or possibly France."

Ingrid was no longer smiling.

"And then Roberto added almost as a postscript, softly, 'And you will *never* marry again.' He verbally underlined the never."

Ingrid was momentarily stunned into silence, but not for long.

She couldn't believe he had just said that, he who had just brought a pregnant young woman back from India, a married woman, having Roberto's child, but not married to Roberto.

Ingrid raised her voice, which she didn't do very often.

"How can you ask that? You, who have just brought Sonali, who is almost half your age, back from India with you?"

Ingrid was so upset, she had spoken English with him. He was so upset, he responded in English.

"But you have the children to take care of. That should be enough for you."

Ingrid did not go on with the discussion, which was about to degenerate into an argument. There was nothing Roberto liked better than an argument to get his juices flowing, while an argument depleted her.

The six-month-old son Sonali Das Gupta had brought with her from India was the son of her husband, an Indian film producer. The child, Gil, grew up regarded by Rossellini as his son, and the child returned that feeling. Though Rossellini's new Indian family was the most immediate cause for the end of Ingrid's marriage, she was always fond of young Gil.

Gil Rossellini told me that many years later, he was unexpectedly in New York at Christmas time, as was Ingrid. "There was a Christmas party at Pia's and everyone was getting Christmas gifts. No one had known I would be there until that day, but that was enough time for Ingrid. My name was called out, and I was given this beautiful package from her. It was a wonderful passport holder which became my most treasured possession. It's here with me now."

Four

꩜

INGRID AND THE WORLD

Someone," Ingrid said, "I don't remember who, a woman, told me, 'You can't have it all,' especially a woman can't have it all. Well, I did. I had it all—even if I did muddle some of it.

"Sometimes I hurt myself. That's the way life is. I took the risks. Happiness is good health and a bad memory.

"If I had any regret in life, it would be if I hurt anyone else. I never wanted to hurt anyone, especially those most dear to me. I can't give Pia back her childhood.

"I can't regret the loss of years in which I might have made films to which I could have brought more than I was able to do with my little body of Italian work, and some of those films would exist and bring pleasure. But there would be no Isabella, no Ingridina, no Robertino.

"I have no regrets. I would be afraid to change anything in the past.

"And I wouldn't give back any of the years of my life to be a year younger.

"I learned so much from my husband's way of working. Roberto was so definite. He never showed any hesitation. I thought that meant he never *felt* any hesitation. I'm certain he didn't feel it much. He wasn't a hesitant person at all. I noticed that particularly because I have always been a hesitant person. I consider myself cautious. I relive it all, wondering how I could have done better. I don't think Roberto ever did that—relived the past. He was always in the present."

"Mum always needed a husband to encourage her and to support her, emotionally," Isabella told me. "I think she only felt very secure about being an actress, and she didn't need anybody's advice about that, but for everything else about life, she needed a man to help her, with the finances, to tell her what to do.

"I remember once that she had to buy a new television set, and she anguished over it. I said, 'Well, what is there to it? You have that table, and you see how big a television set can fit it.'

"She said, 'No, there is General Electric and Sony and Panasonic, and how do you know which one to buy?'

"I said, 'Well, *nobody* knows. You just go more or less with a brand that is known, and hope for the best.'

"This would throw her into a complete state of insecurity. So she would call her husband, even her third husband, Lars. Even after they were divorced, Mother would call him with this mundane little thing. 'What television should I buy?' or, 'The key to my door is broken,' or, 'How do I do that?' And yet, on the other hand, she had great courage as an actress. She always said that Father gave her courage, because Father so loved life and was so courageous. And I mean not just loving life as a warrior. I mean, compassionate, too.

"But being an actress is hard on the soul. Even my mom waited by the phone."

Lars Schmidt was born in 1917 in Gothenburg, Sweden. His family was well-to-do, his father a career military officer.

Young Lars was interested in the theater, but his family encouraged him to prepare for a more secure career, so in his teens he went to Wales to study shipbuilding, but he was still more interested in the theater.

Shortly before World War II, Schmidt went to London and participated in some theatrical projects, but World War II limited possibilities in London. Anxious to go to New York, he took a Finnish ship, but it was hit by German bombs and sank. He was rescued by a British ship, and weeks later arrived in New York without baggage or money.

With the money he earned from doing menial jobs in the theater, he eventually saved enough to buy the European rights to *Arsenic and Old Lace* at a time when the foreign rights to Broadway hits could be had for very little. Subsequently, he became the European producer of *Two for the Seesaw, Twelve Angry Men, My Fair Lady,* and *Cat on a Hot Tin Roof.*

When Kay Brown introduced Ingrid to Lars Schmidt in 1957, she thought being Swedish in Paris and both being alone, and "being two very nice people," as she told Ingrid more than once, they should know each other.

Ingrid was awaiting an annulment of her marriage to Rossellini, since in Italy divorce was impossible. Ingrid and Lars were soon romantically involved.

Schmidt owned a small island off the southwest coast of Sweden that he loved, called Danholmen. He wanted to marry Ingrid, but he had a condition: that she not work in July because he wanted her to be with him on his island for that month.

He took her to see Danholmen, saying that if she didn't like it, they shouldn't marry, because he didn't think he could be happy with someone who didn't feel about his island the way he did. She loved Danholmen.

•   •   •

In July of 1957, Pia arrived alone in Paris after having visited Sweden with her father. Ingrid and Pia had their first reunion in six years.

Pia was eighteen and beautiful. Ingrid was concerned about how her daughter would feel about the sudden attention that would be certain to accompany Pia's arrival and their meeting.

The paparazzi turned out, but Pia was not disturbed. In fact, she found the attention exciting and even enjoyed it.

Ingrid showed Paris to her daughter, and then they drove through Italy. In Rome, the young Rossellini children immediately fell in love with their older half-sister. "They thought Pia was wonderful," Ingrid remembered, "and Roberto liked her very much, too." At the end of the summer, Pia had to return to college, and Ingrid encouraged her to come back the next year.

When Pia returned in 1958, she stayed for three years. She moved into what was known as "the children's apartment," which was maintained by a housekeeper and staff, and was where the young Rossellini children lived in Rome. It was furnished with carousel horses, one of Rossellini's passions.

Ingrid was with Lars just outside Paris, in Choisel, while Rossellini was in Rome with Sonali and her children, Gil and the baby, Raffaella. Rossellini would come to the Rome children's apartment to visit his and Ingrid's children at lunch.

When Pia expressed the desire to pursue a film career, Rossellini tried to help her. She had a few parts in Italian films, including one scene in which she was kissed by Marcello Mastroianni. She returned to the United States in 1966, became a television interviewer and critic in San Francisco, and then a television personality in New York.

Rossellini often went to visit his children when they were in Paris with Ingrid, always bringing with him fascinating and unique gifts. A baby monkey and a baby kangaroo were among the more striking surprises Rossellini brought with him to the Raphael Hotel. They dazzled the children, who never ceased to be amazed by their extraordinary father, who seemed to them a wizard or a magician.

"Father was never down-to-earth," Isotta Ingrid ("Ingridina") told me. "When he brought us a baby kangaroo to the Hotel Raphael, it was an example of his wonderful sense of humor.

"Mama was *so* practical. She said, 'Why didn't you bring new clothes and shoes for the children?'"

The Raphael, however, could not imagine a monkey swinging in the hotel, or worse, a kangaroo jumping about. The fondness of the Raphael Hotel concierges for Rossellini did not extend that far.

Schmidt had to take the monkey to Choisel, but eventually it was sent to a zoo where he could have some simian companionship. The kangaroo had to be sent directly to the zoo.

Ingrid had to go to court to force Rossellini to permit her to take their children with her to Schmidt's Swedish island. The court's decision favored Ingrid. Rossellini was angry and distraught.

When Robertino, Isabella, and Ingridina were delivered to Ingrid for the trip, it was quickly discovered that the children had been sent without their passports, and Rossellini had alerted the Italian police and Italian emigration to the fact that there would be an attempt to take the young Rossellinis to Sweden, passport-less. Rossellini was a famous and exceedingly well-connected person in Italy.

Ingrid knew her former husband well. There was little he would stop at when it came to his passionate desire to hold on to his children. She was, however, a step ahead.

As might well be imagined, she knew the Swedish ambassador to Italy. A call to him produced three Swedish passports, one for each of the children of their famous Swedish mother. The children departed with Ingrid and Schmidt for their summer Swedish island holiday.

Ingrid felt that all of this caused tension in the children, "but at least they knew one thing: They were wanted."

As soon as Ingrid heard from director Stanley Donen that Cary Grant wished to make *Indiscreet* with her, she said yes, even before she heard what the film was about. She arrived in London on November 10, three days before filming.

Indiscreet (1958)

Anna Kalman (Ingrid Bergman), a famous actress, is having an affair with Philip Adams (Cary Grant), a successful financier who claims to be a married man. When she finds out that he is only pretending to have a wife in order to maintain his cherished bachelorhood, she exclaims, "How dare he make love to me when he isn't a married man?"

While she plots her revenge, he has a change of heart and decides to get a "divorce." When he arrives to tell her, she pretends to be having an affair with her chauffeur (David Kossoff). A few days later, Philip returns to call it off for good, but finds he can't and asks her to marry him.

The success of *Indiscreet* proved beyond any doubt that Ingrid could still be a box office attraction in a Hollywood-style film, especially if co-starred with Cary Grant. She received $75,000 plus a percentage of the gross and tax benefits. Ingrid also had it in her contract that she could go to Rome for a week to spend Christmas with her children. First, she and Lars Schmidt planned to be married.

There were complications, however, because of Ingrid and Roberto's proxy marriage in Mexico. It proved difficult to get a divorce from a marriage that was not recognized everywhere.

Finally, just before Christmas, on December 21, Lars Schmidt and

Ingrid Bergman were married in a civil ceremony in London. Lars wanted it to be secret. They had lunch at the Connaught Hotel, and in order to confuse onlookers, they would say "Happy Birthday" with each toast. After the lunch, they left for France and Choisel. Sidney Bernstein, Ingrid's producer and friend from *Under Capricorn*, and his wife were witnesses at the wedding. Since he owned Granada Television, Bernstein asked if he could make the announcement on Granada's six o'clock evening news as Ingrid and Lars were arriving in France. They agreed.

The news was heard in France before they arrived at their Choisel home outside Paris, where they found the press in force with their ubiquitous cameras. Ingrid simply wanted to let them take their pictures of her with her handsome new husband. Then, when they had their photographs, they could just go away. Lars would not have that.

He called the local gendarmes. When they arrived, it was suggested by the police that the simple thing to do was to step outside the house for a few minutes and permit the photographers to take their pictures and leave.

Schmidt was adamant. No pictures. He would not have his wedding night spoiled in that way. It didn't seem to Ingrid that it would spoil *her* wedding day, but she certainly wasn't going to begin her marriage by arguing about it with Lars.

She couldn't help but remember her wedding day in Sweden, twenty years earlier, at Petter's family home when he had become infuriated by the young girl photographer who had concealed herself in the bushes to get a photograph of the couple. It had seemed to Ingrid at the time that it was an inappropriate rage, considering the wonderful occasion and the minor trespass, but she attributed it to "wedding jitters."

Later, as the marriage ended in a blaze of notoriety, she remembered Petter's sensitivity, "oversensitivity," to what he regarded as an invasion of their privacy. Her way would have been to let the young journalist take the picture.

Petter remarried in July 1957, and lived in Pittsburgh where he was a neurosurgeon. His wife was also a doctor. He was forty-seven, she twenty-six.

When Petter married Dr. Agnes Rovnanek, Ingrid hoped his bad feeling toward her would fade. "Roberto told me Petter hates me so much because he *loved* me so much," Ingrid said. "That doesn't make very good sense to me, but I suppose Roberto understood Petter better than I do.

"Carrying a grudge is a heavy burden. We give the power to others to hurt us if we keep reliving in our thoughts what we feel they did to us.

"Hating always seemed to me a waste of one's life, more damaging to the one who's hating than to the one who's being hated, although I must say, feeling that Petter, who had been my *dear* Petter, hates me, *does* hurt.

"But I have to believe that Pia doesn't feel that way, that she at least *likes* me. I hope she forgives me and loves me."

"When Pia had her son," Isabella told me, "Mother thought she would do what grandmothers do. She knitted a little sweater for the baby.

"Mama didn't knit very well because she was out of practice. It was the knitting she learned as a little girl in Stockholm, a simple stitch. It was a very deformed sweater. It had a little waist, not like a baby's waist. and one sleeve longer than the other. Pia treasured it and kept it."

Director Mark Robson wanted Ingrid Bergman for *The Inn of the Sixth Happiness,* and he flew to Paris where he found she had read Alan Burgess's *The Small Woman,* the book on which the movie was based. She liked the part, but she was glad that the title of the film would not be *The Small Woman.*

The film was eventually shot in Wales, and all the Asians who lived anywhere near Snowdonia were recruited for the Chinese background.

The Inn of the Sixth Happiness (1958)

Gladys Aylward (Ingrid Bergman), an English domestic inspired to become a Christian missionary, travels to China at her own expense. An unsympathetic mandarin (Robert Donat) sends Gladys out as a foot inspector whose duty it is to be certain women's feet are not being bound. She does this job with enthusiasm and humility, finally winning the respect of the mandarin, who allows her to return as a missionary.

A Chinese army officer, Lin Nan (Curt Jürgens), arrives to warn the populace of the impending danger of a Japanese invasion. Gladys helps him in his efforts, and they fall in love. Before Lin Nan leaves, he presents her with a jade ring and declares that they will meet again.

When the Japanese do invade, Gladys leads a hundred orphans to another mission. Before she leaves, the mandarin converts to Christianity, his tribute to her.

Lin Nan dies, and Gladys's chance at love, romance, and marriage is finished. She will never be able to give Lin's ring to their eldest son because there will never be that son.

At a mission in the interior, Gladys is offered permanent shelter, but she declines. Looking at the jade ring, she realizes that her destiny lies with the people she has left.

Robert Donat, who was the unforgettable hero of Hitchcock's *The 39 Steps,* became ill before the final dubbing and, while struggling to complete the film, died a few days later. Though it never showed on-screen, he had suffered from severe asthma.

The film was a popular and commercial success.

•   •   •

"At Danholmen on a summer vacation," Isotta Ingrid told me, "we would all get up very early and put out the fish nets, and clean the house with Mama, who enjoyed cleaning."

"It wasn't like Italy," Isabella added. "Everybody worked. And in Sweden, they had a different custom when we went swimming than people in Italy. In Sweden, it was not unusual for us to swim nude if we were with family or friends."

"Men liked this swimming without trunks," Ingrid said. "In the privacy of our home, when we were alone, Lars went swimming nude. I wore my bathing suit only because I felt more comfortable that way, and in my family, we did not swim without our suits. Even when I went swimming alone with my girl cousin Britt, who was two years younger than me, we wore our swimsuits.

"When the children were with us, Lars and I were very careful to be certain that they were far away, especially the girls, when Lars went for a swim.

"One day, we were not careful enough, although at the time we didn't know it. I think the children had been plotting and planning this little escapade for some time. They didn't know what they were going to see, but they knew it was something they weren't supposed to see. They were probably led by Isabella, who was likely to be the chief instigator when there was mischief. They hid in the bushes, behind the rocks, and usually they weren't that quiet, but they made the effort this time.

"Well, Lars stood on this little hill, as was his custom, totally naked before he went into the water. Lars is a very handsome man.

"In Italy, it was totally different, especially when it came to modesty. Little boys wear swim trunks by the time they are one year old. When the children went back to Italy to be with their father, they reported what they had seen. They had seen Lars naked.

"Well, Roberto was livid. He couldn't go into one of his full rages in front of the children, but he saved it for me. He found it terribly shocking, he said, because I had allowed our little girls to be exposed to this—a naked man. Of course, for Roberto, it was much more terrible that the naked man was Lars.

"But the worst of it," Ingrid remembered, "was what Robin, our young son, said. 'Papa, he's much bigger than you are.'

"Robin's small gesture left no doubt as to what he was saying. I don't think Roberto ever got over this."

After blocking Rossellini's attempts in French and Italian courts to gain full custody of the children, Ingrid flew to New York with Lars. There, she made her American television dramatic debut in an adaptation of the 1898 Henry James novella, *The Turn of the Screw*. The ninety-minute taping was part of a series aired in 1960–61 on NBC called *Ford Startime*.

"I loved being in New York," Ingrid said, "but I was unhappy with my performance. I didn't have time to prepare properly." She played an English governess, and the production was shot in one night after a week of rehearsals. Nonetheless, for her performance, she won an Emmy for "outstanding single performance by an actress." The director was John Frankenheimer, early in his career.

The Turn of the Screw (TV, 1959)

A governess (Ingrid Bergman) takes over the care of two small children, Flora (Alexandra Wager) and Miles (Hayward Morse), after the death of their previous governess, Miss Jessel (Laurinda Barrett). The new governess and children are sent to live on an isolated country estate tended only by a housekeeper (Isobel Elsom).

Increasingly, the governess senses that the children seem to be possessed by the ghosts of Miss Jessel and a steward, Peter Quint (Paul Stevens), and she begins to see their apparitions, too. She is horrified by their leering faces, their expressions of malignant evil, soon mirrored on the children's faces. The children deny seeing the ghosts while at the same time appear to be fully aware of them.

In her hysterical attempts to protect the children, the governess terrifies them, and Miles dies in her arms. In the dark background, Peter Quint grins malevolently.

While Schmidt was preparing to produce *My Fair Lady* in Europe, he arranged with CBS for Ingrid to appear in a film for television. *24 Hours in a Woman's Life* was adapted from a story by Stefan Zweig. It was produced by Schmidt for Revlon, and aired as a ninety-minute videotaped program on CBS, March 20, 1961. Ingrid was pleased with her role of a woman at different ages in her life, and she said she liked young Rip Torn, "a fine actor and a jolly fellow."

24 Hours in a Woman's Life (1961)

Young Helen Lester (Helena de Crespo) comes to her grandmother Clare (Ingrid Bergman) with a problem. She wants to marry an erratic young playboy who has been to jail for passing bad checks, but her family objects, even though he swears he is reformed. What does Grandmamma think?

Clare says that as far as she is concerned, Helen is free to do as she likes, but she asks the girl to listen to the story of a day in her grandmother's life many years before.

As a wealthy English widow on holiday in Monte Carlo, Clare met a moody young American playboy, Paul (Rip Torn), of self-destructive tendencies who was also a compulsive gambler. She fell in love with him, and he professed his love for her, but his heavy gambling debts prevented his staying in Monte Carlo.

She paid the debts, but he left anyway.

Never again did she make this mistake, and she hopes that her granddaughter won't have to make it the first time.

• • •

Rip Torn, who co-starred with Ingrid in *24 Hours in a Woman's Life*, talked with me in New York, in September 2006, just before the New York Film Festival opening of his new film, *Marie Antoinette*.

"Ingrid was a warm woman, a lot of fun. We were always laughing together. I told her a lot of jokes. I thought sometimes a producer would look at us in a funny way, like maybe we were laughing too much and having too good a time.

"In New York, I lived on Tenth Avenue, in the Hell's Kitchen part. It was a pretty rough neighborhood. I dressed down. I wasn't slovenly, but sometimes I didn't shave.

"I'd been a first lieutenant in the military, and there was a tremendous emphasis on neatness when you weren't in battle, and I was supposed to be in charge of that, so maybe I had kind of a reaction against all that neatness.

"When it was time for me to make my entrance with my hair that had been worked on to have just the right coiffure and all my Victorian clothes, I saw Ingrid looking at me. She had a rather pensive expression, even a little sad. Then, she said:

"'Whatever happened to my old bum?'"

Françoise Sagan's novel *Aimez-vous Brahms?* was published under that title in the United States, but changed to *Goodbye Again* for the film. It was suggested that many Americans would not know who Brahms was and might not understand the French. The change in title didn't help the film in America, but it was successful in Europe, especially in France.

Goodbye Again (*Aimez-vous Brahms?*, 1961)

Interior decorator Paula Tessier (Ingrid Bergman) has passed forty without being able to convince her longtime lover, Roger Demarest (Yves Montand), that they should marry. Instead, Roger is paying less attention to Paula, and she correctly suspects he has found another, and younger, woman.

Paula finds another man, Philip van der Besh (Anthony Perkins), but he is fifteen years younger than she. She wouldn't consider such a relationship except she welcomes the attentions of another man, and he won't leave her alone.

Roger becomes infuriated when he finds out, and pursues her with a renewed vigor until he thinks the younger man is out of the picture, and then he goes back to his old ways. Paula retaliates by allowing Philip to move in for a full-time affair.

Even more angered, Roger tries to forget Paula with other women, but cannot. He begs Paula to take him back. Paula, realizing that her relationship with the younger man cannot be permanent, dismisses Philip and resumes her affair with Roger, whereupon he once move goes back to his old ways.

Paula sadly realizes that she has lost both men and faces a bleak future.

Ingrid did not feel she "connected" well with either of her leading men. Montand told her that he preferred to be a singer, not an actor. As a singer, he could "hear" his performance, but as an actor, he couldn't judge his own work. While Ingrid regarded Perkins as a fine actor, "he never created any magic." Perkins was by this time burdened with his Norman Bates persona, the phenomenal success of which he spent the rest of his life trying to leave behind him.

In 1962, Schmidt produced *Hedda Gabler* on the stage in French with Ingrid at the Théâtre Montparnasse in Paris. The next year, he, David Susskind, and Norman Tutherford produced the Ibsen play in

English for BBC Television, again with Ingrid starring. She appeared with Michael Redgrave, Ralph Richardson, and Trevor Howard. After playing on BBC, it was rebroadcast in America on September 20, 1963.

Hedda Gabler (TV, 1963)

Hedda Gabler (Ingrid Bergman), daughter of a general and a charming but selfish woman with expensive tastes, marries a college professor, George Tesman (Michael Redgrave), who cannot support the life to which she is accustomed. She confides her dissatisfaction to a male friend, Judge Brack (Ralph Richardson). Meanwhile, Tesman, alarmed by the expenses incurred by Hedda, applies for a government appointment. Tesman is warned by Brack that his chief competitor is a successful author, Eilert Lövborg (Trevor Howard), who was once intimate with Hedda.

Hedda resents Lövborg because he was able to overcome alcoholism to become a famous writer through a satisfying relationship with Thea Elvsted (Dilys Hamlett). Hedda spitefully vows to destroy Lövborg's happy life.

By accident, the sole manuscript of his latest book comes into her hands, and she destroys it. Her motive is not only one of malice, but also the belief that she is removing a serious obstacle in the path of her husband's career advancement. Believing he will be pleased, she tells him what she has done, and he is appalled.

Lövborg, unable to admit to Thea that he has lost the manuscript, tells her he destroyed it during a drunken binge. Hedda, understanding that Lövborg is contemplating suicide, presents him with one of her father's dueling pistols, implying that a noble death is preferable to an ignoble life. Lövborg kills himself.

Judge Brack recognizes the general's pistol and confronts her with his suspicions. Hedda realizes that when the truth comes out, everything will be lost for her. She, too, commits suicide.

Meanwhile, Tesman and Thea are busily piecing together fragments of Lövborg's book.

The CBS telecast received a rave review from *Variety*, but *The New York Times* thought the commercials broke the Ibsen mood.

Michael Redgrave asked Ingrid to appear in a play he was directing at Guildford, *A Month in the Country* by Ivan Turgenev, and she instantly agreed. Later, the play moved to the Cambridge Theatre in London where, during 1964, it played for eight months.

Ingrid, unlike many actors, liked acting on a movie set as much as she liked performing live theater. With Lars, she had more opportunities to appear on the stage, usually in classics or revivals.

Ingrid invited Alfred Hitchcock to come to have dinner with her and Lars at Choisel. He accepted, and she thought about what she could do to share a wonderful treat with him. Ingrid loved to eat, and so did Hitchcock. It was one of the bonds they had. Ingrid decided to have her favorite meal—crayfish. It was a great Scandinavian treat during crayfish season, and Ingrid had managed to obtain a quantity of the finest crayfish just outside of Paris.

It was important to her that the arrangement be perfect. She had her memories of eating crayfish in Stockholm, always with a bib because they were very messy and could ruin clothes.

There should be bread and butter and beer to drink and cheese for dessert.

When Hitchcock arrived, Ingrid took him into the dining room to show him the elaborately piled crayfish. "Our dinner," she announced proudly.

Hitchcock looked at it, aghast.

"How disgusting!" he said. "Totally revolting. I never eat shellfish."

Everyone ate crayfish, but not Hitchcock. A small steak, salad, and potato were hastily prepared for him.

It was Anthony Quinn who persuaded Ingrid to play opposite him in *The Visit*, which he was co-producing. He had met her in Hollywood, but it was in Italy that she had changed his life by persuading Fellini to star him in *La Strada*. *The Visit*, by Friedrich Dürrenmatt, had been performed on Broadway in 1958 by Alfred Lunt and Lynn Fontanne. Bernhard Wicki directed the film version, which was shot in Italy at Cinecittà.

Quinn felt that Ingrid was "too sympathetic" and "too beautiful" in the part. "I, personally, was too in love with Ingrid to be able to criticize her in the film," he admitted. Even more difficult to accept would have been the producers' original choice to play Quinn's character: William Holden.

"Ingrid didn't like the ending of the play, where my character is killed. She thought it made Karla seem too cruel. So, it was rewritten for her, and I got to live," Quinn said.

The Visit (1964)

Karla Zachanassian (Ingrid Bergman) returns to the town in central Europe that twenty years earlier had forced her to leave in shame. Now one of the world's wealthiest women, she seeks revenge against the man who caused her misery, a merchant named Serge Miller (Anthony Quinn). He had seduced her, and then denied he was the father of her unborn child. Finally, he was among those who drove her out of town.

In exile, her child died and she was forced to become a prostitute to survive. Later, she pulled herself out of her misery and finally married the millionaire whose death left her wealthy.

Her revenge is to buy the town for a million marks, and then the life of Serge for another million, to be divided among its citizens. They are at first appalled by such an idea, then, as they regard their own poverty, they wonder. Meanwhile, Serge becomes increasingly terrified, especially when his wife, Mathilda (Valentina Cortese) turns against him.

The desperate plight of a servant girl (Irina Demick) causes the millionairess to change her mind. Serge's life is spared by Karla, who decides not to make a martyr of him. Instead, she prefers that he live out the rest of his days in guilt and remorse.

"Ingrid stayed away from America," Quinn told me, "because she was so hurt. And she was so hurt because she had loved America so much.

"America embraced her so totally with such love and warmth that she never considered that she could go from that to such vilification. Actually, it was because they loved her so much they felt she had no right to disappoint them and break her ethereal image into pieces. She didn't just chip it. She demolished it. From the image of virgin to international tramp.

"America seemed to have turned against her and judged her as immoral. She didn't know if she went back to the U.S. if she would be arrested on some kind of moral turpitude charge or stoned. You can't blame her for not wanting to come back to find out.

"There are a lot of people in America who didn't hate Ingrid, but the haters seem to have more pens and paper, and more time. The greater part of the letters she got were terrible. There were even threats against her and her baby. Some of the worst letters came from people who said they did it from religious principles because she was one of the big-time sinners of all time.

"What could you expect from Rossellini when Ingrid arrived and they were alone together? Or as alone as you can be in Italy. After all, he *was* a man.

"There never was a more desirable woman than Ingrid. No man could have been trusted with her.

"But it was a different time. Now, it's not as easy to become a major sinner because the rules have changed, but too late for Ingrid." I was speaking with Quinn during the 1990s in his Upper East Side Manhattan art studio.

"When I think of Ingrid, there are things I think of simultaneously. Her beauty. The most beautiful woman I ever saw. I've tried to paint her from memory, but I could never do her justice. I'm no Leonardo da Vinci.

"The other part is she was the nicest, the nicest person I ever met in my life. I never met a nicer woman, a nicer person. She changed my life. She and Roberto [Rossellini] and Federico [Fellini]. But it was Ingrid more than anyone else, because it was her idea, and she persuaded Roberto, and he persuaded Federico. She was also a friend of Giulietta [Masina], Fellini's wife, who starred in *La Strada*.

"Ingrid knew part of the secret was to have the most delicious dinner. She loved to eat, and so did Fellini, so she knew the way to his heart."

In the mid-1960s, Ingrid appeared in two anthology films, *The Yellow Rolls-Royce* and the Swedish *Stimulantia*. In the first, she starred with Omar Sharif in the last part of a three-story film directed by Anthony Asquith.

The Yellow Rolls-Royce (1965)

In episode one, the Marquess of Frinton (Rex Harrison) buys the Rolls-Royce as a gift for his beautiful wife (Jeanne Moreau), then disposes of it when he finds out she is unfaithful to him in the yellow Rolls-Royce.

In the second episode, the car is owned by mafioso Paolo Maltese (George C. Scott), who tours around Italy in it with his girlfriend Mae Jenkins (Shirley MacLaine), who is also unfaithful.

In episode three, at the beginning of World War II, wealthy Mrs. Gerda Millett (Ingrid Bergman), an American widow, uses the car to travel from Trieste to Belgrade to visit the Queen Mother. En route, she picks up Darich (Omar Sharif), a Yugoslav partisan who draws her unwillingly into the guerrilla war against the invading Germans. Gradually, she becomes emotionally involved in his conflict and with him, and they fall in love after she has distinguished herself in battle. She wants to stay and fight beside him, but he persuades her to go back to America and warn her countrymen about what is happening.

In spite of the stars and lavish production, *The Yellow Rolls-Royce* was a critical and financial disappointment, for which Ingrid received $275,000 for one month's work.

In 1965, at the age of thirteen, Isabella was diagnosed with a progressive curvature of the spine that, untreated, could have led to painful crippling, horrible deformity, possibly followed by premature death. Years later, over cappuccinos at the Petrossian Café in New York City, Isabella recalled her sickness, unforgettably painful, physically and emotionally:

"A doctor came to our school to examine all of us girls for gym class in Rome. I was not at all concerned and was probably thinking of something else, as I always was when I was in school. I was rejected from gym class. That was only the beginning. The doctor really got my attention when he said I had scoliosis, a deformity of the spine. I heard only one word, *deformity*. I heard the word over and over in my head. I was crushed. Destroyed.

"He told me that I must tell my parents that I had scoliosis. I didn't remember the name. I only heard that one word. I had a *deformity*."

Her twin sister, Isotta Ingrid, was not a victim of the disease that affected Isabella.

On learning the terrifying news, Ingrid canceled all her plans and rushed from Paris to Rome in order to be with her child.

First, Ingrid searched for a cure. She hoped to find it in Stockholm. Then, she asked friends in America to help her find doctors. Roberto's faith, however, was firmly rooted in Europe.

"Roberto and I were in despair," Ingrid told me. "We didn't know what to do. Every choice seemed a bad choice. But we knew that *not* making a choice was the *worst* choice we could make. The decision had to be made, and the sooner the better for any hope of success.

"It was Isabella who made the decision. It was she who said, 'I want the operation. Now.'

"She was very decisive and definite and sure of herself," Ingrid said. "Sometimes with her, I actually felt like *she* was the mother, and *I* was the child."

Ingrid held her daughter's hand during the many weeks of torturous treatment. "I cried and cried. I wasn't very useful," Ingrid remembered. "Sometimes I was sent away because I couldn't conceal my tears, and in my head, I could hear my little girl screaming during the treatments for the rest of my life.

"The terrible suffering of our child was something Roberto and I shared, but it did not strengthen the bond between us. It was shared tension and friction. I wondered if she might have had better care, less suffering if I had found the right doctor in America, but that was something Roberto would never hear about. It had to be Europe and European doctors."

Isabella told me *her* story of that time of anguish. "During the next two years, I *really* became deformed. The miracle we had all prayed for didn't come. My condition got worse rapidly. I tried exercises, but no exercises helped. I began to limp. I couldn't straighten up. I had a bad ache, and it was moving rapidly.

"I did more exercises every day, never missing one day, to prevent my spine from bending more, to keep it from curving. Nothing helped. It only got worse, and very fast. I limped a little more. My rapidly progressing deformity was certain to lead to misshapen crippling, and though it wasn't said in my presence, to my death.

"I was attached to a machine that stretched me in different directions. My neck and hips were pulled in opposite directions. I went into a cast. Then, some weeks later, more of the same, and I wasn't given anything to help the pain because I was told I needed to be alert so they could judge my reaction. It would finish when I fainted. That was how my reaction was judged. The amount of pain I could endure, if sufficient to force my spine straight, would determine whether I would be cured and become 'presentable.' I overheard a doctor use that word. The cast I wore between pullings and stretchings went from my hip to my neck and the back of my head.

"At the end of four months of these procedures, stretching and pulling, the torture, and a brace, there was finally the operation.

"The operation was followed by a body cast to restrict all movement and allow the bones to fuse and a cast on my leg to allow the bone used in the operation to grow back.

"I had to learn to walk again and my muscles had to be reeducated. I couldn't even hold my head up.

Isabella was grateful to her mother for coming to Rome and staying for so long, but for Ingrid, it was all worth it. There was no other possibility. She never hesitated to give up anything she was doing, including being separated most of the time from her husband, Lars, who was in France.

"Though Lars never complained and couldn't say anything about my being in Italy, I feel it took a toll on our marriage.

"I cannot tell you how I felt when it was over, and when I heard her laugh for the first time in so long, to hear her laugh instead of scream. Our young heroine had shown such incredible bravery, but she didn't seem to think it was bravery.

"Always a leader, she was quickly walking around in her cast.

"She even went to a dance with her heavy, terrible plaster cast, and she danced every dance.

"I was so anxious to see my daughter. Once I rushed into her hospital room, and there I saw her poor little body lying there covered by a sheet. I screamed.

" 'You've shortened her! 'You've shortened her!' I was quite hysterical.

"The doctor standing at the bedside said, very calmly, 'This isn't your child.' "

During the more than eighteen months of Isabella's illness, Ingrid accepted only one acting job, two weeks of filming her friend Jean Cocteau's *La voix humaine* (*The Human Voice*) for television. She did the 1930 one-woman play as a tribute to Cocteau, who had just died.

"I thought I couldn't be without acting and that it was the most important part of my life. During those many months, as I sat and held my beautiful daughter's hand through her horrible ordeal, through her pain which became my pain, I found out what was more important.

"She had been so healthy, so energetic, so full of life from the moment she was born. I learned a sad lesson: You cannot take anything for granted."

Isabella was to become a world-famous model and actress. Her career brought her extra pride and pleasure because she knew what her fate might have been and what she had overcome. She had overcome her "deformity" to become famous on magazine covers internationally and on the screen as one of the most beautiful women in the world.

"During this time, my mum incredibly gave up working, which was so important to her, to be at my side all of the time. And it was good and bad. On one hand, I was so grateful to have her next to me, but I felt a little bit of a burden, taking Mother away from acting, which she loved so much.

"I never believed that way about Father. I never felt that Father loved work so much that he felt we children could be any burden. You know, nobody cares if a director has children; but if an actress gets pregnant, she can't work that year. And might stay fat. So, I always felt for Mother that there was a certain amount of sacrifice for her in having us children. I was hesitant to be a burden to my mom.

"When I came out of my illness, and I was sixteen, Mother was very pleased that young boys came home to visit me, playing the guitar, singing to me. I had friends coming, and she thought, 'If only Isabella could have a boyfriend or somebody falls in love with her, this would help her self-confidence, because she is ill and she's been listed as deformed.'

"Father was just jealous. I have to say that I don't think the boys coming around was very helpful to me. I always thought it was Mama's happy Hollywood ending, the kiss that solves it all. Some of the boys kept me company, if they were in a group.

"There was that one who sort of fell in love with me. I didn't trust his feelings, but I didn't know how to chase him away because Mama was so happy. She was so trusting. She was happy because boys were courting me, and it had looked so bad for me for a while.

"Father was as suspicious as Mother was trusting. He didn't say much when I was sick, but as soon as I was up on my feet without my cast, he became very strict, you know; not allowing me to go out without him getting really angry.

"It was similar with Ingrid, my twin sister, but Ingrid is very shy, so my father wasn't as worried about her. Because I was very extroverted, he felt he had to worry about me, and he became quite strict.

"Then I moved to New York, because Mama was in New York in the theater. Mama didn't approve of Papa being too strict with me. She thought I should have many friends and that some of them should be young men. I was eighteen and I became a New Yorker, and stayed with my sister Pia. Mother kept saying, 'Don't go back to Italy and fight with Father, just stay here.' I *did*. I stayed, and I got a little job translating, and meanwhile I wanted to learn English.

"I kept on staying.

"Father found out I had a boyfriend called Mario in New York, and that was it. He refused to talk to me, and he didn't talk to me for, I think, two years.

"In that period when he wasn't talking to me, Father left his Indian companion, Sonali. They weren't married, but they lived together, like being married. They had a daughter together, Raffaella. My father sort of adopted Sonali's son who had come with her. Gil was just a baby, and my father really loved him, and he really loved my father.

"One day in New York, my phone rang. Somebody said, 'I'm Silvia D'Amico.'

"I couldn't place the name.

"She said, 'Can I come and talk to you?' and I said, 'Yes,' and as I hung up the phone, I thought, 'My father's mistress!'

"When the doorbell rang, I opened the door, and I looked at Silvia. She was very little, with short brown hair and brown eyes. Silvia said, 'I used to be tall, with blue eyes and blond, but this is how I became after meeting your father.'

"I fell in love with her instantly."

"Silvia reconciled me with Father. I remember it was at the Algonquin Hotel. She said, 'Your father loves you. I told him he's wrong about not talking to you. It's normal that you have a boyfriend. We'll go together and meet your father at the Algonquin.'

"So I did, the next day or so. And I was *so* frightened, because I was afraid he would get angry again, or something.

"He started to cry. He was so moved to see me, and it moved me *so* much. But he did it to himself, you know. Two years is so long. And then, to show you how charming he was, he hired Mario as his assistant.

"For a very long time, Mario worked with my dad, and I couldn't take any more of the two of them, being together and always talking about work. So I left."

The television adaptation of Cocteau's *The Human Voice* was produced by Lars Schmidt and David Susskind in London in 1966, and broadcast in the United States in 1967. It was shot on tape in two fifty-minute sessions with four television cameras running simultaneously. It was a new experience for Ingrid, to do a one-woman play.

"You have no idea how distracting all of those cameramen and technicians were, talking into their headsets while I was trying to pretend I was talking intimately to someone on my prop phone. I think we got about three minutes of usable footage the first day. Fortunately, the next day I was in better form, and by some miracle, we finished on time. I was happy it all turned out so well, because I intended it to be a memorial tribute to my great friend, Jean Cocteau."

La voix humaine (*The Human Voice*, 1967)
An older woman (Ingrid Bergman) has lost her younger lover to a wife, but she is still emotionally involved with him, and they talk only on the phone. More and more, she understands there can be no happy ending for her, but she is trying to break off gradually, in a way that will not leave her emotionally shattered, and perhaps suicidal.

Ingrid next appeared in *Stimulantia,* an eight-part film featuring Sweden's most prominent actors and directors. The third episode, *Smycket* (The Necklace), starred Ingrid, Gunnar Björnstrand, and Gunnel Broström and was directed by Gustaf Molander. The story was adapted from Guy de Maupassant by Molander. When Molander was approached to direct one of the segments, he said he would come out of retirement for only one reason: "Ingrid."

The film was shot at Svensk Filmindustri in 1964. The same studio had been used for *Munkbrogreven* thirty years earlier. Some members of the original crew were still there, and Ingrid used the same dressing room. Her co-star, Björnstrand, well known from Ingmar Bergman films, had been a fellow student at the Royal Dramatic Theater School.

Smycket (1967)

The wife (Ingrid Bergman) of a minor government official (Gunnar Björnstrand) desperately wants to attend an important reception and ball, but she doesn't feel she can dress well enough to keep up appearances. To make her happy, her husband uses the money he has been saving for something else to buy her a beautiful gown, but she still isn't satisfied. She needs a piece of jewelry. Her husband suggests she borrow it from a wealthy friend (Gunnel Broström), who happily lends her a beautiful necklace the wife has admired.

When the couple returns from the festive evening, the wife discovers the necklace is gone. She has lost it.

After they put together all of their savings and borrow money to buy a similar necklace, the wife returns the replacement, hoping her friend won't notice the difference. She doesn't.

Ten years later, after they have lived a desperate, deprived existence to pay off the debt incurred in buying the replacement necklace, the wife admits to her friend what happened.

The friend laughs and says it doesn't matter. The necklace was only paste.

At the opening of the Greta Garbo Centenary exhibition in 2005 at the Scandinavian Institute in New York, Isabella Rossellini was a highly visible guest. She stood out as the center of attention and was asked many questions. The question most often asked was, "Had her mother ever met Greta Garbo?"

Ingrid had, in fact, met and spoken with Garbo, but only once, long after Garbo had ended her grand film career. The occasion was a luncheon party at a private home in Barbados. Ingrid was there with Lars Schmidt. Barbados was a place both Ingrid and Lars loved.

Ingrid saw Greta Garbo arrive with a small group. "Though everyone knew they were not supposed to stare at the famous guest, or to do anything to make her uncomfortable," Ingrid said, "I sensed a perceptible change in the atmosphere, a kind of unspoken gasp. Years after she had retired, Garbo's aura always traveled with her."

Ingrid watched her go out to the garden, where Garbo chatted with some people, among them Lars. She didn't even consider joining them. She remembered when, in Hollywood, she and Garbo had almost met several times, and Garbo had chosen not to recognize her. "Not even a simple, polite hello," Ingrid remembered.

She understood, however, that if Garbo *had* extended even the most perfunctory of courteous greetings, this would have been an invitation for more, for a greater invasion of Garbo's privacy, which the star so prized and protected. Then, if the press had learned of it, even the briefest meeting of Garbo and Bergman would have been reported as some kind of momentous encounter.

Ingrid went into the garden. She did not approach Garbo, she did not join her husband. She went to a faraway place and sat alone on a bench.

If they spoke, what would she say? Should it be in Swedish? Or should it be English? Years before, it would have been Swedish. Whatever it was, Ingrid was certain it would come out in some strained tone in a voice she would hardly recognize as her own.

None of this fretting was necessary, however. It was Garbo who approached *her*.

"Even though we'd never really met, only briefly passing each other, Miss Garbo did not introduce herself. I suppose she felt no need to say her name. She assumed everyone knew who she was, and she was right."

Garbo had heard from Schmidt that he and Ingrid loved Barbados and were looking at land on which they could build a small beach house.

"Lars and I were thinking of buying some land in Barbados, and building a simple, a very simple house." Garbo spoke in English, and Ingrid continued in what was not a first language for either one.

"Miss Garbo said, 'You are making a very big mistake. Terrible. You will regret it.'

"I didn't understand at all. I suppose my face showed that I was puzzled. Miss Garbo said, 'Do you know why? They will steal *every*thing.'

"I told her that we were not going to build a luxurious mansion, so we wouldn't be troubled. We won't have anything worth stealing because the reason we are coming here is to enjoy a very simple life and to uncomplicate our lives, to take walks and swim, without the burden of possessions. I did not believe anyone would want my shorts and cotton shirts, and Lars would have even less, some trunks and sandals.

"She repeated, 'They steal *every*thing.'

"'My bathing suit?'"

Garbo rose abruptly and departed. She didn't say goodbye to Ingrid, she just left. "I suppose that was her way of saying goodbye."

That was the first and the last time they ever spoke with each other.

"In a way," she said, "you might say her celebrity and my celebrity already knew each other.

"When I was first in Hollywood, I had looked forward so to meeting her. We both came from Stockholm, we went to the same drama school, we knew some of the same people.

"Some people wrote I would be the new Garbo of talking films. I had liked that. Maybe she didn't.

"I suppose I said something that didn't please her, when she just stood up and walked away. I had met Garbo, but a little late.

"I had always considered myself to be an optimist, with faith in people. I felt sympathy for Greta Garbo and wondered how she had come to feel as she did."

Ingrid did not understand why Garbo had walked away from her. Neither could she understand how Garbo could have walked away from acting. "She was so young, only thirty-five." Her last film, *Two-Faced Woman*, was a failure, and Garbo had not had much experience with failure. She did not need money, so she did not have to work. Her earnings had been so well invested by friends in real estate.

For Ingrid, Garbo's life truly seemed to have ended when she gave up acting. Without husband and children, it seemed to Ingrid that Garbo lived a boring and lonely life.

"I always thought Garbo a great beauty and a wonderful actress, and my meeting with the person rather than the actress did not change my appreciation of the actress; but the part she had written for herself in life was not as good as her film parts.

"I should be more generous. Think of all of the people I have disappointed who thought they were meeting Alicia of *Notorious* or Ilsa of *Casablanca*, and all they got was me."

It was director King Vidor who arranged my own meeting with Greta Garbo in her New York apartment. He had known her well in the days she and John Gilbert were going to be married. Vidor was Gilbert's closest friend, and they had planned a double wedding, with Garbo marrying Gilbert, and Vidor marrying Eleanor Boardman. The double wedding never took place, because Garbo didn't arrive for the ceremony at William Randolph Hearst's San Simeon castle.

When the name of Ingrid Bergman happened to be mentioned, Garbo said, "I do not know her personally. We passed each other a few times, but she did not say hello or speak to me. I thought she would, but it did not bother me when she chose not to speak. It saved both of us from saying a few words that meant nothing.

"For years, people have asked me, 'What do you think of Ingrid Bergman?' If I told them the truth, and I did not, I would have said, 'I do not think about her. She is not on my mind. Why should I think about her? Because she is Swedish? Many people are Swedish. I do not meet them all, and I do not want to meet them all.

"I never wanted to meet many people. My life has always been full enough with those people I wanted to have in my life. It is good to have a few friends. Of acquaintances, it is easy to have too many. I had no wish to know the public that only wanted to know Garbo, the movie actress.

"Miss Bergman was also an actress. I never looked among actresses for my friends. Do plumbers look among plumbers for friends?

"I am not what you call a movie fan. When I worked, I had no time. I did not *make* time. I preferred to be out in the air doing something physical. When I stopped working, I preferred other activities, *many* other activities. I would rather be outside walking than to sit inside a theater and watch a picture moving. Walking is my greatest pleasure. I do not find I can get lost in films the way some people *say* they do. I think about all the work, the tension, the jealousy, and everything that is not on the screen, that you do not see. I do not *want* to be lost in a film.

"I do not think I ever saw Miss Bergman in a film. If so, I do not remember it.

"We passed on the way to the parking lot when she came to Hollywood. She did not say hello or speak to me, so I think she felt the way I did. There is no need to be falsely polite.

"I spoke to her many years later at a party. I do not remember what we said."

On September 3, 1967, Ingrid starred with Colleen Dewhurst and Arthur Hill in the American premiere of Eugene O'Neill's *More Stately Mansions* at the Ahmanson Theatre in Los Angeles. Ingrid had vivid memories of meeting O'Neill many years before. The play was staged by José Quintero. In October, it opened at the Broadhurst Theatre on Broadway. A standing ovation greeted Ingrid at each performance, indicating to her that at least *that* audience had forgiven and forgotten.

"We don't choose what we're remembered for," Ingrid told me. "I know what I do *not* want to be remembered for.

"I do not want to be remembered as a participant in one of the biggest scandals of the twentieth century, the personification of the fallen woman.

"I did not always get life right. I lacked the wisdom. I think one needs two lives to get it right."

Because Ingrid felt that her daughter Isotta Ingrid had been seriously neglected during Isabella's illness, she proposed to Roberto that young Ingrid be allowed to accompany her mother during the run of *More Stately Mansions* in California and New York.

"America?" Rossellini thundered. "Absolutely not!" He was adamantly opposed to his daughter being exposed to the hypocrisy of Los Angeles and Manhattan. Ingridina was heartbroken.

About a month later, Rossellini asked Ingrid when she and Ingridina were going to America. Without admitting it, he had completely changed his mind. This was an example of Rossellini's unwillingness to compromise, though afterwards he could totally reverse his position without ever referring back.

"I knew my mother best on stage, more than in the movies," Ingridina told me, "because I was with her when she was in *More Stately Mansions*. I left Rome and went to Los Angeles and New York with her.

"Mama loved being an actress in the theater. I remember her saying, 'Every night is different. Each audience is different. Sometimes an audience is joyful. Sometimes it is reserved, subdued.'

"Since I went every night to see her in the play, I learned the play, especially her part. Mama didn't have a very good memory, and she often made a few mistakes. Every time she said some wrong words, my heart would stop. I was afraid it would upset Mama in her performance. But she always went on perfectly composed, as though she hadn't noticed. I was amazed by how she did that and wasn't upset by her mistake. Then I realized she wasn't aware she had missed the words. Certainly the audience never realized what had happened."

Ingrid always preferred to spend the afternoon in New York before her evening performance very quietly at her Hampshire House suite. Ingridina remembered going into a corner of the living room and reading a book while her mother sat there getting into the mood for her part. "We always went early to the theater because Mother liked to spend time there in the atmosphere of the theater, getting even more into her part."

Ingridina watched her mother onstage and loved it. She found it always fascinating and never got bored with it. "Mama was magical.

"I was very shy. I said, 'Mama, how can you do it? All those people looking at you in the dark?'

"Mama said she was shy like me, and that was how she got out of it—by being someone else. She said that when she was onstage, she was no longer Ingrid, she was whoever she was playing, so she wasn't shy unless she played a character who was shy.

"Well, the logic of it escaped me. If it were me onstage, I would know it was me.

"When I had to leave, to go back for my school exams, I cried and cried, so many tears. I didn't want to leave Mama and life in the theater."

Ingrid cried, too, and had difficulty going on in the play that night.

"Father and Mama had the pressures of the world. They lived a Big Life. I loved them."

Cactus Flower was the first film Ingrid had made on a Hollywood soundstage since *Joan of Arc* in 1948. All of her "Hollywood" films since then were made somewhere else.

The long-running Abe Burrows Broadway play was adapted for the screen by I. A. L. Diamond, who was best known for his many collaborations with Billy Wilder. The film was Goldie Hawn's big-screen debut. Before *Cactus Flower*, she was a popular TV comedienne.

Cactus Flower (1969)

Bachelor dentist Julian Winston (Walter Matthau), wishes to break off an affair with Toni Simmons (Goldie Hawn), a young Greenwich Village bimbo with suicidal tendencies, but Toni is too much in love with him to notice the attentions of the handsome fellow in the next apartment, writer Igor Sullivan (Rick Lenz). Since Julian has lied to Toni about having a wife and children, he decides to make it seem a reality by having his dowdy dental assistant, Stephanie Dickinson (Ingrid Bergman), impersonate a wife.

Stephanie not only plays the part convincingly, but attractively, so that she stirs Julian into the realization that he really likes her better than all of the other women he has been dallying with over the years. Toni, confused when she finds out what is happening, turns to Igor, who is waiting eagerly.

In 1968, writer-producer Sterling Silliphant visited Danholmen, bringing with him an unfinished screenplay based on Rachel Maddux's novel *A Walk in the Spring Rain*. Ingrid liked what she read, and she loved the idea of working with Anthony Quinn again, as well as being directed by Guy Green. Besides being a fine director, Green had been David Lean's cinematographer on *Great Expectations* and *Oliver Twist*. The film was shot on location in Tennessee.

A Walk in the Spring Rain (1970)

On sabbatical in rural Tennessee, Professor Roger Meredith (Fritz Weaver) and his wife, Libby (Ingrid Bergman), drift apart, he concentrating on the book he is writing, and she falling in love with Will Cade (Anthony Quinn), a ruggedly handsome neighbor.

Boy (Tom Fielding), Will's unruly son, sees what is happening and tries to rape Libby. When Will intervenes, there is a fight, and Boy is accidentally killed. The tragedy makes Will and Libby even more dependent on each other.

Roger, finally sensing the relationship between his wife and Will, asks her to go back to New York with him on a family matter, and she agrees, knowing that she is leaving her last chance at love.

In a 1960s TV interview, Anthony Quinn was asked who he thought was the most courageous person he had ever met. Without hesitation, he answered, "Ingrid Bergman." In the decade that would follow, Ingrid sadly earned this encomium.

Five

༄

INGRID AND THE FINAL YEARS

I like to see my mother young in her Hollywood pictures, before I knew her," Isabella Rossellini told me. "I can admire her as an actress, and I can appreciate her beauty.

"I like to drink coffee from Casablanca mugs with her picture. But the truth of it is, at that time she doesn't seem like she really belongs to me. She is Ingrid Bergman.

"I didn't exist yet, and that isn't Mum for me. The person I can remember was much later. When you know the real person, it's not easy to separate that person from the one on the screen. The films that show Mother the way she was that I can remember, those make me feel sad. They are the films of Mama."

In 1971, Ingrid accepted the lead role in a London revival of a little known George Bernard Shaw play, *Captain Brassbound's Conversion*, later to play in New York. When the New York run of the play ended, Ingrid appeared in *From the Mixed-Up Files of Mrs. Basil E. Frankweiler*, a film intended for children that allowed her to play an eccentric woman many years older than her actual age, which was fifty-seven. Like Bette Davis, Ingrid always welcomed the opportunity to play women older than she was, though her celebrated beauty worked against her being cast in such roles.

From the Mixed-Up Files of Mrs. Basil E. Frankweiler (1973)

Two imaginative children, aged ten and thirteen (Johnny Doran and Sally Prager), run away from their boring suburban homes in New Jersey to take up residence in the Metropolitan Museum of Art. There they survive by picking up coins from the fountain, eating at the food shop, and sleeping on period beds. All the while they regard their surroundings with awe.

They meet a reclusive old woman, Mrs. Basil E. Frankweiler (Ingrid Bergman), who invites them into her mansion and offers them wise insights into growing up as sensitive children in an insensitive world.

In the same year, Pia, now a New York TV journalist, married, bringing together Ingrid and Petter for the first time in years. Petter attended the wedding with his wife, Agnes, and their daughter, one of his four children by that marriage.

While I was talking with Sidney Lumet at a dinner for Michelangelo Antonioni at New York City's Museum of Modern Art, our conversation moved from Italian film to Oscars and touched on Ingrid Bergman. I asked him about his experience working with her in his film *Murder on the Orient Express.*

"I showed her the script," Lumet said, "hoping she would consider the important part of Princess Dragomiroff. But that wasn't what interested her. She liked Greta Ohlsson, the old Swedish missionary, and so Wendy Hiller played the aged Russian princess.

"Ingrid told me I would be surprised. She could do a really convincing Swedish accent.

"She had chosen a very small part, and I couldn't persuade her to change her mind. She was sweetly stubborn. But stubborn she was. I tried to persevere and to persuade her to take what was not only a larger part, but I felt a part with which she could do so much more and perhaps even get an Oscar.

"It was no use. She said, 'Well, if you don't want me to be in your picture . . . ' That ended my efforts. I wanted her in it whatever part she wanted.

"Since her part was so small, I decided to film her one big scene, where she talks for almost five minutes, straight, all in one long take. A lot of actresses would have hesitated over that. She loved the idea and made the most of it. She ran the gamut of emotions. I've never seen anything like it.

"Even though she had been a great screen beauty, there never was any effort on her part to glamorize herself. She just played Greta like the funny old character she was. A lot of actresses in her place might have demanded special lighting or makeup or camera angles to minimize her age, but not Ingrid."

Michael York, who loved being an actor in the way Ingrid loved being an actress, was "thrilled," he told me, to find himself in a makeup chair next to Ingrid on the set of *Murder on the Orient Express*.

"Generally, actresses are in the makeup room to be glamorized," he said, "but Ingrid was there to be de-glamorized. The others were there to be beautified, and she was there to be de-beautified.

"Ingrid was there to have her luminosity removed."

Murder on the Orient Express (1974)

On board the *Orient Express* in the mid-1930s, a wealthy man (Richard Widmark) suspected of having underworld connections is murdered. After pursuing many leads and investigating the other passengers and analyzing their stories, private detective Hercule Poirot (Albert Finney) deduces that everyone in the train car who was ever involved with the man is guilty of stabbing him in a ritual murder because of his involvement in the murder of a kidnapped child years before.

In this film, Ingrid was pleased to be in the company of some of the great actors of stage and screen of the time. "I was doing *The Constant Wife* with Johnny Gielgud on the stage at the same time, and he was in the film, too." Also with her in *Murder on the Orient Express* were Wendy Hiller, Lauren Bacall, Vanessa Redgrave, Anthony Perkins, Sean Connery, Michael York, Jacqueline Bisset, Rachel Roberts, Martin Balsam, and George Coulouris, as well as Albert Finney.

"In 1973," Ingrid said, "John Gielgud wanted me to do *The Constant Wife*, a 1927 play by Somerset Maugham. It was a nice play, very funny, but I thought it a bit old-fashioned, and I told Johnny so.

"He replied in that serene way of his, 'What is old-fashioned about *The Constant Wife* is its charm.' I was won.

"I was also won by the idea of working with John Gielgud.

"He was one of the greatest actors who ever lived. That certainly made him an actor's director. He knew just how to bring out the most any actor had to give. He could do that for me. He was as great a director as he was an actor. What I loved was he felt the same passion for the theater I did."

Ingrid could never go home and just go to sleep after a night of performing in the theater. She was, she told me, still at least partly the character she had been on the stage. "Some characters take over more than others. Some stay with me longer.

"When I've left the theater, not only the characters in the play accompany me, but the audience, too. I take them all home with me, so it can be very crowded. I can hear the applause all the way home. There is such a rush of adrenaline that takes me through the performances. It's an indescribable feeling.

"The most difficult thing about being in the theater each night is how to use your day while not doing anything that could tire you and hurt your performance.

"I felt I owed it to my audiences to save all my energy for the play. If I went out to lunch with a friend or by myself to visit a museum for an hour or two, I felt so guilty, I couldn't enjoy it.

"I was so excited after my performances that when I was married to Petter, he gave me a pill he prescribed to calm me. Afterward, I decided I didn't really want to calm down. I wanted to relish the excitement, the elation. I liked sitting at home, very, very late, with a glass of champagne until I was tired enough to fall asleep naturally. Then, I slept well."

One night in London, she had a drink to help her to sleep, and she was turning the pages in a magazine when she saw an article on breast cancer. It recommended self-examination, and without thinking, while glancing at the magazine, she suddenly found a lump. She called Lars, and he told her that she should go to a doctor the next day, but she didn't.

If she had needed an operation, it would have closed the play, because she was not insured, and without her the play could not go on. When she went to a doctor in London, he advised her that she needed to find out about the lump. Then, she agreed to an extension of the run of the play. She also accepted the part in *Murder on the Orient Express*.

When the play ended, she went to New York to see her daughters. Six months later, her American doctor urged her to have a mastectomy, but she found further excuses to delay treatment. Finally, in June 1974, she underwent a mastectomy in London, followed by radiation therapy.

Ingrid said she had tried not to show to others what the mastectomy meant to her. Until that time, she felt that even though she was no longer young, she looked younger than she was, and that she was still attractive. The operation, she said later, took away her confidence in herself as a woman. What remained healthy was her confidence in herself as an actress. As soon as she could, she resumed her career, performing as she had agreed in the U.S. tour of *The Constant Wife*.

In Century City, California, while walking, which she loved to do, Ingrid stumbled and broke a bone in her foot, requiring her to wear a cast. It happened on a Saturday afternoon, just after the matinee.

"In the theater, you know, they have this expression which means good luck, but it doesn't sound lucky to me. They say, 'Break a leg.' I took it too seriously, and I did. Well, not exactly. I didn't break a leg. I broke a bone in my foot.

"I had always said, as a joke, if I broke a leg, I would go on. When it happened to my foot, I did.

"The evening performance, it was sold out, and they had already deposited the money in the bank, so they couldn't refund it all until Monday. I said, 'I'll do it in a wheelchair!'"

While her cast dried, a wheelchair was sought. When they weren't able to find one before the curtain went up, an hour late, she went on sitting in a regular chair after an announcement had been made offering the audience their money back if anyone chose to leave. No one left. Everyone stayed, and they enjoyed the confusion onstage while the actors tried to reblock themselves around a stationary Ingrid. "It was so funny," Ingrid said. "Everyone was bumping into each other. I couldn't help laughing, and the audience joined me in laughter. We had such a wonderful time. I entirely forgot my pain."

Finally, a wheelchair arrived, in time for Ingrid to move around a little in the last act. She continued to appear in the wheelchair in subsequent performances until she was able to limp through her part while her foot healed. No one ever asked for a refund.

"She was an incredibly natural actress," John Gielgud told me. "She went into her character and *became* her, as much, *more,* than any other actress I have ever known.

"Everyone said to me, 'How can she play the part that way, in a wheelchair, and not show the pain she's in?'

"I had thought, myself, that it was remarkable that she could hide her pain that way. And then I realized that the reason was even more remarkable. She *wasn't* in pain, and she wasn't in pain because she was no longer Ingrid Bergman. She had become her character so completely that she didn't have a broken foot because the character she was playing didn't have a broken foot."

Isabella was with her mother when they heard it announced that Ingrid had been nominated for her third Oscar. "It was on the radio," Isabella remembered, "and Mama said, 'Oh, no! Now I have to think of the dress!'"

When Ingrid received an Oscar at the 1975 Academy Award ceremonies for best supporting actress in *Murder on the Orient Express,* she told the audience that she had wanted the award to go to Valentina Cortese, whom she thought should have won it. Ingrid said that she, herself, had voted for Cortese, who had appeared in François Truffaut's *Day for Night.*

Then she saw the faces of the other nominees and immediately she regretted blurting out those ill-considered words. She had embarrassed the other nominees in the category—Madeline Kahn, Diane Ladd, and Talia Shire—causing them additional disappointment. Worse yet, no one was more embarrassed than Cortese, who did not enjoy having been singled out by Ingrid at the expense of the other nominees. "I often spoke first and thought afterwards," Ingrid said. "Oh, well."

In the autumn of 1975, Ingrid returned to Rome to make a film. The twins were there, and it was an opportunity for Isabella to make *her* film debut, as Sister Pia, a nursing nun, and for Isotta Ingrid to participate as a makeup and costume assistant.

In the cast was Charles Boyer, with whom Ingrid would be working for the third time. "He was not only a fine, fine actor, but a truly good person," Ingrid said. "It was so sad to see Charles so lost, so depressed. It was as if all of the life had been crushed out of him. Neither he nor his wife had ever recovered from their only son's death, by accident or suicide. Ingrid understood what he felt. There was nothing anyone could say.

A Matter of Time (1976)

An ambitious but uneducated young provincial girl (Liza Minnelli) comes to Rome hoping to find the good life. Instead, she finds work as a chambermaid in a cheap hotel. There she meets an impoverished old noblewoman (Ingrid Bergman) who encourages her to look after her appearance and gives her valuable advice on living. Soon, the young girl finds herself involved in the old woman's memories, moving back and forth over a half-century period as the Contessa herself. As the old woman dies, the young girl becomes a movie star, largely due to the Contessa's help.

This little-known film was directed by Vincente Minnelli, who was disappointed with what happened to the completed footage after he left Rome. Minnelli, who had looked forward to working with Ingrid and with his daughter Liza, told me, "The finished film was not what I had visualized."

Liza Minnelli told me, "I admired Ingrid Bergman as an actress, and I hoped I would learn something working with her. My father thought she was great.

"We had a crying scene together, and we were both going to be crying. Well, I knew it would come easily to her, and she would know just how to do it, but I didn't know how *I* was going to get tears to flow.

"I went and sat in a corner and tried to go through in my mind all of the sad things that had ever happened to me, which was very unpleasant for me to do, all those sad memories, but it didn't produce a tear. Then, I thought about everything sad that ever happened in the world, which was a lot. Nothing.

"Then I looked over at Ingrid, who had just come in for makeup, and I saw that she was using some glycerin. It *couldn't* be.

"I went over and asked her, 'You're using *glycerin?*'

" 'Of course,' she said. She saw I was kind of shocked. She smiled. She said, 'But we don't tell people our tricks. I don't cry unless I'm really sad, and I'm not sad, and I don't *want* to be sad. The important thing is not whether I am really crying, but that the audience believes my character is crying.'"

Liza did manage a few tears on cue. "But when I looked at the rushes, there was Ingrid crying, so moving, so emotional, so perfect. And I look like I'm getting a cold."

For Isabella, working on *A Matter of Time* was a memorable occasion in her life.

"Mother loved the book very much and was looking for roles, as every actress does when she reaches a certain age and it's harder to find parts. And she was absolutely delighted that the film was going to be done in Rome so she could be with us.

"Because the hours are early in the morning until maybe midnight on a film, she asked to have my sister Ingrid to do makeup so we could be together as much as possible. Not that Ingrid knew anything about makeup, but the Contessa was a crazy lady who put on a lot of makeup and never took it off, and it didn't matter that it was messy. So Ingrid became the makeup artist, but there were other people who helped.

"Mother decided that maybe I could play the little part of this nun who is there nursing her character when the Contessa dies. She's hit by a car and brought to the hospital, and I would play the nun who is there nursing her.

"Liza Minnelli was this maid who has become very close to the Contessa. I have to announce to Liza that the Contessa has just died and tell her the last words, which I heard. I forget now what they were, something meaningful about life, but just a short sentence.

"Liza's character asks me, 'Did she say anything?' and I say, 'Yes. She said something strange,' I tell her, and Liza understands she's referring to her.

"I really didn't want to act then. I wished I could do the makeup or costumes. I was embarrassed acting. The moment I arrived on the set, it was full of paparazzi.

"Mother thought it would be fun to use me as an actress playing the nun because I looked like her. So, when the contessa is dying and looks up at me, she thinks she sees herself as a young woman. Mama thought it was an added little something, another dimension. But mostly, she did it so I could be on the set for three days with her.

"I remember liking the way Mama helped me with memorizing the lines, so I was very well prepared. She not only taught me by repeating the lines, but she gave me the rhythm of how to say them, because I didn't speak English at the time.

"I was embarrassed once I was on the set, because there was so much attention paid to me, but Mama seemed to be happy with her two daughters there. It was one of the things that made me feel at the time that I didn't want to be an actress, because if I ever became an actress, there would be so much attention paid to me, I would never have time to learn.

"You know, there's always the expectation. Is she going to be like her mother? The comparison, and also the excitement all the time. It's too embarrassing, sort of an infantile excitement that people have that makes it hard to concentrate on doing the job. At the time, it was a different kind of attention paid to me than another actor. Not now, but at the beginning when you're young. I was Mama's daughter. I don't know how Liza Minnelli did it with her mum. It must have been dificult, always having the comparison. I always found Liza wonderfully amusing and warm.

"There was a scene in the film where there's a flashback, and Mother looks younger, playing in a casino. So they fixed Mother up. You know how they do it with makeup. They pull back your face, and it's like they're giving you a face-lift. Then the camera has a little filter trying to make Mama look twenty or thirty years younger.

"Liza took some still photos of that day from the set, blew them up beautifully and gave it to Mother as a present. I remember Mama being so surprised, because she wasn't very vain. Mother was not concerned with being young or glamorous. All that sort of embarrassed her. She cared about being the best she could be in bringing her part to life."

"Not everyone who is a star would be the way Mama was," Isotta Ingrid added. "She never had any temperament. Mama was always kind to everybody. She knew everyone on the set, and she would talk with them all. And she understood everything about making a film."

"I tried to be meticulous in sorting and collecting the material which was the story of my life," Ingrid said. "So I was surprised to find a letter that I had never opened. It had been sent from California in 1950, shortly after Robertino was born. I was shocked when I saw that the letter was from Howard Hughes.

"As I read it, I was moved to tears. I understood so much. I understood that I had judged him falsely, in the same way I had been judged falsely. I had allowed the sensation-seeking press and gossips to condition my own thinking. I had appointed myself as the prudish, self-righteous, know-it-all arbiter of his morals without having any knowledge about the kind of man he really was. I had accepted manufactured truth, unexamined, made up just to sell newspapers.

"I had told myself it was my intuition that had made me uneasy with him. My intuition had been wrong. The letter was signed 'Howard'. As I looked at the signature, I realized that I had never thought of him as Howard, but rather as Hughes. I had not really thought of him as a person.

"I, who prided myself on being a polite and considerate person who went out of her way not to hurt people, had been rude and inconsiderate because I had mistakenly judged him as a person without feelings when he was, in reality, one of the most sensitive persons I had ever known.

"Twenty-five years later, with my baby son a grown man, I sat down to answer. So much had happened to him, as it had to me."

In his letter, Hughes had expressed a certain hesitancy in writing to Ingrid because he had not been "fortunate enough" to know her well, as he would have wished to do, but he had held her in his thoughts with admiration for her courage and honesty, for the strength with which she had faced the situation of the scandal. He hoped that by the time her son was old enough to hear what had happened and face the world, another broader-minded attitude would prevail. He said she was not scheming but rather he used words such as "one of the most brilliant and courageous women of the twentieth century."

"What could I say in my letter to him that could possibly mean to him what his letter had meant to me?" Ingrid said. "How could I explain my tardy response? I needed a word stronger than tardy.

"I learned he was living in a London hotel penthouse, and I sent my letter there.

"I knew that he had become very eccentric over the years. Could my letter mean anything to him at this late date? Did he remember me? I had heard such terrible things about what had happened to him, the condition he was in.

"I accepted what I had heard and didn't make the decision to try to see him. Same thing. I was influenced by what I had read and heard. Perhaps he wouldn't like for me to see him the way he had become.

Perhaps he wouldn't enjoy seeing me twenty-five years later, and it was better for him to have intact his memory of me, if he still remembered me."

In Choisel, Ingrid was packing all her possessions. She would be moving. She and Lars were divorcing. "Amicably," Ingrid said. "That's what they call it, isn't it?"

It would be the second time in her life that a husband had ended his marriage to her because another woman, with whom he had a relationship, was expecting his child. Ingrid was shocked. She was stunned by the child, not the mistress.

"It had been a long marriage," Ingrid said, "and he had been patient and understanding when there were long absences. Too many absences. At my age, at my stage of health, I would not be looking for another husband, but I understood Lars's desire for a child of his own, especially a son. Having a child of his own was something he missed, and I was too old." Schmidt's only child, a son, had died before he and Ingrid were married.

"I understood Lars's deep sadness, even though he didn't talk about it. I knew that Roberto never stopped feeling the pain over the death of *his* firstborn son, Romano, long before I knew him. Roberto and I had three children, and he loved them. He loved his son from his first marriage, Renzo, every one of his children, but no one exactly took the place of Romano, because Roberto's mourning for him was deep in his soul.

"When Lars told me about his expectant mistress, I asked him if he wanted a divorce. He said yes. In the same situation, Roberto had said yes, too."

Even though Ingrid had not found her dreamed-of lasting romantic relationship that her father and mother had shared, she would not have been the one to ask for a divorce.

"In my head, I knew that I had been away so much with my career and then with Isabella's long, grave illness, too, that when my charming, handsome Swedish producer husband had to travel, I couldn't accompany him. I understood that he was lonely, and women I knew warned me that I could lose him. In my head, I could imagine they were right. In my heart, I couldn't imagine it. Not really. Not until it happened.

"I should not have been as surprised, as shocked as I was. I tried to keep at least the appearance of composure, though I didn't feel composed. I didn't want Lars to feel guilty. I didn't feel he *was* guilty. I was.

"It was a surprise to him when he learned his mistress was pregnant. It was a bigger surprise for me. I didn't know he had a mistress. One is supposed to be an adult about those things, but though I tried to be civilized, very adult, I didn't feel that way. It made me feel like a lonely little girl, and I didn't know how to cope. Lars had done much of the coping for me. In this situation, I couldn't very well turn to him.

"I didn't want to lose Lars, and I knew I would miss him very much in my life. I knew he would never completely leave my life. We didn't have the bond of youthful discovery or of children together, but we had our love of theater, of his Swedish island, so many bonds.

"And so it was. We were divorced, but never out of touch. Because of the phone bills, it was more expensive than being married. What was so wonderful was that I felt totally free to call him about anything big in my life, but more important, I could call him about any *little* thing. He never made me feel that I had bothered him with something small or unimportant."

Ingrid told me that she considered the greatest loneliness to be loss of intimacy with someone to whom you had once been close. "Separation from those you care about is difficult, but the most terrible loneliness is that of being with them and finding that you have lost the ability to connect.

"It happened to me in my three marriages—with Petter, Roberto, and Lars. Even when one keeps a friendship, which is what I always wanted to do, there is a depth of intimacy which is notable for its absence.

"You talk about things of medium importance, and you try to think before you speak, to get it right. That is a terrible feeling, when you feel you have to be careful when you are speaking to your life's companion. The big things in your life you eventually bring yourself to speak of. The most difficult is the trivial. You don't have anyone to tell about the little things in your daily life, which is really most of what life is made up of. I couldn't say what naturally came to mind because after the veil of separation, I felt like a foolish child when I said little things to Petter, Roberto, and Lars.

"My life," Ingrid told me, "was very much concerned with finding and holding on to love.

"I had been a lonely child after my father died. Petter cured my loneliness for a number of years, before we married and for a time afterwards. Even when World War II separated us, I felt secure because he was in the world, *my* world.

"I think no matter how many friends you have, or *feel* you have, you need to have one *special* friend, who ideally is your mate, your soul mate, the person who you want to spend your life with.

"For me, Petter was that friend who combined everything I needed and wanted, and very important, he felt that way about me. He didn't just say everything, the way I did, but I could feel it. He didn't have to say it. I felt I was the luckiest person in the world because we found each other, and we loved each other. I knew it would be forever.

"Roberto was very much like Capa, with a gambling spirit, though in Roberto, it wasn't so obvious.

"The difference was Capa was an overt gambler. He knew what he was, and made more of it, rather than less of it.

"Roberto did not call himself a gambler, but I feel he was.

"Lars certainly did not consider himself a gambler. He considered himself a businessman, but he was in a risky business—the theater.

"Petter was not a gambler. He always knew what he wanted and what was possible, and he pursued the course that would take him to his goal. Nothing he did was a gamble except maybe marrying me, only he didn't know it at the time.

"My Dr. Petter Lindstrom," Ingrid said, "was a perfectly consistent person when I had come to desire some inconsistency.

"My Roberto Rossellini gave me inconsistency at a time when I cherished consistency.

"My Lars Schmidt always seemed consistent, but perhaps I took his consistency too for granted.

"*My*? Why do I say 'my'?

"Because each of them was *mine*, if only for a while."

While working for RAI, Italian television, in New York, Isabella interviewed director Martin Scorsese. He was instantly attracted to the beautiful young woman whose father was a great Italian director whom Scorsese admired, and whose mother was the legendary Ingrid Bergman.

Early in the courtship that followed, Scorsese asked Isabella to marry him. When they traveled to Italy together, he wanted the wedding to be there. In Rome, they met Federico Fellini, who was always happy to see the daughter of his mentor.

Isabella remembered Scorsese asking Fellini if he knew of a romantic, private place where they could be married, quietly, away from the paparazzi.

"Yes," Fellini said. "Stromboli."

"The wedding," Isabella told me, "was a civil ceremony in Rome. Bob De Niro was Marty's witness. Mama was there. My witness was

Argenide, who was called our housekeeper, but she was like our family, and we all loved her. The Taviani brothers were there because I was making a film with them. We had a small party at a local castle. I put a knight's armor headpiece on Marty and sent that photograph of him to everyone as our wedding picture."

Scorsese valued privacy, and Isabella hadn't cared about a photograph, or *thought* she didn't. One photographer, however, learned of the nuptials and managed to sneak in and get a picture, which was published in *Oggi*, the Italian newspaper. Later, Isabella was happy to have it.

It was at the café-bar of the Hampshire House in New York City that I met with Roberto Rossellini. I hadn't written my first book yet, *Hello, I Must Be Going*, which would be about Groucho Marx. I also hoped to write a book about people who love their creative work.

It was Ingrid's favorite hotel in New York, and his, too. I had been warned by Henri Langlois that I should bring along something to read, because Rossellini was inclined to tardiness. It wasn't that he was inconsiderate, just that it was a part of him that had to be accepted, and that he couldn't help it. The advantage of that personality was, I was told, that once he arrived, he would "not measure out a stingy ration of time." It was suggested that I not leave, no matter how long I had to wait, because I would never be disappointed in Rossellini.

Langlois was right about my not being disappointed, but wrong about his coming late. Usually, I arrived early, but because of what I was told, I arrived not quite as early as I might have, only to find Rossellini already sitting there. His tendency to tardiness seemed to have been greatly exaggerated.

Our first subject of conversation was the horses and buggies that could be seen outside the window, on Central Park South. "I was looking at the horses pulling the carriages through the park," he said, "and it made me think of Ingrid.

"When I showed her Italy for the first time, on our way to Stromboli, she was always thinking about the horses and donkeys we met, and worried about them. Did they get enough water? Did they get enough to eat? Why did they have to work so hard? When she saw one of them being beaten by his owner, she wept. I must say Ingrid wept easily, I was to learn later.

"At that time, many of the poor farmers did not treat their horses well, but they themselves didn't have easy lives. They took out their frustrations on their horses and donkeys. Whenever Ingrid saw a horse being beaten, she insisted that we stop, and she would tell the person to stop beating his horse. If he didn't stop, she screamed at him. Of course, she was speaking English. I did not at that time understand English very well myself. She would say to me in French, 'Tell him in Italian.' I understood what she wanted. I did. I got up out of the car and told them what Ingrid told me to say in the most authoritative tone I could achieve, which, at that time, was very authoritative.

"They always did what I said and they stopped beating their animals. We drove on. I wondered if, as soon as we were out of sight, they didn't start beating them again even more brutally. Sometimes Ingrid reminded me more of Don Quixote than of Joan of Arc."

As we ate, Rossellini asked me, "Do you know why I am fat?" He didn't wait for an answer. "The simple answer is I enjoy eating, and I enjoy it *too* much. But I believe there is more to it than that.

"Someone mentioned this theory to me many years ago, and I ignored it at the time, but it stayed in my head long after I had forgotten who put it there. This extra fat is like a suit of armor that protects me and hides the real me, which is deep inside and makes the me that is inside less vulnerable.

"The artist puts himself on trial all the time, his performance, his work, his creation. It is pleasurable to receive the laurel wreath, but no positive reward is felt as intensely as the thumbs turned down, the throw-him-to-the-lions response. But a man does not cry, except deep down—underneath the fat.

"People say I talk a lot. Well, they are right. It's true.

"They don't say it to me, because they can't get the words in to say it while I am talking. They think it is my way of being on the offensive.

"They are wrong. It is my defense. I found out as a boy that I was invulnerable when talking. My tongue was my sword.

"For the book you are writing about people who love their work so much, I think perhaps Ingrid is a better subject for you than me. She loves her work, being an actress, more than anyone I ever knew. I love my work. True. *Very* much. But when I saw each of my films, I was proud and I was ashamed. I saw some beauty. Also, I saw defects. When I held each of my children, I never saw any imperfection. Immediately, I loved each one, beautiful and perfect."

"Mama loved to make wonderful celebrations for holidays and special occasions," Isotta Ingrid told me. "She would make the best Christmas, Easter, and birthdays."

"I remember when Father became seventy," Isabella told me, "Mother came to Rome to visit us. We were all adults, and she was going to leave a few days before May 8th. Mother said to us, 'You have to give your father a big birthday party.'

"Mother gave the most wonderful little birthday parties, not a big party with famous people, but little party with lots of surprises. She had a real knack for it. There were speeches that were wonderfully funny, fake telegrams from Mao Tse-tung, Indira Gandhi, all those kinds of people. She would do wonderful things. So we begged Mother to stay and help us do *this* party.

"Mother started by pretending to have a dinner with Father on the

6th of May because she had to leave. She said she wouldn't be able to be with him on the 8th, and then she surprised him on the 8th, early in the morning, appearing at his house with my sister, me, and all of us, singing songs, full of flowers, you know, flowers on our heads, singing and giving him breakfast. And then Mom said, 'Roberto, I'm sorry I have to leave now. I postponed my trip for a couple of days to be here for breakfast, but I am leaving now. I have to catch the noon flight. I know you're having dinner with Ingrid and Isabella.'

"And then Mother was at the dinner.

"My brother Robertino came dressed as a waiter, which was my mother's idea. She had him come from Paris to do it. My father didn't even look at him until Robertino said, 'Papa,' and only then, Father looked up and recognized him. We invited Marcella, my father's first wife. I mean, *everybody* was there. Everybody was invited.

"Father was so amused and delighted, probably to see Mama the way he knew her when they were first married and Mother *would* give him a little party. Mama had such charm.

"I found out a little later on, after Father died, that they *did* see each other. When Mother got sick with cancer, she was quite in despair, and they spent an evening at the Raphael Hotel, which they both loved. I don't think it was as lovers in any way. I think it was an evening spent talking. I thought it was a very important moment for my family. My mum told me she spent that one night with Father talking to her, giving her the courage to confront the illness.

"Mother told him that Ingmar Bergman had offered her a film. She was sure that Father was going to be really mad, because Father would consider Bergman too psychological, too bourgeois, too something. Instead, Father wanted to cheer her up, and felt so happy for her, that she could work and have something to engage her beyond the illness. They were friends. They *did* see each other. They never told us children, but I'm sure there were phone calls, long phone calls, and a lasting friendship."

• • •

Ingrid was feeling worried about facing the future when that spring night in 1977 she needed to talk with someone close. That night, Roberto was there for her. It seemed a chance happening that they should both find themselves at the Raphael in Paris, but Ingrid felt it was destiny. "In a way," she said, "we were never closer." She wanted his companionship, his compassion, his good advice. Ingrid remembered that she did almost all the talking, and she was able to confide in someone who cared and who knew her and understood her.

After being with Roberto, she felt so much better. Roberto could always make her feel better. They had lunch, too. Ingrid was reminded of the way it had been for her with Roberto when she first arrived in Italy. She had loved what Roberto said, but it also meant a great deal to her that Roberto really listened.

Later, that dinner and the lunch of the next day took on new meaning for Ingrid. When Roberto Rossellini died, that dinner and lunch became the last time she ever was with him.

At first, she had regrets. She wished that she had used the time together to say something meaningful, even though she didn't know what that might have been. She might have told him she loved him, but he knew that. She might have talked about happy memories shared. She might have told him that she had no regrets about going to Italy. She had never quite put that into words.

If she had known, she said, she probably would have cried the entire time. "Roberto hated it when I cried. He said it made him feel useless. He didn't know what to do, and that always frustrated Roberto and made him unhappy. It's better I didn't know."

June 3, 1977, Ingrid told me, was one of the saddest days of her life.

She was in Chichester, England, doing *Waters of the Moon* on the stage. She had lunch at a pub with her friend, former Selznick diction coach Ruth Roberts, who was staying with her. When they returned from lunch, there was a message to call Fiorella, Roberto's niece whom Ingrid regarded as a daughter.

The message said that Ingrid should call Rome immediately, but added, "The children are okay."

Once she knew nothing was wrong with her children, Ingrid could catch her breath. She was grateful that Fiorella had included the reassuring postscript about her children, and that the maid had taken the time to carefully write it down. Nothing could be so terribly wrong she thought. But it was.

Fiorella told her that Roberto had died. It was a terrible blow. Ingrid knew that not only had he meant so much to her in her life, but that he still did. The pain seemed as great as if it had happened in the early days of their love.

For Ingrid, the world would be a much emptier place with Roberto gone from it. "When I first learned that Roberto had died," Ingrid said, "it was like a part of me had died. It was at that moment I knew how much I still loved him.

"As long as he was still in the world, it was a different world for me. I didn't have to call him, but knowing I *could* call him made all the difference. After speaking with Fiorella, I put down the phone and felt an indescribable emptiness. I knew I would miss Roberto every day as long as I lived."

Ingrid's first thought was that it must have been an automobile accident, her longtime, deeply-felt fear, but it was a massive heart attack.

Ingrid was so stunned that she didn't hear the rest of what Fiorella was telling her.

When the heart attack occurred, Rossellini was in his apartment in Parioli. He was glad to be back in Rome after having been president of the jury for the Cannes Film Festival. He saw more films than he wanted to in a short space of time, but, all in all, he was glad he had done it, appreciated the honor, and considered it a valuable experience. On the way back to Rome, he had the chance to drive, which he always enjoyed, and to be with Sonali's son, Gil.

Gil was now a young man, and Rossellini felt it was really his first opportunity to speak with him not as a child, but as a man. "He wanted to talk about things men talk about," Gil told me.

That morning, Rossellini had reread the newspaper article he had written, which he was just about to turn in.

"He had little time," Isabella told me, "but he called Marcella, his first wife, who lived just across the street. She ran to him, but there was nothing she could do. He died with her there, in her arms."

In Chichester, Ruth Roberts knew it was getting close to the time of Ingrid's performance. She said, "Ingrid, it's time to go to the theater."

Ingrid felt she couldn't do it. How could she play the part of a gay and wealthy woman onstage when she wanted only to talk with her children, and to others, who were close to her, and cry.

Then she thought maybe her character, Helen Lancaster, could help her. If she could be Helen Lancaster for a few hours, it would be a relief from the pain.

When Ingrid arrived at the theater, everyone knew. They looked sad, but no one said much because they knew she was going onstage. Being actors, they understood how Ingrid was feeling and that what she needed to do was to get into her character.

She went onstage, and there she was, no longer Ingrid Bergman. She was Helen Lancaster. There would be time, later that night, to be Ingrid and cry.

"There are aspects of a man," Ingrid told me, "which may capture your imagination and stimulate your romantic fantasies during courtship, but not when you have to live with them over a long period of time. Roberto loved cars long before I met him, long before he loved me, from the time when he was a boy. He told me that he had to wait until he was nine before an aunt taught him how to drive.

"I remember my first ride with him. I feared it might be a last ride, the last ride for both of us. He laughed. He said he was driving slowly, so I wouldn't be worried. Too late. He should have told me that before. Not that it would have made any difference. It was the one thing I never enjoyed with Roberto, being with him when he was driving, although I must say, he followed rules and kept his attention on the road. I had admired the grip of his wonderful hands on the wheel. I'm told that racing car drivers do this.

"I especially couldn't bear it when Roberto drove with the children. They weren't frightened the way I was. Robertino wanted to be exactly like his father, and it seemed he was anxious at only three or four years old to begin driving, perhaps just like his father, fast. I hoped time and good sense would temper that passion in my very young son. I knew from the first that I was too late to influence Roberto.

"Roberto was already himself. I don't know at what point he became Roberto. Certainly he was himself at an early age. Perhaps he was born Roberto.

"Indulgence was part of what created Roberto, and most especially indulgence by women. Roberto had been appreciated from the moment he was born and he took it as his natural due. I agreed that it was and made my own contribution.

"But I could never adjust to our children being in the car when Roberto drove, even though I understood he was a wonderful, wonderful driver. Having been a racing driver, he told me many times that he would not have been alive to meet me if he did not know how to be careful and when to be careful, which was *always*. He said no matter how great your own skill is, you never know what another driver will do. You have a good idea about what a racing car driver will do, but an ordinary fellow on the highway, you never know and must be ever alert.

"One day our little Robertino, who was about three and a half at the time, got up onto the bed where his father was sitting. He crawled over, stood up, and with all of his three-and-a-half-year-old force, struck his father across the face.

"Roberto was very stunned, but he tried not to show it. Our little boy was, as they say, the apple of his eye. I don't remember if the phrase was apple of his eye or apple of his eyes.

"So Roberto asked, 'Why did you do that?'

"Robertino stalwartly stood his ground on the bed, and said, 'Because you made my mommy cry.'

"I couldn't bear the sound when Roberto left the house and shot off in his Ferrari. My heart stopped. It was a sound that particularly horrified me every time. I never lost the feeling of having been stabbed. Sometimes, my eyes filled with tears.

"Fortunately, my hair did not turn white. It could have. I was always afraid *that* was how Roberto was going to die. Roberto thought that he would die in an airplane crash, and he didn't like the idea of flying.

"In the end, when I heard that Roberto was dead, I thought it must have been in his automobile. But it wasn't. And it wasn't as he had *thought* it would be, in an airplane.

"It was a massive heart attack.

"It had been sudden, and it was over in minutes."

Isabella told me that, learning of Roberto's death, her mother wrote to Jean Renoir and his wife, "Roberto died fast, the way he drove."

Isabella, who admitted to not being objective about her father, said, "Not everybody thought my father was perfect, though I did. I *do*.

"Not everyone thought he was a genius, but he *was* a genius, I think.

"My father's films revolutionized cinema.

"For me, June 3, 1977, was the saddest day of my life. I was Daddy's girl."

Isabella remembered being very small and hugging her father. Her little arms didn't go very far around his ever-increasing girth. People said to her father, "You have to lose weight. You are getting too fat. You must go on a diet."

Little Isabella didn't like that at all. She liked her father just the way he was. He was perfect. There was more of him to love. She didn't want to have less of him. She knew her arms would grow longer, the better to encircle him.

The last time I talked with Rossellini, he told me, "I admit you cannot totally ignore the critics, though I would certainly like to. I just don't want to be influenced by them. They should make their own movies, and leave mine alone.

"I would never try to please them, and if by some miracle they ever praised a film of mine, I would worry a lot about it.

"There are critics who, dressed like everybody else, in civilian life seem like people you could know. But as soon they put on their critic's robes, they become something else. Then they are not only unwilling to like something, they are *afraid* to. They have to show their superiority by showing your inferiority."

Ingrid told me that Roberto didn't care at all about critics, that he didn't read them and didn't want to know what they said, exactly the opposite of the way she felt. She believed critics were important, and she admitted that when they wrote negatively about her acting, she was pained.

"Bad reviews can take away your opportunities to work in the future," she said. "They can cost the producers, who gambled on you, their money. They can shape the way audiences perceive what you do, as good or bad."

On the death of his father, Renzo Rossellini, as Rossellini's eldest surviving son, was called upon "to undress and then re-dress" his father's body for the funeral. As he undressed him, he found his father's wallet. The wallet had no money in it, which certainly did not surprise Renzo. There was a tiny glove of his brother, Romano, which Roberto had carried with him since the death of his first son in 1946. Besides this, Renzo told me there was only a carefully folded, deeply creased, yellowed newspaper clipping.

Renzo carefully unfolded it. The clipping obviously had been carried for many years by Rossellini, and it had taken on the shape of the wallet. Unable to imagine what it could be, Renzo read it.

It was a critique of *Paisan*—a very, *very* bad review. "Imagine, my father had kept this review with him, had carried it with him, this insult, for more than three decades!"

It began, "From the obscure mind of the film director . . ."

Renzo realized that even *he* hadn't completely known Roberto Rossellini, the private man, his father.

The funeral of Rossellini brought out all of Rome, the rich and the poor, intellectuals, those with little education, the right, the left, the royalists, the communists. Many of those who turned out had never seen even the masterworks, *Rome: Open City* and *Paisan,* of the father of neorealism, but everyone knew one of Italy's great persons of all time had died.

"Father left no will because he didn't need one," Isabella told me.

When Rossellini died, he left for his six children an estate of a little more than $200 and a key to a safe-deposit box.

"We did not expect Dad to leave much money," Isabella continued, "so his small estate didn't surprise us, but when we found the key to a safety-deposit box, we were curious and thought there must be something interesting in that box. There was. We thought it might be a letter of instructions to us children about life.

"The entire contents of the box was one very soiled handkerchief. A lady's handkerchief. What else! It was much used and not washed before it was put away.

"We learned the story of it from a man who was a friend of Father's. It was obviously true because it was so in the character of our father to choose this as his treasure.

"It was the handkerchief of a mistress who was leaving him, and she may not even have been very important in his life, but it was an emotional scene of high drama, which my father fortunately appreciated, because there had been quite a few such scenes in his life. Father was the subject of many years of ladies' tears. I can understand it. Even though he was not the most handsome man, women like a genius.

"This particular lady had left her handkerchief behind. Dad had found it several days later. It was still wet from her tears. He felt it was a miracle that it was still damp from the tears, so off to the safety-deposit box.

"My father died so very poor and full of debts that all of us, his children, decided to give up our rights to inherit the money, because there was no money. There was no real estate, no cash, nothing. The only one who couldn't do that was Renzo. It was much more complicated for him to renounce Father's estate.

"Renzo is the only heir of Father's estate, for what it is worth, because he had worked so much with Father. He couldn't really give up all of his claim to his own work.

"I remember when I was still married to Martin Scorsese, I told Marty very proudly that Father died full of debt, and a friend of Marty's said to me, 'Why do you seem to be proud of *that*? Isn't it terrible that he didn't pay his bills?' It was the first time that I looked at this problem of not paying bills that way.

"Father didn't pay his bills, but he never really made individual people suffer. For example, he would go to a big hotel, generally the Hotel Raphael in Paris. He would tip enormously the doorman and the waiter and the bar attendant, the elevator operator, but maybe he would not have enough to pay the bill for the room. The hotel had to wait, but he did not create any bankruptcy for the Raphael and he made all the employees so happy.

"He lived financially longer than his seventy-one years. So, it was the first time that rational thinking entered, with this friend of Marty's, who said, 'Aren't you ashamed? Why are so proud of it?' That was the beginning of my understanding of life in the way society, people generally, understand it."

"With each of my three husbands," Ingrid said, "I let them make financial decisions. I really never enjoyed business, and I didn't like to talk too much about money. I believed I could always earn what I needed, and I didn't need so much as long as I could make long distance calls without worrying about it. It was also nice to travel first class and to buy the best food.

"If it hadn't been for the children, I would have thought even less about money, maybe not at all. But I wanted to leave my children provided for the best I could. I wanted to do for them what my father had done for me. I knew I could not take care of them for their whole lives, but I could give them some feeling of security.

"If you have a feeling of security, you can live your life differently and dare to do so much more.

"The one thing I couldn't bear was debts. Roberto believed debts were a good thing. He had a way of explaining why debts were good. He never was able to make it clear to me. I knew how *I* felt.

"Roberto believed it would be a terrible thing to die and leave behind money that could have brought pleasure. He need not have worried. He missed by only one day—leaving enough money behind him to live one more happy day."

Rossellini told me, "An artist shouldn't speak about money. He shouldn't even think about it. Money should be used for buying time and life and for the satisfaction of whims, the luxuries which are not really luxuries, because one person's luxuries are really another's needs.

"One should never regret spending money which brought pleasure because you may not be able to buy that at a later date, or it may have too high a price. What you bought should be judged not only by its value, but by the happiness it brought at that moment."

Ingrid remembered her father had said something like that to her, that money was only for the happiness it brought. "But," she added, "my father was never in debt."

With his wife, Enrica, at the Hotel du Cap in Cap d'Antibes, Michelangelo Antonioni talked with me about Italian films in general and about Roberto Rossellini and Ingrid Bergman in particular. Antonioni started out in films as a writer, and one of his earliest scripts was done with Rossellini. It was 1941, and the film was *Un Pilota Ritorna* (A Pilot Returns).

"Roberto was a kind and helpful person, and he was always ready to share his judgment, his ideas, or his connections. He was greedy for life, but not greedy about his work. He was never petty, nor jealous of anyone. He was a package wrapped up in himself, and I say that in a good way. He didn't mind anyone else's business, because he had so much of his own to mind.

"He was a great director. Just after the war, when the chaotic world we found ourselves in needed someone to interpret it for us objectively, he did it. Later, he adjusted to the need to internalize our feelings. I should say he 'tried,' since internal feelings are so difficult to treat objectively.

"That was with the Ingrid Bergman films. If you only looked at Roberto, you wondered why this *so* beautiful woman chose him, but if you knew his mind, you understood. Later, there was television, which Roberto thought would change the world for the better. I disagreed, but it was the ultimate neorealism, since it was a new kind of reality that wasn't real at all, but an illusion of reality.

"The appearance of Ingrid Bergman in a Rossellini film was more incongruous than Laurel and Hardy encountering a gorilla on an Alpine rope bridge. The fact that it worked at all was a tribute to Rossellini's infinite resilience and Bergman's extraordinary persona. I believe that these films, as well as all the others that have been overlooked in Rossellini's canon, will in the future be reappraised as much more valuable than now.

"I don't think Roberto was capable of making a film that was without value."

Many years after they had more or less drifted apart over a relatively trifling disagreement, Fellini remembered Rossellini as an inspirational and encouraging mentor early in Fellini's career when he needed it most.

"I showed a print of *The White Sheik* to Rossellini before I had finished editing it. Robertino was very encouraging. It meant a great deal to me. I respected him as a director, and his praise at this crucial, early moment in my career was important to me. Shortly afterwards, I told him that someday I hoped I would be able to repay him for his generosity. He said that I could repay him by encouraging someone else. Someday when I was in the position of being one of the most important Italian directors, which I surely would be, he said that I should remember him and help someone younger than myself."

"As I watched *Cinema Paradiso* with its director, Giuseppe Tornatore, I liked it very much. It was wonderful. Like with *The White Sheik,* this wasn't the final edited version, but I could see the director had a wonderful future. I remembered Rossellini, and I was reminded of that time long before when I, a young, worried hopeful, showed my own film to a director whose position was much ahead of mine at the time. Roberto Rossellini had been there for *me*. I thought of his words to me, telling me I would someday see in the future someone younger who was at a critical moment in his career. Giuseppe Tornatore was that person for me.

Ingrid told me, "Federico would say to me, 'I learned so much from Roberto. He was my mentor.' So I would ask him *what* he learned, if he could put it into words. He said Roberto created an aura, and you had to give yourself up to it. He said you could not copy Roberto because he offered inspiration rather than tutoring, and then, if you could, you had to create your own world.

"Federico certainly did that. He created his own world. I would like to have gone into that world with him to make films. I admired his pictures, and he had his own style. He was a unique creator. I looked hard to see the influence of Roberto in the Felliniesque films. Perhaps *La Strada*. It was a film I know Roberto would have been proud to make."

When Swedish director Ingmar Bergman met Ingrid at the Stockholm airport, after a brief greeting, the first words she had to tell him were about how encouraging and enthusiastic Roberto had been about her making a film with him.

Even though Roberto was no longer her husband, she knew he was capable of making a terrible uproar when she just mentioned the name of another director with whom she planned to make a film. He might be especially displeased when she showed great enthusiasm for the director.

At the mention of Ingmar Bergman's name, however, Roberto had shown great pleasure and had totally encouraged her. Very specifically, he had told her that he thought it would be a great experience for her to work with Ingmar Bergman.

What Ingrid didn't tell Bergman was that she believed that Roberto had reacted that way because he had so desired to see her distracted from her illness and from her disappointment in her marriage to Lars, that he was tremendously pleased for her that she had something in life she could look forward to doing.

Roberto's words and the feeling they conveyed had meant a great deal to her. She saw from Bergman's emotional reaction that the way Roberto had felt meant a great deal to Ingmar Bergman, too.

Liv Ullmann worked in twelve Ingmar Bergman films before *Autumn Sonata*. She and Bergman had a unique professional and personal rapport. They had a child, a daughter, Linn, who played her mother as a child in *Autumn Sonata*. Ullmann and Bergman remained the greatest friends, but didn't marry.

Coming from a conservative family living in a conventional Norwegian community, Ullmann could well understand what had happened to Ingrid when the world learned she was having Roberto Rossellini's child.

Ullmann has enjoyed an illustrious acting career, which she expanded into a successful directing career, and she also became a best-selling author in America and around the world.

Autumn Sonata (Höstsonaten, 1978)

After many years, world-renowned concert pianist Charlotte (Ingrid Bergman) comes to visit her daughter, Eva (Liv Ullmann), who has married a country parson. It is an uneasy meeting, since Eva feels her mother has neglected her and her sister, Helena (Lena Nyman), who suffers from cerebral palsy, in the pursuit of a concert career and various affairs. For her part, Charlotte cannot seem to summon up maternal feelings for her daughters. Helena's distorted grimaces upset her. After quarreling and making up several times, and after an hysterical fit by Eva, they part, not truly having come closer.

"Well, I must say that I really appreciated and love Ingrid Bergman, who I met for the first time when we did *Autumn Sonata*," Liv Ullmann told me. "I learned a lot from her about acting, but more about being a woman. I used to sit in the studio and watch her, feeling very proud to be a woman. And that was because of the way she handled the people around her, the way she listened, the way she wanted to do what was asked from her, but at the same time doing what she felt was right.

"Now, Ingmar Bergman and she did not have the best of relationships, which she would say, and I believe he would say it, too. It was because she asked questions. The way he liked to work was that we read the script and made our own answers from our own experience and fantasy, but Ingrid was not like that. So, even on the first reading of the script, she would start every other sentence with, 'Well, Ingmar, what do you mean by that?' Or, 'Do you really want me to say it that way?' Or, 'Wouldn't this be better?'

"So, after that first reading, Ingmar wanted to say, 'No more films,' and he was literally crying, when we were alone. He said, 'I don't know how I can continue.' But, of course, he *did* continue.

"Ingrid really showed her stamina. We didn't know from the beginning that she was very much cancer-affected, very ill. She never talked about it to anyone. She was the first one to come to makeup. She was the last one, almost, to leave the studio in the evening. Each evening, after shooting, she and some of us girls would sit together. We would have drinks, and we would laugh, and we would talk about the day. Not a word about her misery. I can even remember one day she was asked by Ingmar to lie on the floor and talk about her past. And she would stretch out her arms behind her head. I heard later when you have the operation she had had, on her arms and her breasts, you cannot do that. But Ingrid did that.

"Then one evening, she did tell the makeup girls and me what had happened to her and how she felt. She talked about how much she loved her children. She said she was going to go on, and she was going to have a full and worthy life, as long as she possibly could.

"I remember that we went out and had dinner that day, and she was talking about her past and she said, 'Oh, you know, I've been through difficult things before.' She talked about the time when she left the United States, and she couldn't see her child until much later, and the children with Rossellini, and how she couldn't have them with her as she wished, and how she was attacked in the Senate and she couldn't come back to America. And I was looking for, you know, the victim, I was looking for the tears. I was looking for what would be natural, some self-pity. Never. She was telling the whole story with some laughter, with a smile. 'Ah, maybe I should have said this, maybe I should have done that. But you know, I was in love.'

"Everything she did, the whole story, which must have been *terrible* for her, losing her daughter Pia, not to be able get in communication with her because the father wouldn't let Pia talk to her, and Ingrid couldn't come back to the United States. It was a *horrible* situation. Not *once* did she say, 'Oh, poor little me.'

"I remember a note that José Quintero sent her. He congratulated her for how she accepted that Oscar. When she, for the first time in years, appeared onstage at the Academy Awards in Los Angeles, people leaped up and applauded and applauded, but she just stood there. She didn't bow, she didn't do anything. She accepted it, but she would not give in and say, 'Thank you, thank you for taking me back.' She was a really proud person. And then there were the times when Ingmar wanted to do something that wasn't right for her, and she wouldn't accept it.

"Each Wednesday, when we were shooting, Ingmar's tradition was to show a movie. It's been the tradition with him for years and years and years. He selected the movie, and we all went. Sometimes we liked the movie, sometimes we didn't, but they were *his* favorites. So he said, 'Ingrid, we'll have a drink first, and then we're all going to see the movie.'

"We go to the movie, and then, after five minutes, Ingrid gets up and says, 'I don't have time for this,' and she leaves.

"As you can imagine, that did *not* endear her to Ingmar! I don't remember what the movie was anymore, because I was so shocked! But in my heart, I admire a woman like Ingrid.

"I belong to a club in Norway. It's a women directors club. We have gone on now for almost forty years. We had seven members, but some of them are dead by now, because I'm the youngest, and I'm sixty-seven. We never have a guest, but when Ingrid was there, we wanted Ingrid.

"When she came, we told her, 'You are our first guest. You mean so much for us, and we admire you,' and whatever. Then, we had a wonderful meal with wine, and talked about theater, films, and so on. At the end, Ingrid got up and said, 'I just have to tell you women,' there were seven then, 'what it meant to me, that you allowed me to come, because so much has happened in my life, and as you have told me, many successes. But I have never really been part of a group of girlfriends, and this is kind of my first meeting with girlfriends. That, I think, is wonderful, and I thank you.'

"After that, I think she lived only two years or three years. When we had our meetings, very often we would call Ingrid and say, 'Here we are. How are you doing? and we miss you so much.'

"But with Ingrid, to get back to *Autumn Sonata*, this is the last story of how she did not endear herself to Ingmar, the most important example. It is a scene where I, the forty-year-old daughter, am blaming my mother because my life was so miserable, and Ingrid is my mother, the pianist, who chooses to go out and give the world part of her creativity and her talent. In the world's eyes, men can do this all the time, and a woman will serve them and help them. But in this case, it was a woman doing it, and Ingmar was very negative about the woman who made that choice instead of staying home with the children.

"Ingrid and I, we went to Ingmar before the shooting, and we said, 'Can't we change a little, you know, in the script, because it's so unclear and doesn't seem right for our characters?' Ingmar said no. He doesn't like to change the script. I know that. Then we said, 'Can we play a little against the work the way it is?' He said, 'Sure, you're actors.' I gave myself forty-year-old glasses that I didn't really need, and Ingrid made herself the most beautiful and aware woman that could be. We had to fight what we were saying because we couldn't change the lines.

"In this long scene where, finally, the daughter really explodes against the mother, it was a long night, and I had a long monologue. I think it was three or four pages where I just call Ingrid's character the horror I feel she has been. I tell her how she has ruined her husband, and her little child, me. I tell her why I can never be anything because of her. And I go on and on and on and on.

"But when you're forty, you're somehow responsible for your life. This woman didn't understand that. It was her mother's fault. In the end, Ingrid was to say something, like, 'Please hug me. Please love me,' something like that. When I read it, I thought, this is so wonderful. And I thought if I were to do it, oh, I'd make people cry, because I'd say like a victim, 'Oh, please hug me, please love me,' you know, and I almost envied her the part she was playing.

"Anyway, they took all my monologue first because I had so much. It was a long night, and the day was coming before the camera was turned on Ingrid, when she is supposed to say, 'Please hug me, please love me.'

"So, we did all of the monologue. I was finished, and we turned the camera on her, and she said, 'I'm not going to say that. I'm going to slap her face and leave the room.'

"Oh, Ingmar! And he screamed! And she screamed back. Then they realized they couldn't scream in front of us. So the crew and the actors, we went out in the hall. And we heard the screaming.

"Then the door opened, and they came in and they were quiet, the crew first, and then the actors. And, of course, the crew went on, and the camera was turned to Ingrid, when she was to say, 'Please hug me, please love me,' and in that moment, her face was the face of every woman who has been forced to say, 'I'm here. Please like me. Please do this, please do that.' It was Nora of *A Doll's House,* it was anyone who, behind those wonderfully people-pleasing words, shows the anger. That is what she did. She showed a face for the daughter that was full of anger.

"I thought that was fantastic, because I would have made it a sweet, emotional scene, but she didn't do that. She spoke for all of us women who have been brought up not to be like this woman, so people will not think we have balls.

"That reminds me, what she did there, of many years before when I was interviewed by Barbara Walters. It reminds me because of the way men look at women if they show strength. She said to the crew, 'Oh, that light there. You have to turn that light there. It isn't good on Liv, and I want that light there,' and so on. So professional. I admired her. My press agent, who I was with, said, 'Did you hear Barbara? Oh, my God, what balls she has.'

"We are supposed to be these sweet little people, but when we get a little tired of it, they don't like us. That wasn't Ingrid. She didn't have time anymore. She didn't have time, and that was the biggest lesson I learned. And I'm there, too, now, although I have probably more time than she had. I don't have time anymore, either, and I know that was a lesson I learned from Ingrid. So, that's what I was thinking of. I'm living a little like Ingrid told me: There is no time just to people-please."

I asked Liv if Ingrid seemed different in Swedish, which was the language they always spoke together.

"Maybe she was," Liv said. "She was closer to her roots. English was a learned language, and I believe she learned it later than most of us, because I don't know how much she learned in school. So, probably she wasn't so alive as she was in Swedish.

"I've just remembered another thing. For the dubbing of *Autumn*

Sonata, we did it together in New York City, and she was so *quick.* Then, when we were finished, I was going back to Sweden, I know she was meeting her daughters, and we were standing on the street corner, and we had a green light. I would have liked to stand there and to make the goodbye a little longer, because, who knows when do we see each other again? Not she.

" 'Bye, Liv,' and there she went. She didn't have time to make a big emotional scene, she didn't have time for that. Usually people will turn, especially when they know they may not see each other ever again. Ingrid never turned. Crossed the street and she was gone. That was the last time I was with her. She knew it, and I knew it. I never saw her again.

"I spoke to her once on the phone, because Ingmar renegotiated her salary. He called me and said, 'Do you agree to this?' I said, 'I'll do whatever Ingrid says.' She agreed to do it. She said, 'Life is too short.'

"I really loved her. It's the best experience I ever had with anyone, because I learned so much about being a human being. I learned there isn't enough time, be honest, don't be a victim, and don't blame other people. I never heard her say a bad word about Dr. Lindstrom or Rossellini. Never. She didn't gossip about people.

"You know, lately I've heard people say she was very tough in Hollywood. I've heard bad stories, you know. I just don't believe it. She came, and she won. She looked *beautiful,* and she *was* beautiful, and it's a wonder to watch her. Unfortunately, some didn't get what they wanted, but she got it. They implied she sort of slept her way to it, but there's no way. I'm sure she slept with as many as anyone else, but not to get parts."

Paavo Turtiainen, a young Finnish friend who was working for Lars in France, accompanied Ingrid to a film in Paris. The theater was so crowded that they couldn't find seats together.

They had gone to the cinema to see one of Ingrid's favorite actors, favorite directors, and favorite friends, John Gielgud.

"He was in a part Ingrid didn't care for in a film she didn't care for," Paavo remembered. "At the end of the film, I looked for Ingrid, but she wasn't at the seat where I'd left her. I went out into the lobby, and I found her there with her book. Ingrid usually brought something with her to read. She hadn't liked the film. She hadn't expected to like the film, but she couldn't not go because of her friendship for Gielgud.

"Once there, Ingrid knew after fifteen or twenty minutes that it was not a film she wanted to see, so she took her book and sat in the lobby waiting to meet me. Ingrid didn't like to waste time pretending she was being entertained when she wasn't. She would never hurt anyone's feelings, if she could avoid it, but John Gielgud wasn't there, except on the screen."

I remember walking with Ingrid in Paris, along the Rue Faubourg Saint-Honoré, to the Hermès store. She said she wanted to show me "a wonderful purse that matches a belt I've owned for years."

She asked the salesperson if she had three purses exactly alike. This would be a purse to be passed on for more than one generation, so with three daughters, she felt she would have to buy three purses.

Though obviously tempted, she decided that she should save the money for her children to spend on what *they* chose. "I don't have enough life left myself to amortize the purchase, and the belt probably doesn't fit anymore."

As the purses were put away, Ingrid recalled her Aunt Elsa, "Tante Mutti," shopping without buying anything. As a little girl, Ingrid promised herself never to look at a lot of things and then leave the salesperson with the work of putting everything back, and perhaps hurt feelings. She bought a beautiful silk scarf, which she tied around her neck and wore as we left Hermès.

One afternoon in London, Ingrid and I met at Fortnum and Mason for tea. She was carrying some shoe boxes.

"It's so wonderful," she said. "I've found a boutique with the most beautiful flat shoes I've ever seen. I'm too tall to wear high heels."

As we had tea, she opened the boxes to show me her purchases. "I'm certain the designer is going to be very famous," she said. "His name is Manolo Blahnik.

"I've always enjoyed shopping for shoes because buying clothes is such a big responsibility. I could never *really* imagine myself in evening clothes or cocktail and party dresses in my personal life. I could only imagine myself in suits or simple print dresses or sports clothes. Even when I looked at myself wearing a dress that had seemed very elegant on its hanger in the shop, I'd put it on and, in the mirror, it seemed like someone else was looking back at me."

During our conversation, after a brief discussion of which cheeses were best at Fortnum's and which were best at Harrods, Ingrid reminisced a bit wistfully about her later career.

"It was not the same for me after Italy. I returned as a woman past forty, older, with a different image after all that scandal and notoriety. Because very few people had seen me in any of the Italian films, I came back on the screen as someone different, someone they didn't know so well. People said Ingrid Bergman could never return to her pedestal after leaping off. And the opportunities for parts were more limited for 'a woman of a certain age.'

"I have always wanted to be a working actress doing something 'important,' but it was only late in my life that I understood that entertaining people was important and, if you were lucky, it would be having the opportunity to entertain as many as possible."

After tea, Ingrid insisted on paying. She remembered that I had paid the last time, months before.

When the check came, she asked me what I thought she ought to tip. I suggested a pound, even though a service charge had already been included. Ingrid never knew whether people recognized her or not, but when they did, she thought a bigger tip was expected, "the price of fame." She left two pounds.

As we were leaving, a woman said to her, "Do you know, you look just like Ingrid Bergman."

Ingrid smiled. "Yes, I know. Many people have told me that."

On January 28, 1978, Ingrid opened in London with a revival of N. C. Hunter's 1950s play, *Waters of the Moon*. Her co-star was Dame Wendy Hiller. By June, the cancer had spread, and Ingrid underwent a second mastectomy when the play closed in July.

During one of her last performances in *Waters of the Moon* (1978) on the London stage, Ingrid "went up" on her lines, momentarily forgetting them. After the curtain fell, she was distraught, while her co-star, Wendy Hiller, endeavored to reassure her, to persuade her that the audience loved her and hadn't even noticed.

Ingrid said, "You're right, Wendy. It's only a play," paraphrasing Alfred Hitchcock's words to her, whenever he thought she was taking herself too seriously: "It's only a movie."

"Once people know you are sick, everything is different," Ingrid said. "No escape. They feel they must constantly ask how are you, and you know it's nothing casual. It has deeper, darker implications. They mean well. What can they do? They can't ignore that you have aged ten years in one. But when you see *that* look on their faces, it is so terrible. If other people do not know or not many do, I could pretend a little better for myself.

"I much prefer not to say anything, so I don't have to relive bad news every time I see anyone. They are hearing it once. I am saying it a dozen times, which means every time I say it, I hear it."

Ingrid once told me, "What I think is important is to appreciate every bit of happiness that comes your way, not to wait to celebrate the big happiness when it comes, but the more frequent little happinesses.

"Little pleasures are so important. Big pleasures usually come with burdens, responsibilities. There's nothing like licking an ice cream cone as you walk in the park in the summer with flat shoes and no stockings.

"I am always sentimental on New Year's Eve. A part of it may be looking back at the year that was, in which I never seem to have accomplished all that I thought I would, and looking ahead to a 'Happy New Year,' even though one never knows what the new year holds. So, perhaps my tears are for something of the unknown.

"It is like a birthday. You don't get a year older in a day, but still, even though my head knows that, my heart doesn't. I never minded being a year older on a birthday, which, for me, in my mind, was always a happy occasion.

"New Year's Eve is different. I feel a bit wistful, and sometimes even slightly apprehensive. I tell myself a year doesn't go in a day, but I am always glad to be with people on New Year's Eve, and we drink champagne. Champagne bubbles always make me optimistic."

The American Film Institute honored Alfred Hitchcock at its gala tribute on March 7, 1979. The scene was the Beverly Hills Hilton Hotel, with stars, directors, and studio heads in attendance.

There was no one Hitchcock was happier to see than Ingrid, his close friend over the years and the beautiful star of three of his films, *Spellbound, Notorious,* and *Under Capricorn,* who had flown in from London to be mistress of ceremonies for the evening. When he heard she was coming, Hitchcock knew he *had* to do it. She was going to be there for him. He *had* to be there for her.

Hitchcock was terrified before the event, fearful that his knees might buckle. He had been offered the opportunity to be seated at his table with his wife and Cary Grant, as the guests entered, but he did not want to do it differently from the way all of the honorees of past years had done it. Hitchcock had great pride, and he did not want to call attention to his physical problems, even though they were so severe that he no longer was ever without pain. Remaining seated, "planted there," he said, "would be unmanly and rude."

Rather than appear "disabled," his word, he chose to enter and make the long walk to his seat, passing along the aisle barely separating him from the assembled guests who closed in to greet him as he passed.

Hitchcock said that before the event, he had waking dreams, not sleeping dreams, because he couldn't sleep, in which he fell down in front of the whole assemblage as he entered.

He knew that Ingrid wasn't well, but he had no idea just how seriously ill she was.

Toward the end of the evening, Ingrid, onstage, said:

"Now, there's just one little thing I'd like to add before we finish this evening. Do you remember that agonizing shot when you had built some kind of elevator? It was a basket or something with you and the cameraman, and you were shooting this vast party in *Notorious,* and you came zooming down with your elevator and your poor pull-focus man, all the way down, into my hand, where you saw the key in a close-up. So, that was from an extreme long shot to close-up, just the key that we saw. You know what? Cary stole that key after the scene, and then he kept it for about ten years. And one day, he put it in my hand, and he said, 'I've kept this long enough. Now, it's for you for good luck.' I have kept it for twenty years, and in this very same hand, there is the key.

"It has given me a lot of good luck and quite a few good movies, too. And now, I'm going to give it to you with a prayer that it will open some very good doors for you, too. God bless you, dear Hitch. I'm coming to give you the key."

Ingrid left the stage and walked past the tables to where Hitchcock was seated. When she reached him, he rose, unassisted, though not without difficulty. He accepted the key, and they embraced tenderly in what was an emotional moment for both.

They were both ill, and there was only a little time remaining for them to be together.

After the show ended, I was standing near Ingrid and Cary Grant as they chatted. "Was that *really* the same key we used in the film?" I heard her ask him.

Grant smiled and shrugged.

Hitchcock told me, "I am in mourning for the films I would have made with Ingrid Bergman, the films that never were. When she left for Italy and stayed, it was a loss to me, to the world, and to her."

Ingrid said that for years Hitchcock had never said anything to her about Roberto, though she understood he wanted her to be in his movies, not in Italian films.

"Finally, after several years," Ingrid told me, "when I was visiting Los Angeles, Hitchcock said to me, 'It's a shame. He ruined your career.'

"I laughed. 'Oh, no, dear Hitch. Roberto didn't ruin my career. I ruined *his.*'

"I didn't belong in those pictures of his."

In spite of Hitchcock's regrets about Ingrid having left Hollywood—and him—for Italy, he had the greatest professional respect and admiration for Rossellini and his work. "Those Italian fellows—Rossellini, Fellini, and Antonioni—are a hundred years ahead of us," Hitchcock said.

Ingrid was to make only one more appearance in California, for charity, for the Variety Clubs. They used a Casablanca theme, rebuilding Rick's Café at Warners.

She wore a floor-length white gown with long sleeves and a high neck, and a Cartier necklace Lars had given her.

She decided to show the film that her father had made of her as a baby and child, and that David Selznick had restored and preserved for her. It was a great success.

When Ingrid checked out of the Beverly Wilshire Hotel, it was to go to San Diego with writer Alan Burgess, who had written the book *The Inn of the Sixth Happiness* on which the film was based, to visit Petter.

She saw Petter's wife, and three of his four children for the first time. She hoped to wipe away all of the old sadness and bitterness, but that was too much indeed to accomplish after all those years. Though the visit did not produce the magical anodyne for which Ingrid had hoped, she was glad to have tried. She always preferred to actively try rather than to be passive. She had done the best she could.

When Ingrid was offered the part of Golda Meir in a television miniseries, she couldn't imagine herself playing a familiar world figure whose physical appearance was so totally different from her own. Isabella described Ingrid's surprise at even being offered the part:

"I remember Mama laughing and laughing, and saying, 'How can they ask a big Swede, a Protestant Swede, to play Golda Meir?' And then she said that the director had insisted. He came and talked with her, and he said, 'It isn't that you are Protestant and glamorous, but it's that you come across as believable. People believe you and trust you, and this is what I want, because Golda Meir had the trust of the people.' Now *that* was interesting to Mother.

" 'I'm too tall,' she told the producer.

" 'And I'm Swedish,' she said again. But the producer was still hopeful."

Though she held out no hope to the producer, she did make a trip to Israel, inviting her cousin Britt to accompany her. She read some books about Golda Meir, and she listened to recordings of her voice.

Golda Meir's voice would be a challenge, "but at least my voice wasn't too tall," Ingrid said.

Finally, she was persuaded by producer Gene Corman that Golda Meir was "a grand-scale person," one that people would assume was much taller than she actually was. Ingrid well knew that height could be camouflaged on the screen. She hoped, however, that everyone else in the scenes would not have to stand on boxes.

Ingrid's rapidly deteriorating health was a more serious problem. Insurance for Ingrid was impossible. Not only did she have cancer, but it was spreading, and if anyone had known how bad it was, no one would have gone on with the project.

Ingrid was not one to complain. She considered herself to have been too lucky a person to have any right to complain about anything. "I would like to live my life as fully as I can until the last possible moment, discussing my personal health problems as little as possible," Ingrid had told me.

"At some point, you have to make peace with adverse circumstances. Fighting is a very tiring thing. At a certain point, when it is futile, you have to bend. Bending is a part of life."

"My mum," Isabella told me, "never complained in front of us children or to anyone except her husband. After Lars wasn't her husband anymore, she still saved up her complaints about producers, about life, for him on the phone or when she would see him."

When Isabella and Lars visited her mother in Israel, Ingrid was standing at the Wailing Wall, and Lars was just behind her, "Mom turned to him and said, 'Lars, how does it feel to be between *two* wailing walls?'"

Gene Corman, an American who had produced some films in Israel, persuaded Paramount to go forward with the project, even though Ingrid could not be insured.

It was all too clear to Ingrid that she did not have a long career ahead of her, that her career and her life were largely behind her. She would never play the old witch onstage as she had once jokingly predicted she would be doing when she was ninety. She would never be ninety.

It was probable that Golda would be her last part. Her greatest concern was, once she began work on the film, would she be able to complete it? Everyone would be depending on her, and she must not let them down.

Ingrid asked for a screen test. She was told it was not necessary, not for her, not for Ingrid Bergman. She insisted. "Oh, no, Miss Bergman. A star of your magnitude does not have to have a screen test." But Ingrid still insisted. She knew what she wanted. The screen test was not for them. It was for her.

She had been offered all kinds of makeup. She had been told they could give her Golda's exact nose, and, oh, what miracles could be done with chins! They offered her a "spectacular" double chin.

Ingrid wanted to bring to life the essence of the character, Golda's spirit, "not with a gimmicky putty nose."

She put on a gray wig, and she wore no makeup at all.

"My mother liked to find some unknown key to the character she was playing," Isabella remembered. "It made her feel very secure about playing the character when she found this key, an insight. She found two of them through Golda's assistant.

"Mama learned that Golda had a secret. Very late in life, she had had a manicure, and she discovered that she liked it very much. She loved it. She enjoyed it at the time, more than she could ever have imagined liking such a frivolity. Then she was pleased with the way her hands looked. She felt proud. She had never been a vain woman, but she found herself holding her hands out on the table, more than was necessary.

"For Mother, this was the key to Golda's character, the real person under the public exterior. Then, Mama felt much more secure being Golda.

"Then Golda's assistant told Mother about the way Golda Meir wore her bra. She always wore it over her slip.

"The assistant didn't know why. I guess she wondered, but she never felt it appropriate to ask, which it wasn't. I don't know if Mum ever figured out why. But that Golda Meir did it, that probably was enough.

"Mama loved that detail about the bra. It revealed to her some of the psychology, the sense of values of Golda. She loved the way she received people in the kitchen, even when she was prime minister. That created a whole different and informal atmosphere for talking politics.

"Mama was able to change her look just by putting on that gray wig that was so different from her blond hair. Her own hair never turned at all gray or white. She said she wanted to achieve Golda's look 'by just being bare.'

"When I saw her performance, I saw a mother that I'd never seen before—this woman with balls.

"She never showed herself like that in life. In life, Mum showed courage. She was always a little vulnerable, courageous, but vulnerable. Mother had a sort of presence, like Golda. I was surprised to see it.

"She couldn't show that side to Father, or to Lars, or to us children. She loved to show her enthusiasm and joy, to make things fun. What she was feeling inside, especially if it was negative or sad, she didn't want to show that.

"I admire Mama and when I saw her in the part, I understood she had the strong presence of Golda, and that she had balls, too."

Ingrid could not have selected a more challenging farewell role. It also had a special significance for her.

During World War II, Ingrid felt guilty because she had so misjudged the situation in Germany when she was there filming *Die vier*

Gesellen (The Four Companions), just before the war. She had considered the Nazis only a temporary aberration, "too foolish to be taken seriously." She believed Germany would not start a war. "The good people there would not permit it." She had been wrong, not that there would have been anything she could have done about it. There was also something more personal.

At about the age of eleven, Ingrid was spending her annual summer holiday in Germany with her mother's family when she was told a family secret by her Aunt Mutti (Elsa Adler). It was a profoundly serious subject for her aunt.

She cautioned Ingrid that what she was about to tell her, she must promise never to tell anyone else. She said that Ingrid's father already knew because Friedel had told him, well before they married.

Ingrid remembered that before her aunt spoke, Aunt Mutti took a deep breath. Then, in a hushed tone, she said, "There may be a little bit of Jewishness in the family, some Jewish blood." She again cautioned Ingrid that she must never tell anyone, especially since there might be some difficult times coming.

She need not have worried. Ingrid didn't really understand what her aunt was saying nor did she see any great significance in it. Her aunt continued:

"It's not that there's something wrong with being Jewish, but there are some who think it's a very bad thing, so you must not say a word about it ever, and keep our secret."

Ingrid had no trouble keeping the secret because she didn't quite understand what it was her aunt was talking about.

She immediately forgot what she'd been told, but not quite.

Ingrid remembered her aunt's words again when she became closely involved with Robert Capa, whose life had been shaped by being a Jewish refugee. She told Capa that she might be "a little bit Jewish." She hadn't ever told anyone but Petter, who had shrugged if off. Capa asked her if she remembered any more of what her aunt had said, but Ingrid didn't. Her aunt never mentioned the subject again. Ingrid felt guilty all the rest of her life because when she was in Germany at the end of the war, she had been afraid to go with the others to witness the atrocities of the Nazi extermination camp.

Near the end of filming, Ingrid requested that she be allowed to redo a scene. "Mother had seen Golda Meir make a gesture in a newsreel," Isabella told me. "When she was elected, Golda Meir covered her face with her two arms, with the two hands. Mother said, 'This is an image that we've seen so much on television, that I have to redo exactly the same gesture.'

"But she couldn't raise her right arm. She physically just couldn't do it. She had a very huge arm after they did the mastectomy and had to remove some lymph nodes, and the circulation of the lymph nodes was severely damaged, so that the right arm—and she wrote with her right arm—became huge. She kept it covered with a large shawl. It was a huge thing, and she started to refer to it as something that didn't belong to her, like a Great Dane that she had to walk in the street every day. She called the arm 'my big, overgrown, ugly, sick dog, and I have to take it for a walk like I would any big dog.'

"So she stayed all night long with her arm suspended so that fluid would go away, and she couldn't sleep at all, just to be able to do that gesture. Otherwise, the arm was so big. You know, she had to hide it most of the time during the filming.

"Mum sympathized totally with Golda Meir, who always felt some guilt when she had to leave her husband and family in order to carry out the responsibilities of her office. Since her early twenties, Mama had felt some guilt over the conflict between her work and her home. She, like Golda, had to learn to deal with the inability to be in two places at the same time."

A Woman Called Golda (1982) presented the life of Golda Meir in four hours. The young Golda, a teacher in Milwaukee, was played by Judy Davis. This two-part television film was shown in the United States on April 26 and 28, in 1982. Each segment lasted 120 minutes.

Ingrid was frequently ill during the filming, though she struggled never to complain nor to show how sick she was.

Four months after the filming was completed, she died.

It was after Ingrid's death that her daughter Pia accepted the Emmy for Ingrid's performance as Golda Meir.

Asked who most resembles her mother, Isabella said, "Probably the actress in the twenty-first century closest to my mother's persona is Julia Roberts. She is 'natural,' the word everyone used to describe Mom. She is beautiful, but not intimidating. She's not pretentious, and people like her."

On June 15, 1982, Ingrid left London for New York to be there to celebrate the thirtieth birthdays of her twin daughters. All three of her daughters were living in New York, and she was accompanied on the flight by her son, Robertino. Ingrid stayed at the Wyndham Hotel, and the party was at Pia's home.

The birthday of her daughters was something to which she had looked forward and something for which she had planned extensively. Ingrid indulged herself with an entire new wardrobe, a great splurge for her, designed by her favorite dressmaker in London in her style. Outfits were created especially to conceal how much weight she had lost and to hide her swollen arm. Ingrid planned her wardrobe, dresses, suits, coats, and accessories for each day and night and every event she could imagine, not only the party, but for restaurant lunches, the theater, whatever might occur. Ingrid stayed a few days longer than she originally had planned, so she repeated a few of her outfits.

The birthday party was thought out with the help of Paavo Turtiainen, her Finnish friend who had come to New York and become a successful chef, caterer, and party planner.

Ingrid wanted an unforgettable smorgasbord for the occasion, including the absolutely best herring available. She had always taken birthday parties seriously, and planned them with great care and imagination.

As birthday gifts for Isabella and Isotta Ingrid, Ingrid brought for each one a necklace that had belonged to *her* mother.

Though Ingrid was gravely ill, she managed not to show it. She didn't want her family at the party to have their good time spoiled. She knew that this would be the last time she would be celebrating the birthday of her twin daughters.

When she returned to London, Ingrid called Lars and told him that she would like to visit Danholmen and then go on to Stockholm. Both of them understood that this would be her last trip to Sweden.

She had great affection for Lars's Swedish island, and she was sentimental about memories of summers there. She told Lars she wanted to have one of those dinners of fresh crayfish, one of her favorite foods.

When she arrived, she was too weak to walk and had to be carried; but a few days there, with the wonderful air, seemed to restore her so that she could walk a short distance and sit on her favorite rock.

Despite the tremendous exertion it would entail, Ingrid wanted to go on to Stockholm and be there a few days before returning to London. She wanted to be in Stockholm for what she knew would be the last time, to walk the streets she had walked as a girl.

Lars left the island the day before Ingrid, while Paavo and her cousin Britt stayed on with Ingrid to close up. Ingrid would not fly to Stockholm because she knew the press would somehow find out and be there, something she couldn't face. She did not want anyone taking pictures of her as she looked, and especially photographing her huge arm.

Paavo, talking with me in 2006, remembered the trip as if it had been the week before.

He, Britt, and Ingrid took a small boat to where Paavo's Citroën was parked. Despite the pillows and blankets they had taken along to make her travel more comfortable, every bump on the road jolted Ingrid's arm. "It was a trip of utter misery," Paavo recalled, lightened only by the stop for the picnic lunch he had carefully prepared, and which Ingrid was able to enjoy.

Ingrid stayed with Britt in Britt's Stockholm apartment, which was very near to where they had lived as girls, and they took some of the same walks together that they had enjoyed in their childhood.

As Ingrid passed the building where she had lived briefly with Aunt Ellen, she experienced that same nagging doubt, as she had over the years, that she had failed her aunt, the night Aunt Ellen had died. She might have done something more on that terrible night. If only she had remembered to open the window, so she could hear her cousin calling, and throw the key out the window . . .

The image that came to her when she was reminded of her kind, if strict, aunt was not of Aunt Ellen taking her to the bakery, or coming on Sunday morning to wake her for early church service, but of Aunt Ellen turning blue, gasping for air, unable to breathe. Ingrid, so near the end of her own life, knew she could not return to that moment no matter how fervently she might wish it, that moment when she didn't throw down the key.

The last night, Ingrid went to visit Greta Danielsson, her girlhood companion, who was living near Stockholm with her doctor husband. Ingrid remembered how good Greta had been to her and what Greta had meant to Ingrid's father.

Justus Bergman had returned to Stockholm when he knew he didn't have long left to live, and Ingrid was doing the same.

Ingrid went back to London less than a week before her sixty-seventh birthday.

Isabella learned from Britt about Ingrid's extraordinary vision on the last day of her life.

"The morning of her sixty-seventh birthday, Mama awakened early in her London home. Even before she opened her eyes, she felt this awesome presence in the room, and she knew immediately who it was, almost as if she had been expecting her.

"She knew she was dying, because she saw her own mother sitting at the makeup table, her back to Mama. Though Mama didn't use makeup, occasionally after she was so ill, she used a little rouge for a visitor, and she enjoyed the look of her vanity table, with her well-used hairbrush.

"She asked her mother, 'Have you come to take me?'

"Her mother was facing the mirror, and she didn't turn. She was young and lovely, in her early thirties, as Ingrid knew her from photographs and film taken by her father before Friedel's early death.

"The mother Mama never really knew was there, and Mama understood why.

"Mama felt reassured. Her mother had been a joyful young woman there to rejoice at Mama's first birthday, and she was there to be at Mama's last birthday, to make it easier for her.

"Mama said, 'My mother has come for me, to take me with her.'

"That night, Mama died, the night of her sixty-seventh birthday."

Isabella had wanted to be there in London for her mother's birthday. Having seen her in New York for the recent birthday of herself and her sister, she had hoped her mother might not be as sick as she feared, as the doctors said. When she called, she was told her mother's birthday party might not be in London. She wasn't told how near the end it was. Isabella knew she could rush to London on the Concorde and arrive in a few hours, but she regretted afterward that she waited in New York for word from her mother or about her mother and hadn't just gone to London to see for herself.

The day after Ingrid's death, Isabella was in London to say goodbye to her mother.

"When I arrived," Isabella said, "the body was still in the bed. I remember the lights were very dim. It was difficult to recognize her face as dead. You know, when people die, you don't believe it.

"The face no longer seemed like Mum. I could no longer recognize her. It looked like the face of a woman who was 300 years old. I could only recognize her hands. But Mother still had her natural blond hair, no white. Everything else looked so surreal.

"Then they removed the body. And guess who had the service to remove the body? Harrods! Harrods, the department store, also has an undertaking service, and Harrods was my mum's favorite shop.

"My mother had always loved the store, especially the food halls. When she was looking for a home in London, the only stipulation she made was, she had to be very near Harrods.

"That was a requirement, for food mostly, I think. She didn't shop much for clothes. It was fun to go to Harrods.

"And now, it was Harrods for the last time, their undertaking service. Mum would have loved that. She would have laughed her wonderful laugh."

It was *la ronde.* Ingrid had died on her sixty-seventh birthday. Those who knew her knew how she felt about birthdays and believed that through a great force of her strong will, she had remained alive that long. She had no strength and no reason to fight to survive for another day. The pain and suffering had cruelly tested her endurance and finally overwhelmed her.

Isabella said she had been shocked to have someone ask her if her mother had committed suicide, saying she must have, because she had died on her birthday.

"Even if the life she had left was no longer a life she could love, Mama would never, never have committed suicide, because it would have meant scandal. She would never have wanted us children to have to face more scandal.

"We sort of grow up when we become our parents' parents, as they need us the way we once needed them. I wished I could have done more for her, but the last time when she was ill, Mother never wanted us to overstay our visits. Overstay meant seeming bored, or worse yet, to show pity. She wasn't accustomed in her life to being pitied, and she didn't plan to get used to it.

"I thought it was so like Mama to die on her birthday. She was very orderly, and it was a tidy thing to do.

"Mom loved life so much. She never wanted to let go of it, even after she was too sick to work. She struggled, but the sickness always got worse. The sickness and her battle against it continuously weakened her, but she wouldn't give in. She took what pleasure she could, even in those last months, weeks, days."

Ingrid chose Danholmen as the place from which her ashes would be strewn into the waters beyond the island. "We were going to scatter her ashes there," Isabella explained, "but summer was over, and it was going toward winter, the sea was very tempestuous. Then it froze."

The following June, Lars took a boat out with Isotta Ingrid, Robertino, Pia, Fiorella (Rossellini's niece), Ingrid's cousin Britt, Paavo, and the ashes, mixed with wildflowers, were scattered amidst the waves. Ingrid had loved summer. Isabella couldn't be there. Her daughter, Elettra, was born only a few weeks later.

The urn that had contained the ashes was buried in the Swedish cemetery, next to the graves of Ingrid's parents.

This was to cause some confusion in future years. Many believed that it was Ingrid who was buried there, rather than just the urn. Visitors came to stop at the supposed gravesite and occasionally a newspaper story appeared about Ingrid being buried there.

Everyone gathered for the reading of the will, which was a lengthy handwritten letter Ingrid had composed with the help and guidance of Schmidt, since lawyers and contracts were his forte. The original document had given half of Ingrid's estate to Schmidt, as her husband. Isabella described what happened:

"When Mother died, she had her way, in a sweet, wonderful way. When you die, the law says that everything you own, fifty per cent, goes to your husband, and then, the remaining fifty per cent is divided among your children. Mother left a will, written by hand, in the old-fashioned way. When we went to open the will, the lawyer said, 'I'm sorry, Lars, but Ingrid erased your name.' Lars said, 'I don't believe it,' and the lawyer showed him the will. Lars Schmidt's name was crossed out.

"Of course, they were divorced, and he wouldn't have been automatically entitled. But she really wanted to make sure that she left nothing for him. Revenge from the beyond! She didn't like to argue, but she had the last word. I loved it, because it was very actress-like. Charming. Even Lars had to smile."

Schmidt was rich, and Ingrid wanted to be certain her four children were well provided for. Ingrid was intensely committed to taking care of her children after she was gone, just as her father had provided for her. What he had done had protected her and given her more choice and comfort. It had made possible her trying out for drama school, which changed her entire life. Very important to her, it demonstrated his caring and his desire to protect her.

In her late years, when I saw her in London, she said she felt "guilty" buying luxuries that she didn't really need, because she was so determined to create the maximum estate she could provide for her children.

"After my parents died," Isabella told me, "I had a recurring dream. My mum was reclining on a sofa and seemed to be asleep, and when I tried to wake her up, she said, 'Oh, I'm dead. Let me be dead. Don't call me back. I had a wonderful life. I'm content.'

"But for my father, it was quite different in my dream. I've always dreamed of him coming back, sometimes even like a zombie. He's very desperate about being dead and about being in a decaying state, because he hadn't finished living. He had more things to do.

"I think that Mother was ready to die. She had been suffering, and more important, she knew she couldn't work anymore. Her death as an actress was terrible for her. It was like dying twice. She had always loved life, but she had lost interest in living.

"My father's death was a heart attack, with no warning. It was so very fast. He had been healthy and energetic, full of projects.

"Mother was a more delicate person. She always felt comfortable with acting, but everything else seemed to make her uncomfortable.

"Mum always said, 'I feel more myself when I am being someone else.'"

When Isabella received a $25,000 check from Diet Coke, she thought, "It's from Mama," and she was very touched. Diet Coke had used *Casablanca* as the film being watched on television by a young couple while they were drinking Diet Coke. The company had paid the studio that owned the rights and sent $25,000 to each of Ingrid's children. It was good to receive the money, Isabella said, and it was very moving to feel "it was Mama watching over us after all this time."

Isabella thought about what she wanted to do with the $25,000. "I decided to give it to Wesleyan University for Jeanine Basinger's archive for Mother, and, of course, for what there is of Father's material, too. Mother kept all of her things and put it all together for us, and Father did the opposite.

"My mother kept everything, everything of hers, of her parents, of her grandparents. She began saving the souvenirs and memories of her life from the time she was a very young girl. In the last years of her life, she put a great deal of time and effort into organizing her papers and scrapbooks.

"When she knew she didn't have long to live, she made a special effort to put everything in order. She selected three dresses and had them dry-cleaned, hand-pressed, and wrapped in plastic, one to represent each of her three marriages. She pinned a note on each with a safety pin to identify it.

"One day, I asked her, 'Mama, why have you saved everything?'

"Her answer was that she always knew she was going to be famous.

"I was shocked because the answer seemed arrogant. It was totally out of character, because Mum was never arrogant. I wish I'd asked her more about it right then, but I didn't, and she didn't live long after that, so I never got the chance.

"Mama was an orphan. Her mother died before Mum was three and her father died when Mama was twelve. Maybe she had a kind of orphan psychology, and clinging to the ties of the past gave her a feeling of belonging.

"Or maybe it was a way of keeping them alive, her family that had gone, their presence. For Mama, maybe it was a little like throwing the people away to throw away what they had left behind in the world."

"The death of memories is the saddest thing I know," Ingrid told me.

"It's not easy to pass on memories, but only some of us are lucky enough to have memories anyone wants to share and preserve after we are gone.

"I am so lucky to have these memories to pass on, that my memories are wanted. It's a privilege.

"I do not like to live in the past, but I cannot imagine being without the past. The past has something to say to me."

Looking back on her life, Ingrid told me, "I believe that I was greatly influenced by the romance of my parents.

"As I heard about it from my father, my Aunt Mutti in Germany, and others, and especially as I shared their intimacy when as a young woman I read their love letters, I had the vicarious experience of a great love.

"Without consciously thinking about it, I believe I spent my life in search of that romance. Perhaps my high expectations even worked against my finding it or, more important, against my holding on to it.

"I know I felt certain that the warmth of this bond would be mine, that a great love would find me, as it had my parents. Words would be nothing. Feeling is everything. It cannot be explained to others because it is so personal a bond of intimacy that it can only be known to the two who are blessed by the warmth of it.

"It was to my father's enthusiasm for my pretending and my acting as a little girl that I owe everything. I was acting before I could read, even if I was only playing a flowerpot. I owe my career to him. He was the perfect man in my life. It was because of his encouragement I found my real home—the film set and the theater.

"The thing I missed most in my life was being able to show my father my films and my stage performances. My father had such high hopes for what I would do, and I know I didn't let him down. I think he would have been very happy to know of the career of his 'little Ingrid.'"

FILMOGRAPHY

Munkbrogreven (*The Count of Monk's Bridge*)

Svensk Filmindustri, 1934, released 1935. Producer: AB Fribergs Film-byrå. Directors: Edvin Adolphson and Sigurd Wallén. Screenplay: Gösta Stevens, from the play *Greven fran Gamla Stan* by Arthur and Siegfried Fischer. Cinematographer Åke Dahlqvist. Editor: Rolf Husberg. Music: Jules Sylvain. Cast: Valdemar Dalquist (the Count), Edvin Adolphson (Åke), Ingrid Bergman (Elsa), Sigurd Wallén, Eric Abrahamsson, Weyler Hildebrand, Artur Cederborgh, Tollie Zellman, Julia Caesar, Arthur Fischer, Emil Fjellström, Viktor "Kulorton" Andersson. Running time: 83 minutes.

Branningar (*Ocean Breakers*)

Svensk Filmindustri, 1935. Producer: Film AB Skandinavien. Director: Ivar Johansson. Screenplay: Ivar Johansson, from an idea by Henning Ohlson. Cinematographer: Julius Jaenzon. Music: Eric Bengtson. Cast: Sten Lindgren (Daniel Nordeman), Ingrid Bergman (Karin Ingman), Carl Ström (her father), Tore Svennberg, Bror Olsson, Knut Frankman, Karin Swenson, Weyler Hildebrand, Georg Skarstedt, Henning Ohlsson, Vera Lindby, Viktor Öst, Emmy Albiin, Wiktor Andersson, Helga Brofeldt, Carl Browallius, Olle Granberg, Holger Löwenadler, Erik Rosén. Running time: 70 minutes.

Swedenhielms (*The Family Swedenhielm*)

Svensk Filmindustri, 1935. Producer: AB Svensk Filmindustri. Director: Gustaf Molander. Screenplay: Stina Bergman, from the play by Hjalmar Bergman. Cinematographer: Åke Dahlqvist. Music: Helge Lindberg. Cast: Gösta Ekman (Rolf Swedenhielm), Karin Swanström (Marta), Björn Berglund (Rolf, Jr.), Håkan Westergren (Bo), Tutta Rolf (Julia), Ingrid Bergman (Astrid), Sigurd Wallén, Nils Ericsson, Adele Söderholm, Mona Geijer-Falkner, Hjalmar Peters, Sven Jerring. Running time: 88 minutes.

Valborgsmässoafton (Walpurgis Night)

Svensk Filmindustri, 1935 (U.S., 1941). Producer: AB Svensk Filmindustri. Director: Gustaf Edgren. Story and Screenplay: Oscar Rydqvist and Gustaf Edgren. Cinematographer: Martin Bodin. Cast: Lars Hanson (Johan Borg), Karin Kavli (Clary), Victor Sjöström (Frederik Bergström), Ingrid Bergman (Lena Bergström), Erik Berglund, Sture Lagerwall, Georg Blickingberg, Stig Järrel, Richard Lund, Linnéa Hillberg, Marie-Louise Sorbon, Gabriel Alw, Carl-Gunnar Wingard, Aino Taube, Torsten Hillberg, Anders Henrikson, Torsten Winge, Greta Berthels, Åke Uppström, Linnéa Hillberg, Ivar Kåge, Lill-Åcke, Olåf Widgren, Hjalmar Peters, Pecka Hagman, Harry Hednoff. Running time: 75 minutes.

På Solsidan (On the Sunny Side)

Svensk Filmindustri, 1936. Producer: Aktiebolaget Wivefilm. Director: Gustaf Molander. Screenplay: Oscar Hemberg and Gösta Stevens, from the play by Helge Krog. Cinematographer: Åke Dahlqvist. Music: Eric Bengtson. Cast: Lars Hanson (Harold Ribe), Ingrid Bergman (Eva Bergh), Edvin Adolphson (Joakim Brink), Marianne Löfgren (Kajsa), Karin Swanström, Einar Axelsson, Carl Browallius, Erik "Bullen" Berglund, Eddie Figge, Olga Andersson, Wiktor Andersson, Eric Gustafson. Running time: 92 minutes.

Intermezzo

Svensk Filmindustri, 1936. Producer: AB Svensk Filmindustri. Director: Gustaf Molander. Screenplay: Gustaf Molander and Gösta Stevens, from an original story by Gustaf Molander. Cinematographer: Åke Dahlqvist. Music: Heinz Provost. Cast: Gösta Ekman (Holger Brandt), Ingrid Bergman (Anita Hoffman), Inga Tidblad (Margit Brandt), Hans Ekman (Åke), Britt Hagman (Ann-Marie), Hugo Björne (Thomas Stenborg), Erik "Bullen" Berglund, Emma Meissner, Anders Henrikson, George Fant, Folke Helleberg, Millan Bolander, Margit Orth, Carl Ström. Running time: 93 minutes.

Dollar

Svensk Filmindustri, 1938. Producer: AB Svensk Filmindustri. Director: Gustaf Molander. Screenplay: Stina Bergman and Gustaf Molander, from a play by Hjalmar Bergman. Cinematographer: Åke Dahlqvist. Music: Eric Bengtson. Cast: Georg Rydeberg (Kurt Balzar), Ingrid Bergman (Julia Balzar), Kotti Chave (Lt. Louis Brenner), Tutta Rolf

(Sussi), Håkan Westergren (Ludvig von Battwyhl), Birgit Tengroth (Katja), Elsa Burnett (Mary Johnstone), Edvin Adolphson (Dr. Johnson), Gösta Cederlund, Erik Rosén, Carl Ström, Axel Högel, Millan Bolander, David Erikson, Erland Colliander, Nils Dahlgren, Gustav Lagerberg, Richard Lindström, E. Dethorey, N. Dickson, Aina Elkman, Hester Harvey, Helga Kihlberg, Allan Lindner. Running time: 78 minutes.

En Kvinnas Ansikte (A Woman's Face)

Svensk Filmindustri, 1938 (U.S., 1939). Producer: AB Svensk Filmindustri. Director: Gustaf Molander. Screenplay: Gösta Stevens, from *Il Etait une Fois* by François de Croisset. Cinematographer: Åke Dahlqvist. Cast: Ingrid Bergman (Anna Holm), Georg Rydeberg (Torsten Barring), Anders Henrikson (Dr. Wegert), Karin Carlsson-Kavli (Fru Wegert), Tore Svennberg (Magnus Barring), Bror Bügler, Karin Kavli, Magnus Kesster, Erik "Bullen" Berglund, Gösta Cederlund, Göran Bernhard, Gunnar Sjöberg, John Ericsson, Hilda Borgström, Sigurd Wallén. Running Time: 104 minutes.

Die vier Gesellen (The Four Companions)

UFA, 1938. Producer: Universum Film-Aktiengesellschaft. Director: Carl Froehlich. Screenplay: Jochen Huth, from his play. Cast: Ingrid Bergman (Marianne), Sabine Peters (Käthe), Carsta Löck (Lotte), Ursula Herking (Franziska), Hans Söhnker (Stefan Kohlund), Leo Slezak, Erich Ponto, Heinz Welzel, Willi Rose, Karl Haubenreiber, Wilhelm P. Krüger, Lotte Braun, Hugo Frölich, Rudolf Klicks, Max Rosenhauer, Ernst G. Schiffner, Hans-Jürgen Weidlich. Running time: 96 minutes.

En Enda Natta (Only One Night)

Svensk Filmindustri, 1939 (U.S., 1942). Producer: AB Svensk Filmindustri. Director: Gustaf Molander. Screenplay: Gösta Stevens, from the story "En Eneste Natt" by Harald Tandrup. Cast: Edvin Adolphson (Valdemar Morsaux), Aino Taube (Helga Mårtensson), Olof Sandborg (Magnus von Brede), Ingrid Bergman (Eva), Erik "Bullen" Berglund, Marianne Löfgren, Magnus Kesster, Sophus Dahl, Ragna Breda, John Eklöf, Tor Borong, Wiktor "Kulorten" Anderson, Ka Nerrell, Folke Helleberg, Nila Nordstähl. Running time: 90 minutes.

Intermezzo: A Love Story

Selznick International–United Artists, 1939. Producer: David O. Selznick. Director: Gregory Ratoff. Screenplay: George O'Neil, based on the Swedish screenplay by Gustaf Molander and Gösta Stevens. Cinematographer: Gregg Toland. Editor: Francis D. Lyon. Music: Heinz Provost. Art Director: Lyle Wheeler. Special Effects: Jack Cosgrove. Costumes: Irene, Travis Banton. Cast: Leslie Howard (Holger Brandt), Ingrid Bergman (Anita Hoffman), Edna Best (Margit Brandt), John Halliday (Thomas Stenborg), Ann Todd (Ann Marie), Douglas Scott (Eric), Cecil Kellaway (Charles Moler), Enid Bennett(Greta Stenborg), Eleanor Wesselhoeft (Emma), Moira Flynn (Marianne). Running time: 70 minutes.

Adam Had Four Sons

Columbia, 1941. Producer: Robert Sherwood. Director: Gregory Ratoff. Screenplay: William Hurlbut and Michael Blankfort, from Charles Bonner's novel, *Legacy.* Editor: Francis D. Lyon. Art Director: Rudolph Sternad. Cinematographer: J. Peverell Marley. Cast: Warner Baxter (Adam Stoddard), Ingrid Bergman (Emilie Gallatin), Susan Hayward (Hester), Fay Wray (Molly Stoddard), Richard Denning (Jack), Johnny Downs (David), Robert Shaw (Chris), Charles Lind (Phillip), Billy Ray (young Jack), Steven Muller (young David), Wallace Chadwell (young Chris), Bobby Walberg (young Phillip), Helen Westley, June Lockhart, Pietro Sosso, Gilbert Emery, Renie Riano, Clarence Muse. Running time: 81 minutes.

Rage in Heaven

Metro-Goldwyn-Mayer, 1941. Producer: Gottfried Reinhardt. Director: W. S. Van Dyke. Screenplay: Christopher Isherwood and Robert Thoeren, based on the novel by James Hilton. Cinematographer: Oliver Marsh. Editor: Harold Kress. Music: Bronislau Kaper. Cast: Robert Montgomery (Philip Monrell), Ingrid Bergman (Stella Berger), George Sanders (Ward Andrews), Lucile Watson (Mrs. Monrell), Oscar Homolka (Dr. Rameau), Philip Merivale, Matthew Boulton, Aubrey Mather, Frederick Worlock, Francis Compton, Gilbert Emery, Ludwig Hardt. Running time: 85 minutes.

Juninatten (A Night in June)

Svensk Filmindustri, 1940. Producer: AB Svensk Filmindustri. Director: Per Lindberg. Screenplay: Ragnar Hyltén-Cavallius and Per Lindberg from a story by Tor Nordström-Bonnier. Cinematographer: Åke Dahlqvist. Music: Jules Sylvain. Editor: Oscar Rosander. Cast: Ingrid Bergman (Kirstin Nordback), Gunnar Sjöberg (Nils Asklund), Carl Ström (Dr. Berggren), Olof Widgren (Stefan von Bremen), Lill-Tollie Zellman, Marinne Aminoff, Edvin Adolphson, Aino Taube, Olof Sandburg, Erik Berglund, Marianne Löfgren, Magnus Kesster, Sophus Dahl,

Ragna Breda, John Eklöf, Tor Borong, Gabriel Alw, Olof Winnerstrand, Sigurd Wallén, Hasse Ekman, Maritta Marke, Gudrun Brost, John Botvid, Karin Swanström, Mimi Pollak, Charlie Paterson, Ernst Brunman, Alf Kjellin, Karin Nordgren, Mona Geijer-Falkner, David Eriksson, Douglas Hage, Carl Deurell, Sven-Göran Alw, Richard Lund, Nils Jacobsson, Sol-Britt Agerup, Kerstin Ekwall, Britta Larsson, Viran Rydkvist, Erik Forslund. Running time: 88 minutes.

Dr. Jekyll and Mr. Hyde

Metro-Goldwyn-Mayer, 1941. Producer and Director: Victor Fleming. Screenplay: John Lee Mahin, based on the story by Robert Louis Stevenson. Editor: Harold Kress. Art director: Cedric Gibbons. Cinematographer: Joseph Ruttenberg. Cast: Spencer Tracy (Henry Jekyll), Lana Turner (Beatrix Emery), Ingrid Bergman (Ivy Peterson), Donald Crisp (Sir Charles Emery), Ian Hunter, Barton MacLane, C. Aubrey Smith, Sara Allgood, Peter Godfrey, Frederick Worlock, William Tannen, Frances Robinson, Denis Green, Billy Bevan, Forrester Harvey, Lumsden Hare, Lawrence Grant, John Barclay. Running time: 113 minutes.

Casablanca

Warner Brothers, 1942. Producer: Hal B. Wallis. Director: Michael Curtiz. Screenplay: Julius J. and Philip G. Epstein and Howard Koch, from the play *Everybody Comes to Rick's* by Murray Burnett and Joan Alison. Cinematographer: Arthur Edeson. Editor: Owen Marks. Music: Max Steiner. Art director: Carl Jules Weyl. Special effects: Lawrence Butler, Willard Van Enger. Costumes: Orry-Kelly. Cast: Humphrey Bogart (Richard "Rick" Blaine), Ingrid Bergman (Ilsa Lund Laszlo), Paul Henreid (Victor Laszlo), Claude Rains (Captain Louis Renault), Conrad Veidt (Major Strasser), Sydney Greenstreet (Signor Ferrari), Peter Lorre (Ugarte), S. Z. Sakall (Carl), Madeleine LeBeau (Yvonne), Dooley Wilson (Sam), Joy Page (Annina), Helmut Dantine (Jan), John Qualen (Berger), Leonid Kinskey (Sacha), Richard Ryen (Heinze), Curt Bois (pickpocket), Marcel Dalio (croupier), Ludwig Stössel and Ilka Grüning (German couple en route to America), Dan Seymour (Abdul), Paul Andor (man shot at opening), Lotte Palfi (woman selling jewelry), Lorrina Mura (guitarist), Louis Mercier (gendarme at airport), Charles La Torre, Frank Puglia, Norma Varden. Running time: 102 minutes.

Swedes in America

Office of War Information, 1943. Producer: Office of War Information, Overseas Bureau. Director: Irving Lerner. Cast: Ingrid Bergman and the Charles Swenson family and neighbors of Minnesota and Chicago. Running time: 15 minutes.

For Whom the Bell Tolls

Paramount, 1943. Producer and Director: San Wood. Screenplay: Dudley Nichols, from the novel by Ernest Hemingway. Cinematography: Ray Rennahan (Technicolor). Editors: Sherman Todd, John F. Link. Music: Victor Young. Production designer: William Cameron Menzies. Art directors: Hans Dreier, Haldane Douglas. Special Effects: Gordon Jennings. Cast: Gary Cooper (Robert Jordan), Ingrid Bergman (María), Akim Tamiroff (Pablo), Arturo de Cordova (Agustin), Vladimir Sokoloff (Anselmo), Mikhail Rasumny (Rafael), Fortunio Bonanova (Fernando), Eric Feldary (Andres), Victor Varooni (Primitivo), Katina Paxinou (Pilar), Joseph Calleia (El Sordo), Eduardo Ciannelli, Duncan Renaldo, Alexander Granach, Leonid Snegoff, George Coulouris, Frank Puglia, Pedro de Cordoba, Michael Visaroff, Konstantin Shayne, Martin Garralaga, Jean Del Val, John Mylong, Feodor Chaliapin, Mayo Newhall, Michael Dalmatoff, Antonio Vidal, Robert Tafur, Armand Roland. Running time: 170 minutes.

Gaslight

Metro-Goldwyn-Mayer, 1944. Producer: Arthur Hornblow, Jr. Director: George Cukor. Screenplay: John Van Druten, Walter Reisch, and John L. Balderston, based on the play *Angel Street* by Patrick Hamilton. Cinematographer: Joseph Ruttenberg. Editor: Ralph E. Winters. Music: Bronislau Kaper. Art directors: Cedric Gibbons, William Ferrari. Special effects: Warren Newcombe. Cast: Charles Boyer (Gregory Anton), Ingrid Bergman (Paula Alquist), Joseph Cotten (Brian Cameron), Dame May Whitty (Miss Thwaites), Angela Lansbury (Nancy Oliver), Barbara Everest (Elizabeth Tompkins), Eustace Wyatt (Budge), Emil Rameau (Mario Guardi), Edmund Breon (General Huddleston), Halliwell Hobbes (Mr. Muffin), Tom Stevenson, Heather Thatcher, Lawrence Grossmith. Running time: 114 minutes.

Saratoga Trunk

Warner Brothers, 1945. Producer: Hal B. Wallis. Director: Sam Wood. Screenplay: Casey Robinson, based on the novel by Edna Ferber. Cinematographer: Ernest Haller. Editor: Lawrence Butler. Music: Max Steiner. Cast: Gary Cooper (Clint Maroon), Ingrid Bergman (Clio Dulaine), Flora Robson (Angelique), Jerry Austin (Cupidon), Florence Bates (Mrs. Coventry Bellop), John Warburton (Bart van Steed), Ethel

Griffies (Clarissa), John Abbott, Curt Bois, Minor Watson, Louis Payne, Fred Essler, Adrienne D'Ambricourt, Helen Freeman, Sophie Huxley, Marla Shelton, Sarah Edwards, Jacqueline De Witt, Thurston Hall, William B. Davidson, Theodore von Eltz, Glenn Strange, Monte Blue, Georges Renavent, Alice Fleming, Alan Bridge, Ruby Dandridge, Ralph Dunn. Running time: 135 minutes.

The Bells of St. Mary's

RKO Radio, 1945. Producer and Director: Leo McCarey for Rainbow Productions. Screenplay: Dudley Nichols, from a story by Leo McCarey. Cinematographer: George Barnes. Editor: Harry Marker. Music: Robert Emmett Dolan. Art director: William Rannery. Costumes: Edith Head. Cast: Bing Crosby (Father Chuck O'Malley), Ingrid Bergman (Sister Benedict), Henry Travers (Mr. Bogardus), Ruth Donnelly (Sister Michael), Joan Carroll (Patsy), Martha Sleeper (Patsy's mother), William Gargan (Joe Gallagher), Rhys Williams (Dr. McKay), Dick Tyler (Eddie), Una O'Connor (Mrs. Breen), Bobby Frasco, Aina Constant, Gwen Crawford, Matt McHugh, Edna Wonacott, Jimmy Crane, Minerva Urecal, Pietro Sosso, Cora Shannon, Joseph Palma, Jimmy Dundee, Dewey Robinson. Running time: 126 minutes.

Spellbound

Selznick–United Artists, 1945. Producer: David O. Selznick. Director: Alfred Hitchcock. Screenplay: Ben Hecht, adapted by Angus MacPhail from the novel *The House of Dr. Edwardes* by Francis Beeding (pseudonym for Hilary St. George Saunders, John Palmer). Cinematographer: George Barnes, Rex Wimpy (uncredited). Editors: William Ziegler, Hal C. Kern. Music: Miklos Rozsa. Production director: James Basevi. Art director: John Ewing. Special effects: Jack Cosgrove. Designer, dream sequence: Salvador Dalí. Costumes: Howard Greer. Cast: Ingrid Bergman (Dr. Constance Petersen), Gregory Peck (John "J.B." Ballantine), Michael Chekhov (Dr. Brulov), Jean Acker (Matron), Donal Curtis (Harry), Rhonda Fleming (Mary Carmichael), John Emery (Dr. Fleurot), Leo G. Carroll (Dr. Murchison), Norman Lloyd (Garmes), Steven Geray (Dr. Graff), Paul Harvey (Dr. Hanish), Wallace Ford (drunk in hotel), Bill Goodwin (hotel detective), Art Baker (detective), Regis Toomey (detective), Irving Bacon (train ticket taker), Edward Fielding (Dr. Edwards in dream), Jean Acker, Donald Curtis, Erskine Sanford, Janet Scott, Victor Kilian, Dave Willock, George Meader, Matt Moore, Harry Brown, Joel Davis, Clarence Straight, Teddy Infuhr, Richard Bartell, Addison Richards. Running time: 111 minutes.

Notorious

RKO Radio, 1946. Producer and Director: Alfred Hitchcock. Screenplay: Ben Hecht. Cinematographer: Ted Tetzlaff. Editor: Theron Warth. Music: Roy Webb. Art directors: Albert S. D'Agostino, Carroll Clark. Special effects: Vemon L Walker, Paul Eagler. Costumes: Edith Head. Cast: Cary Grant (T. R. Devlin), Ingrid Bergman (Alicia Huberman), Claude Rains (Alexander Sebastian), Louis Calhern (Paul Prescott), Leopoldine Konstantin (Mme. Sebastian), Reinhold Schünzel (Dr. Anderson), Moroni Olsen (Walter Beardsley), Ivan Triesault (Eric Mathis), Alexis Minotis (Joseph), Wally Brown (Mr. Hopkins), Ricardo Costa, Sir Charles Mendl, Eberhard Krumschmidt, Fay Baker. Running time: 101 minutes.

Arch of Triumph

Enterprise–United Artists, 1948. Producer: David Lewis for Enterprise Studios. Director: Lewis Milestone. Screenplay: Lewis Milestone and Harry Brown, based on the novel by Erich Maria Remarque. Cinematographer: Russell Metty. Editor: Mario Costegnaro. Music: Louis Gruenberg. Cast: Ingrid Bergman (Joan Madou), Charles Boyer (Dr. Ravic), Charles Laughton (Haake), Louis Calhern (Morosow), Stephen Bekassy (Alex), Roman Bohnen, Ruth Nelson, Curt Bois, J. Edward Bromberg, Michael Romanoff, Art Smith, John Laurenz, Leon Lenoir, Franco Corsaro, Nino Pipitone, Vladimir Rashevsky, Alvin Hammer, Jay Gilpin, Ilia Khmara, André Marsauden, Hazel Brooks, Byron Foulger, William Conrad, Peter Virgo, Feodor Chaliapin. Running time: 120 minutes.

Joan of Arc

Sierra Pictures–RKO Radio, 1948. Producer: Walter Wanger. Director: Victor Fleming. Screenplay: Maxwell Anderson and Andrew Solt, adapted from the play *Joan of Lorraine* by Maxwell Anderson. Cinematographer: Joseph Valentine, Winton Hoch, and William Skull. Music: Hugo Friedhofer. Arrangements: Jerome Moross. Art director: Richard Day. Costumes: Dorothy Jeakins and Karinska. Editor: Frank Sullivan. Special effects: Jack Cosgrove, John Fulton. Cast: Ingrid Bergman (Joan), José Ferrer (Charles VII), George Coulouris (Robert de Baudricourt), Richard Ney (a noble), Richard Derr, Ray Teal, Roman Bohnen, Selena Royle, Jimmy Lydon, Robert Barrat, Francis L. Sullivan, Rand Brooks, Nestor Paiva, Irene Rich, Gene Lockhart, Nicholas Joy, Frederick Worlock, Tom Browne Henry, Vincent Donahue, Colin Keith-Johnston, Leif Erickson, John Emery, John Ireland, Ward Bond, Gregg Barton, Henry Brandon, Dennis

Hoey, J. Carrol Naish, Hurd Hatfield, Cecil Kellaway, Ethan Laidlaw, Morris Ankrum, Philip Bourneuf, Shepperd Strudwick, Taylor Holmes, Stephen Roberts, Frank Puglia, Houseley Stevenson, Alan Napier, David Bond, Bill Kennedy, Victor Wood, George Zucco, Jeff Corey, John Parrish, Mary Currier, Aubrey Mather, Herbert Rudley, William Conrad, Frank Elliot, Roy Roberts, Barbara Woodell, Greta Granstedt, Julia Faye, Marjorie Wood, Arthur Space, Eve March. Running time: 145 minutes.

Under Capricorn

Warner Brothers, 1949. Producer: Transatlantic Pictures. Director: Alfred Hitchcock. Screenplay: James Bridie, from Hume Cronyn's adaptation of the play by John Colton and Margaret Linden and the novel by Helen Simpson. Cinematographer: Jack Cardiff. Editor: A. S. Bates. Music: Richard Addinsell. Cast: Ingrid Bergman (Lady Henrietta Considine), Joseph Cotten (Sam Flusky), Michael Wilding (Charles Adare), Margaret Leighton (Milly), Cecil Parker, Denis O'Dea, Jack Watling, Harcourt Williams, John Ruddock, Bill Shine, Victor Lucas, Ronald Adam, Francis de Wolff, G. H. Mulcaser, Olive Sloane, Maureen Delaney, Julia Lang, Betty McDermott, Roderick Lovell. Running time: 117 minutes.

Stromboli

RKO Radio, 1950. Producer and Director: Roberto Rossellini. Story by Roberto Rossellini in collaboration with Art Cohn, Renzo Lesana, Sergio Amidei, and G. P. Callegari. Cinematographer: Otello Martelli. Editor: Roland Gross. Music: Renzo Rossellini. Cast: Ingrid Bergman (Karin), Mario Vitale (Antonio), Renzo Cesana (priest), Mario Sponzo (lighthouse keeper). Running time (in RKO U.S. release): 89 minutes.

Europa '51 (The Greatest Love)

I.F.E. Releasing Corp., 1951 (U.S., 1954). A Ponti–De Laurentiis Production. Producer and Director: Roberto Rossellini. Screenplay: Roberto Rossellini, Sandro de Leo, Mario Pannunzio, Ivor Perilli, and Brunello Rondi, from Roberto Rossellini's original story. Cinematographer: Otello Martelli. Cast: Ingrid Bergman (Irene Girard), Alexander Knox (George Girard), Giulietta Masina (Passerotto), Teresa Pellati (Ines), Ettore Giannini, Sandro Franchina, William Tubbs, Alfred Brown. Running time: 113 minutes.

Siamo Donne (We, the Women)

Siamo Donne Titanus, 1953. "The Chicken," the third of five segments. Director of segment: Roberto Rossellini. Screenplay for segment:

Roberto Rossellini, Cesare Zavattini, Luigi Chiarini. Cinematographer: Otello Martelli. Cast: Ingrid Bergman (as herself). Running time: 17 minutes out of 90.

Giovanna d'Arco al Rogo (Joan of Arc at the Stake)

ENIC, 1954. Producer and Director: Roberto Rossellini. Screenplay: Roberto Rossellini, based on the story and dialogue of Paul Claudel and the oratorio of Arthur Honegger, *Jeanne d'Arc au Bûcher*. Cast: Ingrid Bergman (speaker), Tullio Carminati, Giacinto Prandelli, Augusto Romani, Plinio Clabassi, Saturno Meletti. Running time: 80 minutes.

Viaggio in Italia (Journey to Italy)

Titanus, 1954. Producer: Roberto Rossellini in association with Sveva–Junior Films. Director: Roberto Rossellini. Screenplay: Roberto Rossellini and Vitaliano Brancati. Cinematographer: Enzo Sarafin. Music: Renzo Rossellini. Cast: Ingrid Bergman (Katherin Joyce), George Sanders (Alexander Joyce), Anna Proclemer (prostitute), Paul Muller, Maria Mauban, Leslie Daniels, Natalia Ray, Jackie Frost. Running time: 85 minutes.

Angst (Fear)

Minerva Films, 1954. Producer: Minerva Films. Director: Roberto Rossellini. Screenplay: Roberto Rossellini, Sergio Amidei, and Franz von Treuberg, based on the novel *Der Angst* by Stefan Zweig. Cinematographer: Peter Heller. Music: Renzo Rossellini. Cast: Ingrid Bergman (the wife), Mathias Wieman (the husband), Kurt Kreuger (the lover), Renate Mannhardt (the lover's ex-paramour), Elise Aulinger. Running time: 82 minutes.

Anastasia

Twentieth Century Fox, 1956. Producer: Buddy Adler. Director: Anatole Litvak. Screenplay: Arthur Laurents, adapted by Guy Bolton from a play by Marcelle Maurette. Cinematographer: Jack Hildyard (CinemaScope, DeLuxeColor). Editor: Bert Bates. Art Directors: Andre Andrejew, Bill Andrews. Costumes: René Hubert. Music: Alfred Newman. Cast: Ingrid Bergman (Anastasia), Yul Brynner (Bounine), Helen Hayes (Empress), Akim Tamiroff (Chernov), Martita Hunt (Baroness von Livenbaum), Felix Aylmer (Russian chamberlain), Sacha Pitoëff (Petrovin), Ivan Desny (Prince Paul), Natalie Schafer (Ussenskaia), Grégoire Gromoff (Stepan), Karel Stepanek, Ina De La Haye, Katherine Kath. Running time: 105 minutes.

Elena et les Hommes (*Elena and Her Men*, released as *Paris Does Strange Things* in dubbed English version).

Warner Brothers, 1956. Producer and Director: Jean Renoir. Screenplay: Jean Renoir, based on his story. Cinematographer: Claude Renoir (color). Editor: Borys Lewin. Music: Joseph Kosma. Cast: Ingrid Bergman (Elena), Mel Ferrer (Henri), Jean Marais (Rollan), Juliette Gréco, Marjane, George Higgins, Jean Richard. Running time: 98 minutes.

Indiscreet

Warner Brothers, 1958. Producer and Director: Stanley Donen for Grandon Productions. Screenplay: Norman Krasna, based on his play *Kind Sir*. Cinematographer: Frederick A. "Freddie" Young. Editor: Jack Harris. Art director: Don Ashton. Costumes: Quintino. Music: Richard Rodney Bennett and Ken Jones. Cast: Cary Grant (Philip Adams), Ingrid Bergman (Anna Kalman), Cecil Parker (Alfred Munson), Phyllis Calvert (Margaret Munson), David Kossoff (Carl Banks), Megs Jenkins (Doris Banks), Oliver Johnston (Mr. Finleigh), Michael Anthony (Oscar), Middleton Woods (Finleigh's Clerk), Frank Hawkins. Running time: 100 minutes.

The Inn of the Sixth Happiness

Twentieth Century Fox, 1958. Producer: Buddy Adler. Director: Mark Robson. Screenplay: Isobel Lennart, based on the book *The Small Woman* by Alan Burgess. Art Directors: John Box and Geoffrey Drake. Costumes: Margaret Furse. Cinematographer: Freddie Young (CinemaScope/Technicolor). Editor: Ernest Walter. Production supervisor: James Newcom. Music: Malcolm Arnold. Cast: Ingrid Bergman (Gladys Aylward), Curt Jürgens (Captain Lin Nan), Robert Donat (the mandarin), Athene Seyler (Sara Lanson), Ronald Squire (Sir Francis), Michael David, Moultrie Kelsall, Richard Wattis, Peter Chong, Tsai Chin, Edith Sharpe, Joan Young, Lian-Shin Yang, Noel Hood, Burt Kwouk. Running time: 158 minutes.

Aimez-Vous Brahms? (Goodbye Again)

United Artists, 1961. Producer and Director: Anatole Litvak. Screenplay: Samuel Taylor, based on the novel *Aimez-Vous Brahms?* by Françoise Sagan. Cinematographer: Armand Thirard. Costumes: Christian Dior. Music: Georges Auric. Cast: Ingrid Bergman (Paula Tessier), Yves Montand (Roger Demarest), Anthony Perkins (Philip van der Besh), Jessie Royce Landis (Philip's mother), Jackie Lane, Pierre Dux,

Jean Clarke, Peter Bull, Michele Mercier, Uta Taeger, Andre Randall, David Horne, Lee Patrick, A. Duperoux, Raymond Gerome, Jean Hebey, Michel Garland, Paul Uny, Colin Mann, Diahann Carroll. Running time: 120 minutes.

The Visit

20th Century-Fox, 1964. Producer: Julien Derode. Director: Bernhard Wicki. Screenplay: Ben Barzman, based on the play by Friedrich Dürrenmatt. Cinematographer: Armando Nannuzzi. Editor: Sam Beetley. Art director: Léon Barsacq. Costumes: René Hubert. Music: Hans-Martin Majewski. Cast: Ingrid Bergman (Karla Zachanassian), Anthony Quinn (Serge Miller), Irina Demick (Anya), Valentina Cortese (Mathilda), Ernst Schroeder, Paolo Stoppa, Hans Christian Blech, Romolo Valli, Claude Dauphin, Eduardo Ciannelli, Leonard Steckel, Richard Münch, Marco Guglielmi, Jacques Dufilho, Fausto Tozzi, Dante Maggio, Renzo Palmer, Lelia Lutazzi. Running time: 100 minutes.

The Yellow Rolls-Royce (the third episode)

Metro-Goldwyn-Mayer, 1965. Producer: Anatole De Grunwald. Director: Anthony Asquith. Screenplay: Terence Rattigan. Cinematographer: Jack Hildyard. Editor: Frank Clarke. Music: Riz Ortolani. Cast: Ingrid Bergman (Mrs. Gerda Millett), Omar Sharif (Darich), Joyce Grenfell, Wally Cox. Running time: 46 minutes out of 122.

Smycket (The Necklace)

Omnia Films, 1964, released 1967. (Part of Stimulantia, an eight-part film, each directed by a different Swedish director). Director: Gustaf Molander. Screenplay: Gustaf Molander from a story by Guy De Maupassant. Cinematographer: Gunnar Fischer. Cast: Ingrid Bergman (the wife), Gunnar Björnstrand (the husband), Gunnel Broström (the friend). Running time: 18 minutes.

Cactus Flower

Columbia, 1969. Producer: M. J. Frankovich. Director: Gene Saks. Screenplay: I. A. L. Diamond, from the play by Abe Burrows, based on a French play by Barillet and Grédy. Cinematographer: Charles E. Lang (Technicolor). Editor: Maury Winetrobe. Music: Quincy Jones. Cast: Ingrid Bergman (Stephanie Dickinson), Walter Matthau (Julian Winston), Goldie Hawn (Toni Simmons), Jack Weston (Harvey Greenfield), Rick Lenz (Igor Sullivan), Vito Scotti, Irene Hervey, Eve Bruce, Irwin Charone, Matthew Saks. Running time: 103 minutes.

A Walk in the Spring Rain

Columbia, 1970. Producer: Sterling Silliphant. Director: Guy Green. Screenplay: Sterling Silliphant, from the novel by Rachel Maddux. Cinematographer: Charles B. Lang (Technicolor). Editor: Perris Webster. Art director: Malcolm C. Bert. Costumes: Donfeld. Music: Elmer Bernstein. Cast: Ingrid Bergman (Libby Meredith), Anthony Quinn (Will Cade), Fritz Weaver (Roger Meredith), Katherine Crawford (Ellen), Tom Fielding (Boy), Mitchell Silberman (Bucky), Virginia Gregg. Running time: 98 minutes.

From the Mixed-Up Files of Mrs. Basil E. Frankweiler (also The Hideaways)

Cinema 5, 1973. Producer: Charles G. Mortimer, Jr. Director: Fielder Cook. Screenplay: Blanche Hanalis, based on the novel by E. L. Konigsburg. Cinematographer: Victor J. Kemper. Editor: Eric Albertson. Art director: Philip Rosenberg. Music: Donald Devor. Cast: Ingrid Bergman (Mrs. Basil E. Frankweiler), Sally Prager and Johnny Doran (the children), Madeline Kahn (schoolteacher), George Rose, Richard Mulligan, Georgann Johnson, Donald Symington, Linda Selman. Running time: 105 minutes.

Murder on the Orient Express

Paramount Pictures, 1974. Producer: John Brabourne and Richard Goodwin. Director: Sidney Lumet. Screenplay: Paul Dehn, based on the novel by Agatha Christie. Cinematographer: Geoffrey Unsworth (Panavison, Technicolor). Editor: Anne V. Coates. Production design: Tony Walton. Art director: Jack Stephens. Costumes: Tony Walton. Music: Richard Rodney Bennett. Cast: Albert Finney (Hercule Poirot), Lauren Bacall (Mrs. Hubbard), Martin Balsam (Bianchi), Ingrid Bergman (Greta Ohlsson), Jacqueline Bisset (Countess Andrenyi), Jean-Pierre Cassel (Pierre Paul Michel), Sean Connery (Colonel Arbuthnot), John Gielgud (Beddoes), Wendy Hiller (Princess Dragomiroff), Anthony Perkins, Rachel Roberts, Vanessa Redgrave, Richard Widmark, Michael York, Colin Blakely, George Coulouris, Denis Quilley. Running time: 128 minutes.

A Matter of Time

American International Pictures, 1976. Producer: Jack H. Skirball and J. Edmund Grainger. Director: Vincente Minnelli. Screenplay: John Gay, based on the novel *The Film of Memory* by Maurice Druon. Cinematographer: Geoffrey Unsworth. Editor: Peter Taylor. Production Design: Veniero Colasanti and John Moore. Music: Nino Oliviero. Cast: Ingrid Bergman (the Contessa), Liza Minnelli (the country girl), Charles Boyer (the ex-husband), Isabella Rossellini (the nursing nun), Spiros Andros, Tina Aumont, Fernando Rey. Running time: 97 minutes.

Autumn Sonata (Höstsonaten)

New World Pictures, 1978. Producers: Lew Grade, Martin Starger, Ingmar Bergman. Director: Ingmar Bergman. Screenplay: Ingmar Bergman. Editor: Sylvia Ingemarsson. Production director: Anna Asp. Costumes: Inger Pehrsson. Cinematographer: Sven Nykvist (Eastmancolor). Cast: Ingrid Bergman (Charlotte), Liv Ullmann (Eva), Lena Nyman (Helena), Halvar Björk (Viktor), Georg Lokkeberg (Leonardo), Knut Wigert (professor), Eva van Hanno (nurse), Erland Josephson (Josef), Linn Ullmann (Eva as a child), Arne Bang-Hansen (Uncle Otto), Gunnar Björnstrand, Marianne Aminoff, Mimi Pollak. Running time: 92 minutes.

TELEVISION

The Turn of the Screw

Ford Startime, NBC, October 20, 1959. Executive producer: Hubbell Robinson, Jr. Director: John Frankenheimer. Associate Producer-Director: Gordon Rigby. Teleplay: James Costigan, from the novella by Henry James. Music: David Amram. Cast: Ingrid Bergman, Hayward Morse, Alexandra Wager, Isobel Elsom, Laurinda Barrett, Paul Stevens. Running time: 90 minutes.

24 Hours in a Woman's Life

CBS, March 20, 1961. Executive producer: Lars Schmidt. Director: Silvio Narizzano. Teleplay: John Mortimer, based on a story by Stefan Zweig. Music: George Kleinsinger. Cast: Ingrid Bergman, Rip Torn, John Williams, Lili Darvas, Helena de Crespo, Jerry Orbach. Running time: 90 minutes.

Hedda Gabler

CBS, September 20, 1963. Producer: David Susskind, Lars Schmidt, and Norman Rutherford. Director: Alex Segal. Teleplay: Phil Reisman, Jr., from Eva Le Gallienne's translation of the Henrik Ibsen play. Cast:

Ingrid Bergman, Michael Redgrave, Ralph Richardson, Trevor Howard, Dilys Hamlett, Ursula Jeans, Beatrice Varley. Running time: 90 minutes.

La voix humaine (The Human Voice)

ABC, May 4, 1967. Producer: David Susskind and Lars Schmidt for Stage 67. Director: Ted Kotcheff. Teleplay: Clive Exton, from a translation by Carl Wildman of a story by Jean Cocteau. Cast: Ingrid Bergman. Running time: 50 minutes.

A Woman Called Golda

Paramount Television, April 26 and 28, 1982. Executive producer: Harve Bennett Associates. Associate producer: Marilyn Hall. Producer: Gene Corman. Director: Alan Gibson. Teleplay: Harold Gast and Steven Gethers. Cinematographer: Adam Greenberg. Editor: Robert F. Shugrue. Music: Michel Legrand. Cast: Ingrid Bergman (Golda), Ned Beatty, Franklin Cover, Judy Davis (young Golda), Anne Jackson, Robert Loggia, Leonard Nimoy, Jack Thompson, Anthony Bal Berglas, Bruce Boa, David de Keyser, Barry Foster, Nigel Hawthorne. Running time: Two 90-minute segments for two 120-minute programs.

INDEX